UNIVERSITY OF ST. THOMAS LIBRARIES
WITHDRAWN
UST
Libraries

Computational Thinking in Sound

D1711591

UNIVERSITY OF ST. THOMAS LIBRARIES

Computational Thinking in Sound

Teaching the Art and Science of Music and Technology

Gena R. Greher

and

Jesse M. Heines

OXFORD
UNIVERSITY PRESS

OXFORD
UNIVERSITY PRESS

Oxford University Press is a department of the
University of Oxford. It furthers the University's objective
of excellence in research, scholarship, and education
by publishing worldwide.

Oxford   New York
Auckland   Cape Town   Dar es Salaam   Hong Kong   Karachi
Kuala Lumpur   Madrid   Melbourne   Mexico City   Nairobi
New Delhi   Shanghai   Taipei   Toronto

With offices in
Argentina   Austria   Brazil   Chile   Czech Republic   France   Greece
Guatemala   Hungary   Italy   Japan   Poland   Portugal   Singapore
South Korea   Switzerland   Thailand   Turkey   Ukraine   Vietnam

Oxford is a registered trade mark of Oxford University Press
in the UK and certain other countries.

Published in the United States of America by
Oxford University Press
198 Madison Avenue, New York, NY 10016

© Oxford University Press 2014

All rights reserved. No part of this publication may be reproduced,
stored in a retrieval system, or transmitted, in any form or by any means,
without the prior permission in writing of Oxford University Press,
or as expressly permitted by law, by license, or under terms agreed with
the appropriate reproduction rights organization. Inquiries concerning
reproduction outside the scope of the above should be sent to the
Rights Department, Oxford University Press, at the address above.

You must not circulate this work in any other form
and you must impose this same condition on any acquirer.

Library of Congress Cataloging-in-Publication Data

Greher, Gena R.

Computational thinking in sound : teaching the art and science of music
and technology / Gena R. Greher, Jesse M. Heines.
pages   cm

Includes bibliographical references and index.

ISBN 978-0-19-982617-9 (hardback : alk. paper)—ISBN 978-0-19-982619-3 (pbk. : alk. paper)

1. Music—Instruction and study—Technological innovations.   2. Interdisciplinary approach in
education.   3. Computer composition.   I. Heines, Jesse M.   II. Title.

MT1.G825   2014

780.71—dc23   2013026018

9 8 7 6 5 4 3 2 1

Printed in the United States of America
on acid-free paper

Dedicated to Charles Eugene Saulters II (1984–2012), a student in our very first offering of *Sound Thinking* who encompassed interdisciplinarity all in one person. Charles was a musician, photographer, designer, producer, and artist who grew by finding the beauty in all aspects of his brief life. He was taken from us far too prematurely.

CONTENTS

ACKNOWLEDGMENTS

The work described in this book was supported by the National Science Foundation (NSF) Division of Computer and Network Systems (CNS) under Award No. 0722161, "CPATH CB: Performamatics: Connecting Computer Science to the Performing, Fine, and Design Arts." More recently it has been supported by the NSF Division of Undergraduate Education (DUE) under Award No. 1118435. Within that division, our work falls under the TUES program: Transforming Undergraduate Education in STEM (Science, Technology, Engineering, and Mathematics). Any opinions, findings, conclusions, or recommendations expressed in our materials are ours alone and do not necessarily reflect the views of the National Science Foundation.

In addition to the authors, our CPATH team included Fred Martin of the UMass Lowell Dept. of Computer Science, Jim Jeffers and Karen Roehr of the UMass Lowell Dept. of Art, Nancy Selleck of the UMass Lowell Dept. of English (Theatre), and Sarah Kuhn of the UMass Lowell Dept. of Psychology as our evaluator. S. Alex Ruthmann of the UMass Lowell Dept. of Music joined our CPATH team in the second year of that award. (Alex is now with the Dept. of Music and Performing Arts Professions of the New York University Steinhardt School of Culture, Education, and Human Development.) UMass Lowell student Daniel Gabriel served as a research assistant on this award.

Our TUES team consisted of the authors and S. Alex Ruthmann, Fred Martin, and Sarah Kuhn as above, plus Scott Lipscomb of the Univ. of Minnesota Dept. of Music Education as our external evaluator. UMass Lowell students Brendan Reilly, Angelo Gamara, Matthew Vaughan, and Zachary Robichaud served as research assistants on this award.

We also express our sincere thanks to the many UMass Lowell students who enrolled in *Sound Thinking* and the many college faculty and secondary school teachers who participated in our workshops for the lessons they have taught us about interdisciplinary collaboration, music, technology, and computational thinking.

Of course this book would not have been possible without the vision and expertise of our editor, Norm Hirschy. His support, insight, patience, and guidance made the entire planning and writing process run smoothly. We are also grateful for the wonderful production team of Lisbeth Redfield, Erica Woods-Tucker and Taylor Coe for keeping us and the book on track. We also like to give our thanks to the rest of the production crew.

Last but certainly not least, we thank our families, including our children, grandchildren and most gratefully, our spouses, Bonnie Heines and Larry Berger. They have lovingly supported us and put up with us through the grants, course development, presentations, and the writing of this book.

PREFACE

The intellectual challenge of teaching involves becoming a student of your students, unlocking the wisdom in the room and joining together on a journey of discovery and surprise.
Ayers & Alexander-Tanner, *To Teach: The Journey, in Comics*, p. 113

THINKING AND TEACHING BEYOND OUR DISCIPLINE-SPECIFIC SILOS

In the world beyond the confines of school, we are often confronted with problems that don't have easy-to-solve, one-size-fits-all solutions. This book presents our foray into dissolving the discipline-specific boundaries that inadvertently narrow our worldview, separate us from our colleagues' insights, and inhibit students from making important connections to modes of thinking outside the confines of their majors. We have each come to our current positions in higher education from the business world. Our own experiences working with diverse groups of colleagues, and often having to solve problems outside our own areas of expertise, inform our work with our students, our interdisciplinary course in computing+music that we call *Sound Thinking*, and each other.

While at first glance the pairing of a music professor with a computer science professor in one classroom might not seem to be an obvious collaboration, we have discovered the many commonalities we share in our thinking and goals for our students, as well as how our differences spark rich interactions in the classroom. In our first collaboration, we created, designed, and implemented a website for music education students to help them prepare for the music teacher licensure exam. This endeavor helped us realize that although we each brought different areas of expertise to this project, our combined discipline-specific knowledge, as well as our understanding of the other's field, contributed to the success and usefulness of the website.

Our Performamatics work continues to build on that first collaboration. The first iteration of Performamatics was based on the integration of computing, the performing arts (in our case music and theater), and visual art.

The subsequent development of the *Sound Thinking* course and the inter-disciplinary collaboration detailed in this book grew out of that work as we found a symbiotic relationship between computing and music. Our initial work was enhanced significantly by our music colleague S. Alex Ruthmann, who joined us in the second year of our first grant (the NSF CPATH grant detailed in the Acknowledgments section). Alex has taught *Sound Thinking* with Jesse and has worked with both of us to shape and refine the course as well as our thoughts on computational thinking. As with any worthwhile collaboration, we all continue to learn from each other.

Although collaborators can take many routes toward the development of an interdisciplinary course, and we certainly encourage you to explore alternative approaches to ours, we chose the development of computational thinking skills as the overarching learning objective for our students and our course. We believed that there were parallels between computational and musical thinking and that developing the types of learning processes and thinking skills inherent in this approach would benefit all students, regardless of their major. Our hope is to share with you, the reader, our particular journey into the exploration of computational thinking through music, the effects each discipline has on the other, and why we believe this approach benefits both students and professors.

HELPING STUDENTS LEARN ABOUT TECHNOLOGY THROUGH THEIR INTERACTIONS WITH MUSIC

The link between music and technology is inextricable. Digital technology has and continues to alter the way we produce and listen to music. It is now omnipresent in our culture. As its use continues to increase, the likelihood that musicians and technologists will find themselves involved in collabora-tive projects or work environments also increases. But beyond future pro-fessional collaborations, this interdisciplinary approach has the potential to engage students beyond just the typical music and computer science majors. As our enrollments grow, we are discovering that so are the pools of interested students from other disciplines.

While digital audio is a relatively new technology, the symbiotic relation-ship between music and technology actually dates back centuries. Consider, for example, the influence of technology and scientific thinking on the development of the modern piano. What began as a *harpsichord* with plucked strings and a narrow dynamic range evolved into the *fortepiano*, the pre-cursor to what we have come to know as the *piano*, an instrument capable of producing an extreme dynamic range from *pianissimo* to *fortissimo*, able to hold its own with a symphony orchestra. According to Selfridge-Field [9], at its development, the fortepiano was initially viewed more as a scientific than a musical invention. During the 1500s in Florence and much of Europe, it was not unusual for scientists to theorize about musical doctrine. New technologies, materials, and ideas regarding mechanical principles spurred instrument makers to try new approaches to their craft.

Several years ago, listening to the Carnegie Hall Jazz Band with Jon Faddis performing at Tanglewood, Gena's father (a musician who was for a time a member of Xavier Cugat's Orchestra as well as the orchestras for multiple Broadway shows) remarked that the technical expertise of today's musicians was far beyond anything he had heard in his day. This might be the result of advanced engineering in instrument design, which would help to make certain playing techniques easier to master. On the other hand, with so much recorded music available, musicians might be challenging themselves to master the playing styles they hear on recordings to eventually "best" their predecessors. In either case, there is a definite link between technology and music and it seems to be a positive one.

The abundance of interactive digital devices necessitates a workforce skilled in navigating multidisciplinary environments where computer science and the visual, performance, and literary arts converge to create new challenges and opportunities. Thus began our excursion into the creation of a general education course focused on the intersection of art and technology, exploring how music and sound are integrated into computer applications.

Our goal seemed simple enough: we wanted students to explore the art and science of digital audio. We planned to have them look at basic end-user applications that promote creative expression and thereby "hook" them into examining the underlying code that allows those programs to function.

However, once we began to examine what this meant from a novice perspective and to think about the software we would work with and the projects we would assign, things quickly got complex. We began to reevaluate and question our own assumptions about the purpose of general education courses and the challenges posed by teaching students outside our respective disciplines. We also came face to face with the challenges of creating a course that was truly interdisciplinary.

From the perspective of a music educator, a hands-on, interdisciplinary project approach allows music education students to gain real-world experience in understanding the benefits and pitfalls of implementing—and possibly designing—technology applications for students growing up under the influence of media. From the perspective of a science educator, the interdisciplinary approach allows computer science students to gain first-hand experience in the endless number of creative decisions that need to be made when designing a software program and the emotional impact that music can have on the end user of any application. In both cases, interdisciplinary work forces students to "think outside the box" to which they have grown accustomed, pushing them to see their work through eyes and ears very different from their own.

As our workforce moves to a more collaborative structure, it is important that students learn to work in teams that include people who may not share their skill sets and levels of expertise. They must learn to problem-solve the complex issues that arise when using technology. And as anyone who dabbles with technology can attest, there always seem to be problems to solve. Providing students with real-world learning contexts fosters an understanding of the interdependencies between sound, images, and technology. Interdisciplinary classes can break down the artificial boundaries of compartmentalized instruction that sometimes get in the way of meaningful and holistic learning. While much of schooling at the secondary and post-secondary level consists of very specific, discipline-based content, in our lives outside the classroom most of the issues we deal with and problems we need to solve require the kind of thinking that transcends these artificial boundaries.

HELPING STUDENTS SEE THE CONNECTION BETWEEN TECHNOLOGY AND MUSIC

We encourage you to think of this book as a resource on using technology and the digital arts as a means for constructing knowledge, whether you are an experienced teacher or a teacher in training. It starts at a place of almost universal interest for students: their involvement with music and technology. Technology instruction has traditionally focused on teaching *how* computers and software work and the terminology needed to discuss technology issues. What's been lacking is *context*: a clear understanding of how technology can be applied throughout one's educational, personal, and professional experiences. Many arts majors take a course in "technology" in which the subject is technology itself, devoid of context. In such courses, Woolley notes, the focus is typically on merely learning the "how-tos" of running particular software packages [11]. Yet as far back as 1995, SRI International argued that technology instruction should be structured around challenging tasks that prepare students for a technology-laden world [10].

We encourage anyone contemplating educational software development to consider these points, as well. An understanding of what engages students will give developers insight into how to develop interactive applications from multiple vantage points. If we keep students' interests in mind, we open the door for them to explore further on their own. Educators and educational software designers need to craft those moments where what we think students *should* do and learn intersects with what they actually *want* to do and learn.

TODAY'S COMPLEX PROBLEMS REQUIRE MULTIDISCIPLINARY SOLUTIONS

We often tell our students that once they graduate, they will never again work on a project all by themselves. Instead, they will always be working with others. In addition, their co-workers will often be people with backgrounds and points of view very different from their own.

The problems we face in our professional and personal lives are complex. Such problems often benefit from new ways of thinking, and one way to open students' minds to those new thoughts is to have them work on multidisciplinary teams. Another technique is to put them in situations where they are once again novices. Such situations increase their sensitivity to what it's like to approach a problem from the viewpoint of a "beginner."

Using a learner-centered approach that emphasizes project-based experiences, our goal is to provide you with multiple strategies to explore, create, and solve problems with music and technology. The projects we present encourage divergent thinking and promote divergent outcomes while supporting peer-to-peer collaboration, thereby also tapping into your students' social nature. Broad concepts are explored for each type of software application, and we attempt to present the perspective of the software developer as well as the end-user.

Our objective is to help you devise strategies that have educational value as well as relevance for students in terms of "real-world" applicability. We want to create learning environments that unleash students' imaginations while encouraging them to take risks. We want students to be adventurous in their thinking and creative in their problem solving.

In his book *The Children's Machine* [7], Seymour Papert challenged traditional schools of thought in which only certain types of knowledge are valuable. Through our own interdisciplinary work [4, 5, 6], we have learned, much as Papert suggested, the importance of students working on ideas and projects that are personally meaningful. As noted earlier, most technology instruction focuses on merely how to use technology without connecting the curriculum to the students' interests. We attempt to add that missing link.

COMPUTATIONAL THINKING FOR EVERYONE

Throughout this book we address digital audio issues, end-user preferences in multimedia software development, and the multiple perspectives inherent in an interdisciplinary approach. We provide examples of hands-on activities designed to expose students to current multimedia development tools and to encourage them to explore the basic principles that underlie today's technologies. The first three chapters are designed to frame our work philosophically, theoretically, and pedagogically. In Chapter 1 we explore what computational thinking is and how we operationalize it in our course. We do this by sharing with you examples from our work, along with examples of student work.

Much as the launching of Sputnik in 1957 generated interest in the development of educational projects to spur critical and creative thinking [2, 3, 8], we believe our country's current focus on producing the next generation of technological innovators through STEM (science, technology, engineering, and mathematics) education should include a healthy dose of the types of creative thinking supported by the arts. While the mixing of art and science is not incompatible, we do believe the structural limitations of most school curricula can often impede the best of educational intentions, as we outline in Chapter 2. Yet through our own experiences we remain confident that a good amount of problem solving, creative thinking, and collaborative skills, combined with an open mind toward taking an interdisciplinary approach to teaching and learning, can surmount the challenges.

The term "interdisciplinary" often means different things to different people. Chapter 3 walks you through the various definitions and provides examples of how we view these within the context of our own work. We have experienced several permutations of interdisciplinary teaching ourselves, via what our colleague Fred Martin has named "synchronized" and "hybrid" courses. "Synchronized" courses involve a joint, interdisciplinary project that intersects both of the discipline-specific courses each of us teaches. We detail the challenges and benefits of this model versus the "hybrid" course we ultimately created, which we call *Sound Thinking*. While one often thinks of "hybrid" courses as a blending of online learning and real-time, face-to-face classroom activities, we use the term "hybrid" to mean a general education course that is co-listed in each of our departments and in which both of us are in the classroom simultaneously, teaching together. This is an unusual model, to say the least, but the benefits to each of us have been enormous.

The next three chapters take you through the multiple ways we apply computational thinking in practice. As you will see, we are constantly exploring the similarities between the study of music and the study of computer science, not the least of which are the unique symbol systems and ways of representation employed by each discipline. Chapter 4 explores the theoretical and pedagogical underpinnings involved in learning and understanding these symbol systems through the various transformations of our *Found Instruments* project. In Chapter 5 we explore the new face of personal computing in the 21st century, the many entry points available for student engagement, and basic structural hierarchies, data, and file formats. Our philosophy behind the software platforms we adopt for our classes is explored in considerable detail in Chapter 6. We have found that ease of entry, as well as a low to nonexistent price point, can yield rich results with the right kind of project.

In the final three chapters, we take you through the details of setting up, assessing, collaborating, and sharing from both our own perspective as professors and that of our students. Chapter 7 discusses how to begin an interdisciplinary endeavor with a colleague and provides guidelines for getting a project or course off the ground. The challenges related to assessment are dissected in Chapter 8. When two heads from two different spheres of knowledge must come up with one grade, the challenges can be great. We provide examples of the types of rubrics we use and how we grade our students collaboratively. The final chapter explores the various web-based tools we use to stay connected as well as an overview of how the performance aspect of our Performamatics approach impacts our students and their learning.

It is our sincere hope that this book will help you and your students make connections between the practical applications of computers and the basic fundamentals of music. Together with our companion website, we hope that it will give you the resources and foundation for beginning your own journey into interdisciplinary teaching.

BIBLIOGRAPHY

[1] Ayers, W., & Alexander-Tanner, R. (2010). *To Teach: The Journey, in Comics*. New York: Teachers College Press.

[2] Choate, R. A. (1968). *Documentary Report of the Tanglewood Symposium*. Washington, DC: Music Educators National Conference.

[3] Dello Joio, N., Mailman, M., Halgedahl, H., Fletcher, G., Beglarian, G., & Wersen, L. G. (1968). "The Contemporary Music Project for Creativity in Music Education." *Music Educators Journal* **54**(7):41–72.

[4] Heines, J. M., Martin, F., Roehr, K., Jeffers, J., Greher, G. R., & Strukus, W. (2007). *CPATH CB: Performamatics: Connecting Computer Science to the Performing, Fine, and Design Arts*. www.nsf.gov/awardsearch/showAward.do?AwardNumber= 0722161, accessed 4/19/2010.

[5] Heines, J. M., Greher, G. R., & Kuhn, S. (2009). "Music Performamatics: Interdisciplinary Interaction." *Proceedings of the 40th ACM Tech. Symposium on CS Education*, pp. 478–482. Chattanooga, TN: ACM.

[6] Martin, F., Greher, G. R., Heines, J. M., Jeffers, J., Kim, H.-J., Kuhn, S., Roehr, K., Selleck, N., Silka, L., & Yanco, H. (2009). "Joining Computing and the Arts at a Mid-Size University." *Journal of Computing Sciences in Colleges* **24**(6):87–94.

[7] Papert, S. (1993). *The Children's Machine: Rethinking School in the Age of the Computer.* New York: Basic Books.

[8] Pogonowski, L. (2001). "A Personal Retrospective on the MMCP: A Manhattanville Music Curriculum Project Participant Reflects on Its Innovative Initiatives in Light of Current Curriculum Theory." *Music Educators Journal* **88**(1):24–27.

[9] Selfridge-Field, E. (2005). "The Invention of the Forte Piano as Intellectual History." *Early Music* **33**(1):81–94.

[10] SRI International. (1995). *Technology and Education Reform.* www2.ed.gov/pubs/ EdReformStudies/ EdTech, accessed 3/19/2010.

[11] Woolley, G. (1998). "Connecting Technology and Learning." *Educational Leadership* **55**(5):62–65.

ABOUT THE COMPANION WEBSITE

www.oup.com/us/computationalthinkinginsound

The companion website provides a wealth of material that complements the examples printed in the book. These include pictures, videos, and recordings of student work done in our *Sound Thinking* course as well as examples of teaching materials, skill inventories, and grading spreadsheets. In addition, the authors maintain a website at http://www. compthinkinsound.org with links to materials produced since the book was published, information on their Performamatics project, their contact information, and updates to the book.

 This symbol indicates that there is additional information and/or examples of student work related to the current topic on the companion website.

 This symbol indicates that there are sound samples related to the current topic on the companion website.

Computational Thinking in Sound

CHAPTER 1

Computational Thinking in Music Courses

How to Get Artsy Types to Start Thinking like Geeks and Vice Versa

WHAT IS COMPUTATIONAL THINKING?

When we began to develop our interdisciplinary course in computing+ music, which we call *Sound Thinking*, we made the deliberate decision that computational thinking would be the foundation upon which all of our projects would be based. But what exactly do we mean when we refer to "computational thinking" (CT) and what might it look like in practice? Jeannette Wing coined this term in 2006 [11] to characterize analytical thought processes that are subject-matter independent. She wrote:

> Computational thinking involves solving problems, designing systems, and understanding human behavior, by drawing on the concepts fundamental to computer science. Computational thinking includes a range of mental tools that reflect the breadth of the field of computer science.

While the "mental tools" of which Wing speaks may originate in—or at least be most visible in—computer science, she stresses that "computational thinking is a fundamental skill for everyone, not just for computer scientists." We wholeheartedly agree. Too often we see students attack problems in a hodgepodge manner, devoid of planning, hoping that trial and error will eventually lead them to a solution. When they are lucky enough to arrive at a desired result through random processes, students too often fail to understand or appreciate why a particular approach worked. This makes it impossible for them to generalize the approach and apply it to related problems.

Analytical skills are the essence of computational thinking. What's more, we feel that these skills are just as important to music and other arts majors as they are to computer science majors. Both groups are hampered by habit, which limits their abilities to imagine alternative possibilities. By getting students from disparate disciplines to work together, or at least by getting students to look at things from the perspective of someone whose discipline is different from their own, we aim to break the bonds of those habits and help students learn to think analytically. The desired result is a populace that not only knows how to solve problems and design systems but also one that possesses the "mental tools" to do so across a wide scope of problems. Unfortunately, the path to achieving that desired result is anything but clear. As suggested by Sawyer [9], "Innovation can't be planned, it can't be predicted, it has to be allowed to emerge" (p. 25).

OPERATIONALIZING COMPUTATIONAL THINKING

It's one thing to embrace the concept of computational thinking, but it's quite another to try to put it into practice. How can we demonstrate CT in action? How can we teach non–science majors to think analytically? What activities can we assign to help them discover and hone CT skills?

These questions are difficult to answer. They have been discussed and debated at length in articles, at conferences, and on listservs and weblogs (blogs). Google has attempted to provide "classroom-ready lessons and examples showing how educators can incorporate CT into the K-12 curriculum," but browsing these shows that they are all programming-related [3]. This is not surprising, given that Google defines CT as "a set of problem-solving skills and techniques that software engineers use to write programs that underlie the computer applications you use such as search, email, and maps" [4]. We feel that this definition is a bit narrow and would expand it to include what others call "algorithmic" or "analytical" thinking [7], but there is little agreement in the educational community on the nuances of differences between these terms.

Even Mark Guzdial, the prolific author of arguably the most widely read and certainly one of the most erudite and respected weblogs on computing education, admits that he is "as confused as anyone else [about] what 'Computational Thinking' means" [5]. In his post dated August 12, 2010,

Guzdial related two experiences that "highlighted...one aspect of CT...which I feel is *really* computational thinking" [emphasis in original]. Both experiences involved looking at data: one was his own record of distances he ran each day in an attempt to correlate that with the timing of injuries he sustained, and the other was graphs of Atlanta temperatures to substantiate or refute a reporter's claim that the past summer had been Atlanta's "hottest in 30 years." However, even these relatively straightforward examples generated numerous reader comments expressing wide disagreement as to whether they *really* demonstrated CT, and even more disagreement as to what constitutes CT itself. Here are two of those comments, edited for brevity.

Kevin Karplus [blogging as "gasstationwithoutpumps," actual name revealed with permission], a professor of biomolecular engineering at the University of California Santa Cruz:

I agree with you that getting lots of data is the heart of computational science, but I don't think that it is the "computational thinking" part. The analysis of the data is the CT....I distinguish between computational and algorithmic thinking. Algorithmic thinking concentrates on the method, the steps of the method, how things are done, [etc.]. Computational thinking relies on the existence of algorithms, but does not care much about how they work. [Karplus posted more extensive definitions and a discussion of their distinctions in his own blog (gasstationwithoutpumps.wordpress.com), where he states:] Algorithmic thinking is thinking about how to accomplish a particular end....Computational thinking is thinking about data by using computers to summarize, massage, or transform data into a more easily understood form. [7]

Fred C. Martin, a professor of computer science at the University of Massachusetts Lowell:

I think this is a great example of scientific thinking, and of working with data..., but I don't think it has much to do with CT. [Martin went on to provide his own example and concluded with:] I do think this algorithm is a good example of CT outside of a programming context.

[Guzdial replied:] I completely agree that your example is CT, but I don't see what criteria you're applying such that my example is not CT....What are the criteria by which we decide what is CT and what is not?

[Martin replied:] I think you hit [the nail] on the head with your question....I suppose there are various levels or categories, and really what we're after are lots of real-life examples of CT—especially, in non-programming domains—and then we can go about seeing how they relate.

Martin's point is exactly what we try to do in this book. Some of our examples may demonstrate CT and some algorithmic thinking (using Karplus's definitions [7]), but we don't think that the distinction is particularly important in this context. What is important to us as teachers of CT through interdisciplinary courses is that we get students to start thinking logically and critically, using data and algorithms rather than *only* trial and error to implement solutions that extend their creativity. We do not mean to minimize the value of trial and error, which is an important pathway to the discovery process. We merely wish to emphasize the importance of helping students think more analytically and systematically about processes and the progression of their ideas and actions.

A First Activity to Introduce CT

Here's a fun way to introduce CT in class. Begin by telling students that they're going to write down the series of steps—an "algorithm," if you will—for making a cup of tea, given that they have an empty teapot, a source of water, a working stove, a teabag, and a teacup. They'll quickly give you a sequence similar to this:

1. Fill the teapot with water.
2. Put the pot full of water on the stove.
3. Turn the stove on.
4. Wait for the water to boil.
5. Turn the stove off.
6. Pour the boiling water into the cup.
7. Put the teabag into the cup.
8. Wait until the tea is as strong as you like it.
9. Remove the teabag.

Of course there can be variations. Some students may want to interchange steps 6 and 7, and some may want to include steps for adding sugar or lemon or milk. That's fine. But it shouldn't take long to home in on a series of steps that the entire class can support.

You've now got an algorithmic solution to the original problem. Now tell the students that you want them to solve the same problem, but that they are to begin with a pot full of boiling water. Tell them that if they think of the algorithm they just developed as an atomic piece of data, it's actually possible to solve the problem in just two steps!

Most students will understandably claim that the solution is to skip the first five steps of the original algorithm and complete steps 6–9. But that's four steps, not two. If one thinks of the entire 9-step algorithm as a single piece of data, the two-step solution is to pour out the boiling water from the teapot and reduce the second problem to the first, which has already been solved! Performing the algorithm is then a single step, because you know it works and you don't even have to think about its component steps. Such an approach illustrates that CT involves thinking about all aspects of the problem as data.

Students will argue that the two-step solution is inefficient. They will say that it's crazy to go backward. But we do such things every day. We have all been in situations where we've tried to follow directions and gotten lost and decided that "it's easier to start over." In music, when you're rehearsing and trying to correct errors in a tricky passage, it's often difficult to start in the middle. It's more natural to go back to the beginning of a section or phrase, and then rehearse the passage over and over from there. This type of thinking relies on understanding structure, which is the basis of all data analysis, and which in turn is the basis of CT.

COMPUTATIONAL THINKING IN MUSICAL FLOWCHARTS

How might you demonstrate computational (or algorithmic) thinking in a musical context? Building on the earlier discussion, we suggest that one answer lies in viewing music as data and looking for patterns that we also find in computer programs. In yet another response to Guzdial's post, Charles Severance wrote:

> I think that the key point of your analysis (which I agree with) is that data is a great place to start with when it comes to developing computational thinking as a skill. Each of the examples you used was not only data, but it was data that was about people and/or something you could touch, feel, and see.... Computational thinking begins to grow as soon as they start looking at the information methodically.

Can we use music as data? Yes, we can. MIDI,[1] AIFF,[2] WAV,[3] and MusicXML[4] files can all be treated as data, as well as files in the alphabet soup of audio compression formats such as MP3, OGG, M4A, and so on. However, analyzing these types of data, particularly at the level of individual samples, is probably way beyond the scope of an introductory course. (Analyzing some of them is not, however, as we will discuss when we talk later about our use of MIDI.) In our work, we have therefore moved up to a higher level of abstraction, that is, to songs themselves.

Can songs be data? Yes, they can. It is easy to imagine a relatively simple computer program built from the wealth of "meta" information stored in MP3 files (see Figure 1-1). Students could create a program that builds a list of all the songs in their own music libraries and then "mine" those data using simple sorting and searching techniques to, for example, find all the songs sung by a given artist, written by a given composer, or recorded before a given date. But that's not really working with the *music*; it's working with the music's *metadata*. Such data is information *about* the song, but not the song itself. If you're familiar with iTunes® [1], you might agree that that program has a brilliant, efficient, and user-friendly interface for accessing the contents of one's music library according to the various musical attributes stored in metadata.

The students we teach find it much more interesting to work with the actual music itself. But where's the data in that music? One answer: "in the song's structure." Music students are familiar with describing song structures with letters, such as ABA and ABACA. But to get into CT, we need them to get more fine-grained. We need to get them to work with the notes themselves, to look for patterns in those notes, and to show their connections. A flowchart lends itself very nicely to this approach and leads directly into programming, as we will see later. Our colleague S. Alex Ruthmann

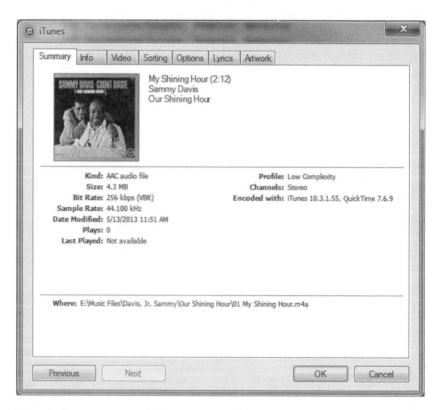

Figure 1-1:
Music metadata displayed in iTunes.® [1]

introduced the idea of having students flowchart songs when he taught *Sound Thinking* with Jesse in the Spring 2010 semester.

Consider, for example, the flowchart in Figure 1-2. Working with a song's lyrics is much more interesting than manipulating its metadata, and those lyrics are an integral part of—or at least a very reasonable handle on—the music itself. It is also easier for students with less (or no) formal music training to work with music that has lyrics. It's not impossible to label flowcharts for music (or a part of a song) that does not have lyrics, but it's a bit harder. You just have to figure out some way to refer to each part or musical chunk.

The beauty of musical flowcharts as an introductory activity or assignment in an interdisciplinary music and computing course is that students don't need to know anything at all about either musical notation or computing syntax to create them. They don't even need to know about standard flowchart symbols. All they need to know is how to draw boxes and arrows, hook them up, and add text to them. These tasks are pretty straightforward for today's students. Of course, much more sophisticated flowcharts can be created, but the important thing is that every student, regardless of background and discipline, can get fully and immediately engaged with CT without the need for an extensive conceptual lecture or a lot of handholding or scaffolding. As always, the examples presented in this book draw on the domains of music and computing, the focus of our course and this book,

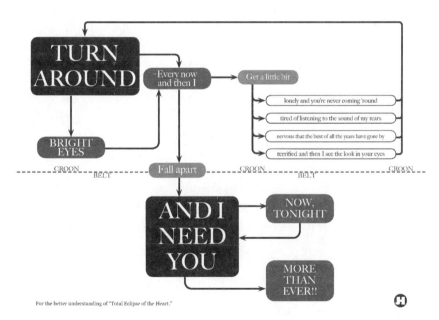

For the better understanding of "Total Eclipse of the Heart."

Figure 1-2:
A flowchart for the beginning of Total Eclipse of the Heart by Jim Steinman, as recorded by Bonnie Tyler. [6, 10] Copyright © 2009, Jeannie Harrell. *Reproduced with permission.*

but similar activities can be designed that cross disciplinary boundaries and encourage CT by students of all majors.

Chunking and Connecting

Where is the CT in musical flowcharts? We think there are two answers: (a) in the size of the chunks, and (b) in the ways they are connected. The former requires thinking about what constitutes a data item. If the chunks are too large, one can't see the song's repetitive patterns. If they're too small, one loses the essence of the song expressed in its phrasing. The latter requires thinking about process, that is, how the sequencing of the chunks contributes to the song's message and reinforces its melodic and lyric structures. Using Karplus's definitions [7], and as discussed earlier, some may classify the former as CT and the latter as AT (algorithmic thinking), but we feel that the distinction is largely academic. Both are equally valuable in helping students develop the "mental tools" (in Jeannette Wing's original definition) that they need to learn to apply to everyday problems.

The goal of the musical flowcharting activity is to have as few blocks as possible, or at least as few different types of blocks as possible. However, we don't state this goal before we turn students loose on the activity. Rather, we try to get them to discover the advantages of this goal on their own. To do that, we introduce the activity quickly and then let students play around with it. After 15 to 20 minutes or so, we interrupt them and ask a few students to show their flowcharts to the class (using an opaque projector or document camera). As we lead the discussion of these initial efforts, students often call out comments such as these:

- "If you move {x} into its own box, you wouldn't have to write it so many times in all those other boxes."
- "The song doesn't really go from {x} to {y}. You missed part z in there, which is really a distinct part all by itself."
- "It's easy to understand two arrows going *into* a box from different directions, but you've got two arrows coming *out* of box {a}. One goes from {a} to {b} and the other from {a} to {c}. How do I know when to follow the first path and when to follow the second?"

Some of these issues can be illustrated by Harrell's flowchart in Figure 1-2, so we will examine that in a bit more detail.

For this activity, we discovered that students will generally gravitate toward familiar songs that have a great deal of repetition. They also tend to work within a musical genre that resonates with them personally, as the following reflection by one student indicates.

> We worked together to create a flowchart to a song we were all familiar with: "Send Me On My Way" by Rusted Root. We had all heard the song before, but now [we] realized exactly how much repetition defined the form. When constructing our flowchart, we first paid attention to the lyrics.

Of course, the easiest place for students to find song lyrics is online, and there are numerous popular lyric websites of varying quality. Here's how the lyrics for the beginning of "Total Eclipse of the Heart" (shown above the dashed line in Figure 1-2) appear on **www.sing365.com** [10].

> *(Turn around)*
> *Every now and then*
> *I get a little bit lonely*
> *etc.*

We've chosen this particular website because the lyrics are well formatted, making it easy to see the patterns and recognize the repetitions. "Turn around" and "every now and then" clearly repeat multiple times, but it's in the fifth and sixth repetitions where "bright eyes" gets thrown in between these two and takes the song to a new emotional level. Thus, it's important that "turn around" and "every now and then" be seen as separate "chunks." Yet a close listening would reveal that on the third repetition of "Turn around," the phrase starts a minor third higher, helping to build toward the intensity of the next section. You wouldn't pick up on this fact just from looking at the flowchart or reading the lyrics. Said differently, it's hard to *see* these patterns when one merely looks at the printed lyrics, but it's easy to *hear* these patterns and subtle changes when one listens to the song. This is one place where it is beneficial to have students work in interdisciplinary teams; some wonderful discussions ensue as they help each other identify the patterns. This was brought out in a comment that a student posted in his reflection:

> The flowchart assignment highlighted how much structure and repetition go into music. Immediately after finishing part of my flowchart, it became apparent that there was a very specific structure to the song. My song ("Poker Face" by Lady Gaga) starts with a musical intro, goes into a verse, then to a pre-chorus and a chorus, then back to another verse.... The structural knowledge that I gained by completing this assignment helps explain how loops, if statements, and broadcasts[5] will be used successfully to create interesting music. We will basically be able to recreate flowcharts of our own songs using the Scratch blocks [8].

In mathematical terms, getting to as few blocks as possible is known as *factoring*. That is, one *factors out* the common elements and isolates them into separate boxes. This is precisely what programmers do when they write functions and subroutines: they take chunks of code that are repeated at various points in a program and isolate them into their own named blocks so that they can be "called" whenever needed. There are many benefits to organizing code in this manner.

- The code is clearer, making it easier to understand.
- The code is smaller, making it not only more manageable for humans, but also more efficient for computers to execute.
- If a bug is found, the programmer can fix it once and this will fix it everywhere that block of code is called.
- If the block is written well and in a generalized manner, the programmer may be able to use that function or subroutine in other programs without any changes at all, saving huge amounts of development and debugging time.

Thus, the analysis of songs through their lyrics and the "chunking" of those lyrics into the repeatable elements are clearly CT skills, as they have direct application in computer programming. As noted earlier, we don't think that all CT skills *have* to have direct analogies in programming, but this one does. Later we will see how these skills can be applied and practiced by programming mash-ups created from actual song chunks.

Once we have our chunks, the next step is to connect them. Here's where the flowchart in Figure 1-2 has a problem: when should one follow the path from "turn around" to "every now and then I," and when the path from "turn around" to "bright eyes?" Likewise, when should one follow the path from "every now and then I" to "get a little bit," and when the path from "every now and then I" to "fall apart?" Harrell's flowchart doesn't help us here. This can be solved by introducing numbers to indicate order when there are multiple possible paths. Given the layout of the flowchart, numbers don't seem necessary to indicate the order of the four phrases that follow "get a little bit," but we will see that even in that sequence there are numbers involved even if they're implicit.

Flowchart aficionados may wish to add diamond-shaped "if" blocks to Harrell's flowchart, and that would be fine, but simply having students add numbers as shown in Figure 1-3 in this situation suffices for us.

The numbering may seem obvious to some, but it is not at all obvious to others, because after you visit ❸ you have to go back to ❶. The key here is

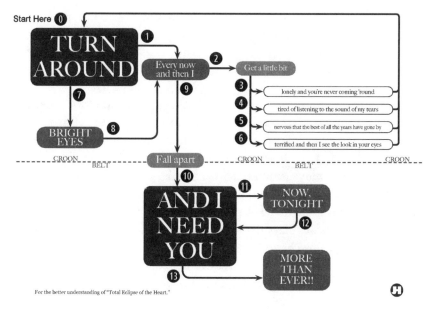

Figure 1-3:
Harrell's flowchart with numbers added to clarify flow.

to number the blocks such that (a) you must follow the arrows, and (b) you must visit every number before following a path to the next higher number, although you can visit numbers you've already visited any number of times. Thus, the paths through this flowchart are these:

❶ ❷ ❸
❶ ❷ ❹
❶ ❷ ❺
❶ ❷ ❻
❼ ❽ ❾ ⑩
⑪ ⑫ ⑬

There are many CT concepts here. Numbers. Counters. Loops. Incrementing. Conditionals. And even an algorithm. Returning to the geeky definition of CT on Google's website [4], we see that it lists "decomposition," "pattern recognition," "pattern generalization and abstraction," and "algorithm design" as specific techniques that are examples of CT. All of these techniques can be introduced using musical flowcharts.

While these concepts may seem simple to those of us who have already grasped them, to many students they are anything but. The most difficult lesson to teach is the meaning of incrementing to non-programmers, especially using a statement such as this one:

counter = counter + 1

That's probably the most commonly used statement in all of programming, yet it can be a real hurdle for non-science majors to get over. Even the seemingly obvious Scratch version of this statement can throw them: `change  counter ▾  by ❶` A musical flowchart can give these students the conceptual boost they need to clear that hurdle.

For example, most students can follow Harrell's flowchart intuitively without needing a lengthy explanation. But when we talk about writing a program that actually plays the song, things quickly get complicated. To connect the song flowchart to a computer algorithm and take the next step in computational thinking, we introduce the concept of a counter for the path (arrow line) to follow. The logic then works like this:

1. Initialize (set) the path counter to 0.
2. Play the chunk that follows the current value of the path counter.
3. Increment (add 1 to) the path counter.
4. Follow *as few paths as possible* to get to the path now in the path counter, replaying chunks previously played along those paths.
5. Go back to step 2.

There are, of course, no right and wrong ways to create musical flowcharts. Getting it "right" is not the point. Rather, the point is to get students to look at their world in a new way and, through music, to begin to think analytically and algorithmically. These aspects of CT are applicable in music as well as in computing, for if one understands a song's structure, it is easier to perform it with appropriate dynamics, expression, and emotion, or to interpret it in one's own way through variation or improvisation.

Added bonus #1 is that students start to see that music can be represented in something other than its standard form, which pays dividends in other interdisciplinary activities that we discuss in later chapters. One student commented on the benefit of this "new" way of representing music as follows:

> The first song that came to my mind was "Stairway to Heaven" by Led Zeppelin. This song is notorious in the musical world (particularly to guitarists) for having phrases that cycle and then change. This makes for an ideal candidate for a flowchart. . . . As I never would have thought, this project allowed me to become even more fascinated with this

legendary song. Mapping a song's progression not only lets you visualize the sequence of events, but forces you to truly listen to what's happening. I'm glad this was our song of choice because I had to replay this song at least ten times before the final chart was completed. And that was fine by me!

Added bonus #2 is that students work with music of their own choice, thereby maintaining interest. Added bonus #3 is that the chunks resulting from this work fit perfectly into future activities and assignments when we ask students to create new compositions from pieces of existing songs. This last bonus is underscored by a comment from one of the CS students in the class:

> As a computer science major, I was able to view the flowchart as a "computer program" as well. I was able to find various programming constructs such as looping and conditionals within the flowchart. This has helped out quite a bit with this assignment because I was able to use the chart to splice up my song.... Through this assignment, I learned to view musical structure in terms of programming. A lot of the concepts in our flowchart could easily be modeled via programming constructs such as loops and conditionals. I learned that I could essentially "block out" parts of the song into their own respective sections, then connect them via some kind of bridge. This is just like executing different blocks of code based on a condition. Having the flowchart made it much easier to see these internal structures, which will come in very handy when trying to unroll the song into Scratch code.

When we grade this assignment, we look, as always, for effort and creativity, but we also look specifically for elegance. That is, we look for flowcharts that are neat and clean and easy to follow, as well as those that have chunks that are truly indivisible "atoms" of the song. We consider how well students chunk the music to its most basic level, handle the song repetitions in a logical intuitive manner, understand the inherent structural hierarchy of the music, and represent the serial and parallel elements of the music.

The same characteristics define quality computer programs, the development of which we see as just as creative an endeavor as composing a piece of music. Thus, we believe that these exercises have real benefits for computer science majors as well as students in non-technical majors. When one gets beyond the restrictions of computer language syntax and grammar, programmers engage in a truly creative activity, crafting elegant solutions to interesting problems. We see that as completely analogous to what musicians do when they create and perform music after mastering the building blocks of music and the mechanics of their instruments.

STUDENT EXAMPLES

Student Jenna created the flowchart in Figure 1-4 for John Lennon's "All You Need Is Love" as performed by the Beatles and released in the United States on *Magical Mystery Tour*.[6] Jenna used simple boxes and lines but added color to differentiate sections of the song and add interest. We were delighted to see that she made the first "Love" block a heart rather than just a simple block. The rendering isn't perfect, but it clearly shows an understanding of the song elements and how they fit together.

Another excellent effort from student Josh is shown in Figure 1-5. This one is missing some words and needs arrowheads, but it succeeds at capturing the essence of the song's flow.[7]

Another approach is illustrated by student Kevin's submission in Figure 1-6. This flowchart also has some musical flaws and lacks arrowheads, but it illustrates what can be done using readily available software tools.

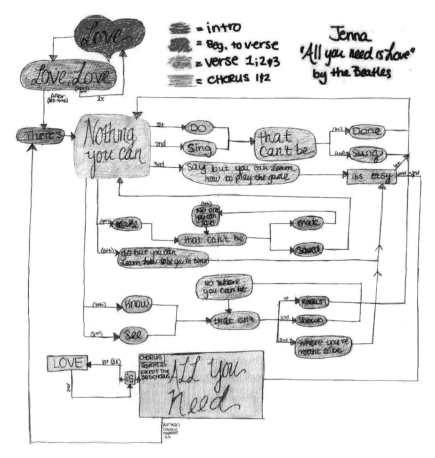

Figure 1-4:
Jenna's flowchart of the Beatles' *All You Need Is Love*.

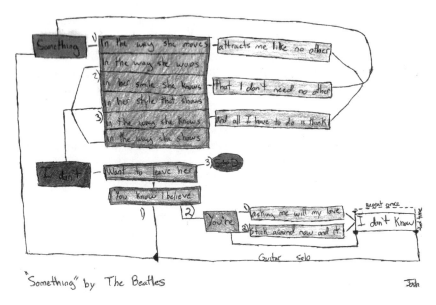

Figure 1-5:
Josh's flowchart of the Beatles' *Something in the Way She Moves*.

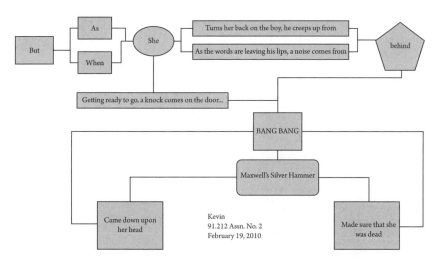

Figure 1-6:
Kevin's flowchart of the Beatles' *Maxwell's Silver Hammer*.

Some of those tools are expensive, but others are freely available on the web. What's most surprising is that one of the easiest to use flowchart-drawing programs is probably already installed on your own system!

 You will see additional student work including flowchart examples, reflections, assignment parameters, and computational thinking inventory on the companion website.

It just so happens that the ubiquitous Microsoft Office products have quite sophisticated tools for drawing flowcharts already built in, and most students can use these with little or no introduction (see Figure 1-7). The tools work especially well in Microsoft PowerPoint, perhaps because that program is more oriented toward working with shapes and lines than the other Office products, such as Word or Excel. For Mac users, many of our students found Keynote equally well suited for this assignment. The really cool thing about these tools is that once you connect two shapes with an arrow anchored to the shapes' side or corner "handles," you can move those shapes and the connector automatically adjusts its position to keep the arrow connected (see Figure 1-8). This saves a lot of time in laying out flowcharts.

A free, web-based program that a number of our students have found easy to use is at **flowchart.com** [2], shown in Figure 1-9. In addition to

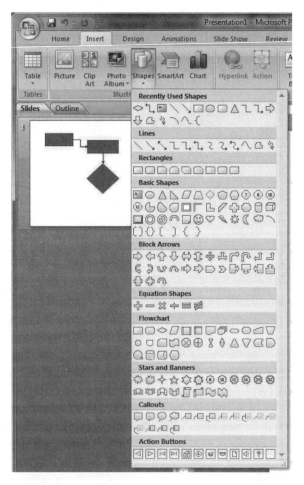

Figure 1-7:
Shapes and connectors in Microsoft PowerPoint.

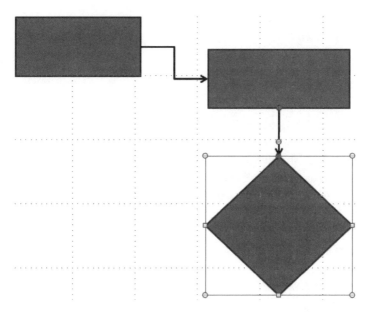

Figure 1-8:
Shape handles and arrow connectors in Microsoft PowerPoint.

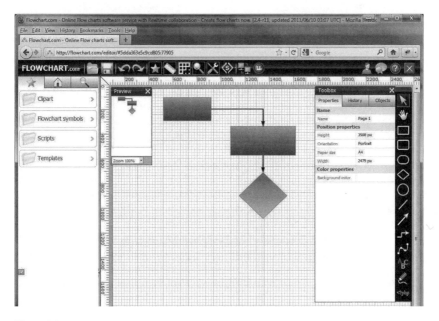

Figure 1-9:
Flowchart.com editor. [2]

providing terrific templates to get you started, an excellent editor, a wealth of clipart you can add to your flowchart, the ability to export your work into Adobe PDF format, and numerous advanced features, **flowchart.com** provides a place to store templates and the ability to share them with others.

LOOKING AHEAD

These examples should give you a pretty good feel for how we teach CT using music, and hopefully they should "prime the pump" of your own thoughts for developing similar activities or adapting ours for use in your courses. There are many more examples to come. The next chapter describes how we get students started even before we do the flowchart assignment and presents more of our approach in context.

BIBLIOGRAPHY

[1]   Apple, Inc. (2011). iTunes (ver. 10.3.1.55).

[2]   Flowchart Software (2011). *Online flow charts software service with realtime collaboration.* (Version 2.4-r11, updated 2011/06/10 03:07 UTC.) flowchart.com, accessed 6/12/2011.

[3]   Google (2011). *Exploring Computational Thinking: Lessons and Examples.* www.google.com/edu/computational-thinking/lessons.html, accessed 6/3/2011.

[4]   Google (2011). *Exploring Computational Thinking.* www.google.com/edu/computational-thinking, accessed 6/3/2011.

[5]   Guzdial, M. (2010). *Go to the Data: Two Stories of (Really) Computational Thinking.* Computing Education Blog. computinged.wordpress.com/2010/08/12/go-to-the-data-two-stories-of-really-computational-thinking, accessed 6/2/2011.

[6]   Harrell, J. (2009). *Koufukuron ("On Joy").* jeannr.tumblr.com/post/165291081/i-made-a-flow-chart-that-we-might-better, accessed 12/25/2009, reproduced courtesy of the author.

[7]   Karplus, K. (2010). *Algorithmic vs. Computational Thinking.* "Gas station without pumps" blog.gasstationwithoutpumps.wordpress.com/2010/08/12/, accessed 6/3/2011.

[8]   MIT Scratch Team (2009). *Scratch.* scratch.mit.edu, accessed 12/21/2009.

[9]   Sawyer, R. K. (2007). *Group Genius: The Creative Power of Collaboration.* New York: Basic Books.

[10] Steinman, J. (1983). *Bonnie Tyler* "Total Eclipse of the Heart" *Lyrics.* www.sing365.com/music/lyric.nsf/total-eclipse-of-the-heart-lyrics-bonnie-tyler/fb0f584f5cd507a448256 9910025c3c1, accessed 6/12/2011.

[11] Wing, J.M. (2009). "Computational Thinking." *Journal of Computing Sciences in Colleges* 24(6):6–7.

CHAPTER 2

Imagination and Creativity

The School-Based Paradox

Those who have been required to memorize the world as it is will never create the world as it might be.

Groch, *The Right to Create,* p. 219

WHO IS CREATIVE AND WHY DOES IT MATTER?

People who are considered "creative" are generally respected and sought after in our society, both in the professional and social realms. Yet among the many paradoxes of our educational system is the strange fact that it does little to encourage a child's imaginative and subsequent creative potential. As discussed by Judith Groch in her book *The Right to Create* [7], one reason might be a strongly held belief that creativity is innate and something one is born with. You either have it or you don't. Another reason might be the difficulty in assessing creativity objectively. Unlike questions and problems with only one right answer, how can you make an objective value judgment on a student's creative output?

But imagine a young Pablo Picasso growing up in 21st-century America and attending a public school dominated by high-stakes testing. According to a case study by Howard Gardner in *Creating Minds* [6], our young Picasso had great difficulty mastering his numbers. Other than his artistic inclinations, which were nurtured by his family, he was an unremarkable student. In most of today's public schools, Picasso would be force-fed a fairly prescribed curriculum that would ensure mastery of test-taking techniques but would be mostly devoid of opportunities for personal self-expression. In fact, in a climate focused on high-stakes testing, little attention would even be given to the arts. Picasso's unique and imaginative vision of the world would probably be squelched for not conforming to the accepted adult views of how one draws the sun, trees, or sky. According to Feldman, Csikszentmihlayi, and Gardner, in *Changing the World: A Framework for the Study of Creativity* [5], creative people are shaped as much by their early experiences as by the natural abilities they are born with. Absent a home life where artistic insights are valued and nurtured, how many future Picassos are walking around America's schools right now who will never know their potential because they will never come into contact with those experiences? How many future inventors, performers, scientists, and composers are currently being stifled by a system that is at odds with providing the conditions for imaginative and creative experiences?

Consider the following scenario. If Gena and Jesse walked into a cocktail party, who would be considered the more "creative" of the two? Why, certainly you would pick Gena. The general perception is that people in the arts are the creative types and by extension the cocktail party attendees would most likely assume that Gena, the musician, would be more creative than Jesse, the computer scientist, and therefore Gena would be the more interesting person to talk to. Yet based on the actual school paths of most music students, the majority of their educational experiences are focused on the *re-creation* of art. They learn to master their instruments by playing someone else's original music. Few, if any, of those school experiences focus on actual acts of creative inspiration, exploration, and decision making. In fact, their music teachers and ensemble directors most likely make the majority of decisions with regard to the music's interpretation. While there is no doubt that a great deal of "doing" music through performance ensembles is taking place, the point is that in a typical music student's education, there is rarely much emphasis on actually creating something original.

Computer science (CS) students, on the other hand, may spend a great deal of educational capital learning programming languages and sitting in lecture classes analyzing algorithms, in what many would consider to be a technical rather than a creative pursuit. Yet at the end of the day the CS students will more than likely be asked to create something from nothing, although admittedly within limited parameters. Their end results may not be monumental in scope, may only be the result of their own personal worldviews and understandings, and may not transform the field of computer science. However, the very act of creating something new from just a germ of an idea is very empowering. In both cases, the music and CS students are being asked to apply what they are learning, which is certainly preferable to just passively receiving content. But the CS student might have the edge in problem solving. Our schools' overwhelming emphasis on external rewards (otherwise known as grades) and quantifying the learning process stifles students' sense of exploration and minimizes the amount of creative, risk-taking effort they are willing to expend.

It may actually be a tie as to who is the more creative person, Gena or Jesse, but you certainly can't assume that a musician will be more creative than a computer scientist or that one field of study is more creative than another. This chapter is in no way making any claims that if you follow our suggestions you and your students will magically be transformed into creative geniuses. However, we do believe in the value for you as teachers to create those conditions that will support a student's curiosity and imagination through risk taking and divergent thinking, even within a system designed more for conformity and convergent thinking. Why should this matter?

THE WHAT AND WHY OF EDUCATION

What is it that we truly hope to teach our students? In reality, how many names, dates, and places do people really need to know in their jobs, in their lives? Facts are facts, and with the proliferation of technology, one can find much of the information needed through a couple of computer keystrokes. The bigger question is *what* should be the purpose of learning these facts, and *why* do your students need to learn them? Just knowing the facts is pretty meaningless unless your students are given a context within which they can explore, discover, and understand how these events and facts affect them.

Unfortunately, over the past few decades there has been a major push to increase the number and types of courses that are fact-oriented, and the number that involve multiple solutions and judgment skills has dwindled. Is the point of all this schooling to turn out a mass array of walking and talking encyclopedias, or are we looking to produce leaders and thinkers who will be able to come up with solutions to problems no one has yet thought of? Elliot Eisner believes that it is through the process of imaginative transformation that human beings are able to conceive what is not, but what will be [3].

Therefore, one of your objectives might be to help your students develop their creative potential and encourage dispositions that will help them experience the world from multiple perspectives. As teachers, you will want to use all means at your disposal to construct the kinds of learning environments that encourage students to take risks, be adventurous in their thinking and problem solving, and unleash the imaginations that our present system tries so hard to stifle. And therein lies the rub! As Sawyer makes clear in *Group Genius: The Creative Power of Collaboration*, "creativity is associated with low pressure work environments" [10] (p. 48). The time constraints built into the very structure of school—with rigid testing and class schedules—work against the type of less-pressured environment that supports creative thinking. And a low-pressure environment is also one that can turn out students who might be motivated more by their own curiosity than by just getting a good grade. Before we explore how you might create those environments, even within the limitations of a typical school day, let's briefly review some of the key points in creativity research and how we view our work within the context of that research.

A BIT OF BACKGROUND

In the early part of the 20th century, researchers linked creativity to intelligence. Behavioral psychologists believed that intelligence and creativity were innate biological traits, unaffected by outside influences. During that time, "intelligence quotient" (IQ) tests came to dominate and impact the educational landscape and were used as a means of sorting students according to their level of "giftedness" as determined by these tests [2, 5, 7, 10]. Groch, however, points out that

> as a predictive measure of "intelligence," the tests, in fact, inspect a narrow range of intellectual performance, placing heavy emphasis on the ability to recall, to recognize, and to solve certain kinds of problems, but ignore other, equally important aspects of intelligence: imagination, innovation, discovery, and the ability to recognize what is relevant. [7] (p. 87)

These were tests of convergent thinking and shaped much of the educational methodologies at that time. By mid-century, tests measuring divergent thinking were introduced, first as developed for adults by Guilford and later modified for children by Torrence [5]. The late 1950s and early 1960s also brought us the Sputnik era, which generated a great deal of interest in creativity tests to identify the most promising young students for intense training in technology and science to help serve the national interest [5]. This fact underscores for us the important role creative thinkers can and do play across all disciplines.

By the mid-20th century, cognitive psychologists began to look at the study of creativity as "a distinctly human process . . . showing that much of what goes into the process of creativity actually comes from outside the individual" [7] (p. 3). This shift toward thinking of creativity as a *process* rather than a *trait* suggests that one can build upon and improve one's innate capacities. This does not, as Feldman points out, deny a person's biology or the fact that some individuals may be more gifted in some areas than others [4]. In this regard, Piaget's contribution to developmental psychology and creativity research cannot be overstated. Piaget developed constructivist theories regarding how one's experiences with the world and how one interprets those experiences can change, impact, and reorganize an individual's knowledge structure over time. He laid the groundwork for psychologists, sociologists, and educators to develop new theories of cognition and development with regard to creativity. Piaget's research led to understandings of creative people as those who have the ability to transform existing bodies of knowledge [4].

Defining what creativity is and how it manifests itself, as well as who—according to those definitions—is creative, has occupied creativity researchers over the years, and for the most part is beyond the scope of this book. For our purposes, however, two views espoused by Feldman, Csikszentmihalyi, and Gardner [5] would be a good place to start. They define creativity as either Big "C" Creativity or small "c" creativity. In their view Big "C" Creativity "refers to achievement of something remarkable and new, something that transforms and changes a field of endeavor in a significant way" [5] (p. 1). They suggest that this type of creativity has enduring value. Feldman, Csikszentmihalyi, and Gardner's framework for studying creativity focuses on three areas [5]:

• The field, which focuses on the job or craft.
• The domain, which centers on a body of knowledge.
• The individual person, who through the acquisition and transformation of knowledge has the ability to affect and change a field and a domain.

Small "c" creativity, on the other hand, is "the tendency to bring a fresh and lively interpretation to any endeavor, whether humble or exalted" [5] (p. 2). While we would be thrilled to have the next Mozart or Einstein in one of our classes, we suspect that other forces that shape those Big "C" Creatives, both internal and external, are probably beyond the capacity of traditional schooling to generate. It is therefore this second view of creativity, the small "c" interpretation, that can more readily be fostered within an educational setting in general, and an interdisciplinary approach in particular.

In fact, we believe that before you can get to the little "c" creativity, you have to first move your teaching closer in practice to Peter Webster's perspective of concentrating on developing "creative thinking" [11]. Webster believes that this way of looking at creativity places the emphasis on the "process itself and on its role in music teaching and learning" [11] (p. 23). Although in this instance Webster is discussing creative thinking in the context of a music classroom, we believe that this perspective is relevant to most classrooms, as he further describes creative thinking as a "dynamic mental process that alternates between divergent (imaginative) and convergent (factual) thinking, moving in stages over time" [11] (p. 28). David Perkins describes the relationship between critical and creative thinking as follows: "The creative thinker has to be critically aware, because creative thinking, except in the simplest situations, involves the generation and sifting of possibilities and reworking them. That has to be a critical process" [2] (p. 15).

Perkins's research has led him to believe that "in general, creative people call upon their minds with questions different from those less creative people ask of themselves" [2] (p. 14). So how might you move the needle in your class toward a culture of creative and critical thinking?

BUILDING A BETTER MOUSETRAP: LEARNING ENVIRONMENTS THAT FOSTER IMAGINATIVE AND CREATIVE EXPERIENCES

Consider a typical lecture-based classroom. The teacher is in the front of the room delivering information. Depending on how engaging the teacher is, the students are either receiving the information through listening or note taking, or they are "tuned out" and counting the minutes until the next class, bringing them closer to the end of their school day. Either way, most of the thinking is being done by the teacher. More likely than not, the students will be assessed through some kind of test rather than being given an opportunity to apply what they are learning. Think of it this way: most tests are designed for questions to have one right answer, not a range of possibilities. This isn't exactly an optimum environment for encouraging those "what if" moments brought about by analytical, critical, or creative thinking, is it? In an overall school culture where your students are programmed to seek the "right" answer, courses designed to let their imaginations take over and to underscore the importance of exploring problems that can have multiple solutions will help prepare them for the reality of a world that is far from neat and orderly.

As you will see in Chapter 4, we have been through a variety of permutations of our Found Objects project. In our synchronized course, students re-purposed jacket zippers, irons, shoes, recyclable garbage, and cereal boxes for musical ends. Over the many offerings of this course we have had several fans and other electronic appliances serve as musical instruments, yet no two compositions or sets of notations have been identical. One student, through exploring the sounds created by the various speeds of her electric hand mixer, discovered that she could play "Taps" on her mixer. Were these students involved in critical and creative thinking? Certainly. Were there some who demonstrated greater engagement than merely fulfilling yet another assignment? Absolutely! Several years ago, in a Music Methods class, a student devised a "recyclophone" from his collection of recycled garbage. He created an inventive notation system that was intuitive enough to allow another student to play the instrument. When that other student began to perform the composition, to everyone's delight we were hearing a quirky rendition of the opening phrases of "The Blue Danube." In reflecting upon this activity, the creator of the "recyclophone" remarked:

> One thing I noticed in this lesson was how unique our "instruments" were and how many different ideas about tone colors and notation we had as a class. Everybody was trying to express a distinctive musical thought with their instruments, whether it was a melody or just a combination of sounds. Playing other people's instruments really made us think analytically and creatively about figuring out how to "break the code." It also made us work together and use each other's ideas.

We can never predict the outcomes of this project and there are always surprises, but on some level we are devising situations that support setting students' imaginations loose.

 Here you will find videos of student presentations as well as assignment parameters and student reflections.

So by now you are probably thinking, "What is the optimum environment?" Just as we wouldn't espouse creating projects with one best outcome, we think there can be a variety of optimal classroom environments. The one that is best for you and your students will ultimately be determined by the goals of your course. For our purposes we think it would have these qualities:

- *Is playful and fun.* While we are serious about our work, we don't necessarily take ourselves so seriously that we come off as unapproachable and/or absolute authorities in our subjects where only one perspective would be considered. All questions are welcomed and multiple perspectives are sought.
- *Is collaborative.* Students are encouraged to ask a lot of questions: of the teacher, of each other, and of themselves.
- *Provides space for exploration and discovery.* You may need careful planning to find the right balance between delivery of content and ample time for your students to mess around with the materials and absorb and apply the information in a meaningful context.

- *Offers support and encouragement of risk taking*, for the students and professors alike. We as teachers need to be comfortable with not always knowing the answers, and sometimes our students may know more about a given area than we do. We must be willing to explore and discover along with our students.
- *Encourages curiosity and internal motivation* without fear of ridicule or failure from either the teacher or fellow classmates.

TOWARD CREATING MEANINGFUL PROJECTS

Let's take a closer look at each of the listed points with respect to some projects you and your students might do.

Playful and Fun

For starters, there is the not so benign aspect of *playfulness and fun*. We believe that there should be a sense of *fun* and *play* in the classroom, even though these qualities are getting a bad rap in educational circles these days. A great deal of research suggests that having fun, a sense of play, and a lack of external controls all contribute to fostering creativity [2, 8, 9]. This is yet another paradox when considering how to teach creative thinking in a school-based environment. If you follow the discourse on the American public education system and its shortcomings, particularly with regard to the push to test students at earlier and earlier ages, you will no doubt notice that recess, playtime, and those subjects where students can express themselves are being squeezed out of the curriculum.

In the *Social Psychology of Creativity*, Beth Hennessey states that "while engaging in a task that they find intrinsically interesting, individuals feel that their involvement is free of strong external control: they get the sense that they are playing rather than working" [8]. In our culture, through listening to our elders' stories and taking our cues from TV shows and movies, we have an image of the worker as a drone, and work as the drudgery one does to satisfy the basic needs of existence. Should we have any energy left, this hard work will allow us to eventually play, provided we have any spare time. On the other hand, Gena's mother, who performed in both professional and amateur orchestras, never said she was "going to work." Rather, she would declare that she was "going to play." To her, working was not synonymous with doing a chore. It was merely what she loved to do, and with any luck, she would get paid to do it. However, in all of the talk about standards and accountability in public education, we can assure you that *fun* and *play* will be noticeably absent from the conversation. We can also assure you that without encouraging fun and play in your class and your projects, intrinsic motivation will be absent as well.

What could be more playful and fun than asking your students to listen to their favorite music and then create 300-second (5-minute) mash-ups that will reveal to the listener something about who each one is as a person? We call this our "audioethnography" project, and we truly require it to be exactly 300 seconds, neither a second more nor a second less. Students get a chance to revisit and explore some of their favorite music and re-mix it to create a musical narrative about their favorite topic: themselves. The real purpose of this assignment is to get them to explore the Audacity program that we cover in Chapter 5. However, to complete this project they will need to play around with the different effects that Audacity offers and hone their editing skills. Those tasks are so far in the background, however, that they never intrude on their personal motivation to create something they are proud to share with the class. We have found that the exact timing aspect of this assignment serves to keep the students organized and their ideas succinct, forcing them to reflect critically on their work and edit it carefully.

 The reader will find the assignment parameters and rubric along with student reflections on this assignment.

Collaboration

The "audioethnography" assignment is obviously not a collaborative project. We believe that before we can ask students to work together on projects, we need to first let them get their feet wet working with music and technology on a couple of solo projects. They then move up to pairs and larger groups. As we point out in Chapter 3, the 21st-century workplace is a collaborative environment, whether people are in the same room or oceans apart, connected via the Internet. Since a great deal of schooling takes place on the individual level, if you build in opportunities for collaboration you will help your students sharpen those skills they will need in the world of work. Being a good collaborator requires many skills, including listening, social interaction, accommodation, teamwork, and being able to critique positively others' work and ideas.

As you may recall from the flowchart assignment in Chapter 1, we required our students to work in pairs or groups of three. This could have been an individual project, of course, but our goal in pairing students with different strengths was to have them teach each other and ultimately produce something together that was better than what they could have accomplished individually. In this case, critically analyzing a piece of music aurally may not be an activity many students are comfortable with, just as creating a flowchart may be a new experience for others. But as our students pointed out in their reflections, in most cases they were each able to contribute something different to the whole.

How did collaborative skills manifest themselves in the flowchart assignment? For one thing, the students first had to agree on a song: accommodation. They then had to listen to the music multiple times, focusing on the lyrics as well as on the music itself. Next, they had to discuss and listen to each other on how they might chunk the music: listening, social interaction, and positively critiquing the ideas of others. Last, they had to practice teamwork. One student noted this in her blog:

> Andy and I, as music majors, were able to listen to the song and analyze the form. We also picked out certain instrumental timbres, such as a whistle or a guiro. Chris, a computer science major, put the flowchart into a document so it looked neat and legible and could be easily followed by one who was listening to the song. Overall, I think we made a good team.

Of course, not every group will have such smooth interactions, and you may find yourself with students unwilling to accept the ideas of others or to relinquish control. You might need to be a mediator for some groups and it might take some trial and error before you find the right groupings of your students.

There are complex social dynamics in play here. While there are certainly challenges to group collaboration, the benefits far outweigh them. This brings us to the *control* factor, which is another educational paradox. Too much control will stifle creativity, while too little will lead to chaos. This is a concern for you as well as for your students. One of the issues Sawyer points out with regard to workplace creativity and group dynamics is that group flow increases when people feel autonomous, which requires members to manage the paradox of needing to be in control while simultaneously maintaining flexibility and openness to the ideas of others [10].

Exploration and Discovery

A space for exploration and discovery in this interpretation refers not to physical space but to carving out enough time to allow your students to freely explore the material just learned. This is of particular importance when you are introducing new concepts either musically or computationally. In one class we introduced two specific musical intervals and their respective inversions,[1] as well as how to represent those intervals within the Scratch program. In this instance, before even getting to those specific intervals, Gena introduced the class to a chromatic scale and how it would look in traditional notation as well as in Scratch. Since each note in a chromatic scale is a semi-tone from the next note, Gena was able to demonstrate how musical intervals such as major 2nds (two semi-tones) and perfect 5ths (seven semi-tones) are formed. While music students are generally comfortable with intervallic concepts, translating these into the language of Scratch made their heads spin. It was equally problematic for the non-music majors. By giving them time and space to explore some simple exercises together in class, ask questions and play around with the program, the students were able to tackle the next composition assignment in Scratch based on the 2nds and 5ths intervals covered in class.

 You can view class demos as well as student examples.

Risk Taking and Curiosity

We will be the first to admit that maintaining a sense of low pressure is challenging when you have a syllabus to get through within a limited time frame and looming deadlines. Perhaps with the right environment and projects your students can get beyond thinking about their grades long enough to let their imaginations and curiosity take over. That's probably wishful thinking, since most of their schooling is focused on grades either positively or negatively. But if you can design a series of tasks and projects that pique your students' interests, as some of the projects we discuss demonstrate, a fair number of them will begin to focus on the questions and problems they are interested in solving, while thoughts about grading hopefully recede into the motivational background.

We are not just interested in creativity as it relates to student output. We also believe that creativity and creative thinking have an equally important role in the teaching process. Your actions as a teacher—both how imaginatively you execute your lessons and how you interact with your students—will by extension affect your students' thinking and creativity. As stated decades ago by composer Warren Benson and equally relevant today,

The creative child could be any child. The teacher's responsibility may not be to separate those who are creative from those who are not, but rather to encourage all students to be creative, to enjoy the pursuit of creation.... To decide that a certain child has a limited future is to shut off the teacher's opportunity to help him achieve a goal that is still unknown to both of them. [1] (p. 40)

In setting the stage for enabling creative experiences for students, both Wiggins [12] and Benson [1] suggest the need for teachers to "get out of their students' way," which we believe is pretty good advice.

Perhaps the greatest creativity paradox built into our education system is the fear of failure. Sawyer emphatically states, "There is no creativity without failure" [10] (p. 55). In fact, most successful people will point to a particular failure of theirs that prompted one of those "ah-ha!" moments leading to their subsequent successful product, project, or business plan. Since most schooling and most high-stakes testing are predicated on questions that have only one right answer, our students are conditioned from an early age to see the right answer as its own reward. Mistakes, whether in answering a question in class or a test, playing a wrong note, or even writing bad code, result in feelings of failure. Reinforcement of those negative feelings will eventually cause students to retreat from speaking out, taking tests seriously, or putting themselves "out there" to try a new idea. It also sends the subliminal message that only certain kinds of ideas are welcome, leaving students to be less willing to take risks in the future. We think that devising a curriculum around meaningful projects that support multiple outcomes and that students can gear toward their personal interests is one way to send a message to our students that their ideas really do matter.

THE YIN AND YANG OF CREATIVITY AND THE COLLABORATIVE PROCESS

Teaching in a manner that encourages students to engage in all manner of imaginative, critical, and creative thinking requires careful curriculum re-envisioning and planning. Changing deeply ingrained systems that run counter to a more constructionist pedagogy that fosters creative thinking may require several iterations before you find the right balance of instructional approaches that you and your students are comfortable with and that match the goals of your class. A good rule of thumb is to consider every class and every project a work in progress, since implementing this type of experience requires you to be open to ideas presented by your students that you may not have thought of yourself.

Becoming an effective collaborator is a learned skill and, like anything else, it takes practice. Putting people together and asking them to work together will reveal an array of character traits and issues that your students will need to negotiate. This is where listening to others, learning to be flexible, and letting go of control are central to positive results. An interesting point raised by Sawyer with regard to the collaborative process and the notion of group brainstorming is that "critical analysis should be put off for later" [10] (p. 60). He cautions that team members should hold off on evaluating ideas until the group has finished generating them. The rationale Sawyer presents is that groups generating a larger quantity of ideas will have a greater chance of finding that one good idea in the mix. In closely examining the issues that prevent our own student collaborators from being successful, we often hear that one member of the group feels as if his or her ideas are being shot down by one or more of the other members. It takes a fair amount of self-control to be able to listen to ideas you don't necessarily agree with while withholding any kind of comment.

As an example of the power of brainstorming, consider the following story that Jesse heard many years ago.[2]

> Several telephone company executives are sitting around a conference table trying to figure out how to remove snow from their telephone lines, which is weighing them down, causing them to sag, and impeding transmission quality. One executive suggests shooting current through the wires to warm them and melt the snow. Another suggests transmitting a high-pitched sound to vibrate the wires until the snow falls off them. Picking up on that idea, a third suggests training birds to fly over the wires while flapping their wings vigorously to knock the snow off. Everyone laughs, but this seemingly crazy idea leads to the ultimate solution: flying a helicopter low over the wires and letting its downwash knock the snow off them.

One way to help your students understand how to develop positive group dynamics is to first model a group brainstorming session in one of your classes. Start with a simple problem where you just generate ideas and make a list. Taking a cue from Sawyer, it's a good idea not to solicit any critiques until all the ideas have been generated. At that point, it's safe to ask students to come up with a positive and negative critique for each of the ideas. When they run out of critiques, it's then safe to start narrowing down the list. Another approach, which thwarts identifying a particular student with any particular idea, is to ask each student to generate a list of ideas, write them down on paper, and put them into an "idea box." That way, every generated idea is anonymous. You can then go through the critiquing process.

As we hope you will discover, creating a work environment that is conducive to letting imagination, curiosity, and creativity flow will yield tremendous benefits to you and your students. We realize that changing your pedagogical approach might take a leap of faith at first, but our own experiences confirm that the benefits outweigh the challenges. We are not suggesting that this will be an easy transition. However, once you find your risk/flexibility sweet spot, like a good brainstorming session, the ideas will just keep flowing.

BIBLIOGRAPHY

[1] Benson, W. (1973). "The Creative Child Could Be Any Child: Drawing Out Inherent Creativity in Compositional Experiences." *Music Educators Journal* **59**(8):38–40.

[2] Brandt, R. S. (1986). "On Creativity and Thinking Skills: A Conversation with David Perkins." *Educational Leadership* **43**(8):12–18.

[3] Eisner, E. W. (1988). *The Role of Discipline-Based Art Education in America's Schools.* Stanford, CA: J. Paul Getty Trust.

[4] Feldman, D. H. (1994). "Creativity: Proof That Development Occurs." In D. H. Feldman, M. Csikszentmihaly, & H. Gardner, eds., *Changing the World: A Framework for the Study of Creativity.* Westport, CT: Praeger.

[5] Feldman, D. H., Csikszentmihaly, M., & Gardner, H. (1994). "A Framework for the Study of Creativity." In D. H. Feldman, M. Csikszentmihaly, & H. Gardner, eds., *Changing the World: A Framework for the Study of Creativity.* Westport, CT: Praeger.

[6] Gardner, H. (1993). *Creating Minds.* New York: Basic Books.

[7] Groch, J. (1969). *The Right to Create.* Boston: Little, Brown.

[8] Hennessey, B. A. (2003). "The Social Psychology of Creativity." *Scandinavian Journal of Educational Research* **47**(3):253–271.

[9] Moran, S., & John-Steiner, V. (1994). "Creativity in the Making: Vygotsky's Contemporary Contribution to the Dialectic of Development and Creativity." In D. H. Feldman, M. Csikszentmihaly, & H. Gardner, eds., *Changing the World: A Framework for the Study of Creativity.* Westport, CT: Praeger.

[10] Sawyer, R. K. (2007). *Group Genius: The Creative Power of Collaboration.* New York: Basic Books.

[11] Webster, P. (1990). "Creativity as Creative Thinking." *Music Educators Journal* **76**(9): 22–28.

[12] Wiggins, J. (1999). "Teacher Control and Creativity." *Music Educators Journal* **85**(5): 30–44.

CHAPTER 3

Interdisciplinary Teaching and Learning

Two Heads Might Actually Be Better than One

YESTERDAY AND TODAY

I n this interconnected, socially networked, 24/7, multidimensional, media-centric culture, your students are doing just fine creating, performing, and making things without your help. Thanks to the proliferation of user-friendly, intuitive software applications to create, capture, and perform music, as well as websites that allow easy showing and sharing of these creations, your students can lead very productive, creative, and expressive lives without the baggage of learning traditional music notation and computer code. This realization sends shudders through some of our fellow professors, but nonetheless it is a reality of our times. You can choose to fight these trends and hold fast to the traditions of an educational system designed for another era and different priorities, or you can meet your students where they are.

Much of education has been about the transmission of subject-specific content with a focus on the individual. This fosters competition for the teacher's attention and top grades. Hierarchical classrooms perpetuate the notion of teachers as authority figures and decision makers while suppliant students wait for the teacher's knowledge to be bestowed upon them. Socialization is rarely encouraged inside the classroom. On the other hand, the modern workplace is flattening its hierarchical structure and becoming ever more dependent upon critical thinking skills, collaboration, teamwork, and shared decision making. In fact, many corporate offices are being designed physically to foster collaboration through shared offices and informal small lounges where workers can gather to brainstorm [4]. Learning to work with others is a lifelong endeavor. These skill sets don't develop in a vacuum. They need to be nurtured through modeling and experience. As suggested by John-Steiner [6], students need to be socialized into the culture of collaborative work and the kinds of creative and critical thinking the new workplace requires.

As you will discover, collaborative work yields processes and results that are far richer than any that a single person's expertise can produce. John-Steiner calls this "creative collaboration": "In collaborative work we learn from each other by teaching what we know; we engage in mutual appropriation. Solo practices are insufficient to meet the challenges and the new complexities of classrooms, parenting, and the changing workplace" [6] (p. 3). However, we found out both by observing the students in their project teams and reflecting on our own interactions as teachers that collaborative work creates a complex dynamic where diverse ideas and opinions are continually being challenged and negotiation is a constant presence. It quickly became clear that creating interdisciplinary assignments and forming multidisciplinary student teams to share the work is not enough. Getting team members to actually learn new skills from their peers in other disciplines simply would not happen without a great deal of mediation and guidance from us, the teachers.

DEFINING INTERDISCIPLINARY TEACHING

So what exactly do we mean when we say that a course is "interdisciplinary"? There are many definitions and variations, some involving one teacher presenting multiple perspectives and others involving team teaching.

Interdisciplinarity is often described as "the integration of disciplinary perspectives" [7], which in our case would be music and computer science. It is often confused with "multidisciplinary," which Spelt et al. [12] describe as "additive," presenting multiple perspectives without the integration of the disciplines or opportunities for students to synthesize knowledge from them. Davis [2] points to the need for "blurring genres" and "synthesizing disparate sources into new knowledge." He claims that the disciplinary focus of much of higher education cannot adequately address the issues confronting 21st-century thinking. Davis is an advocate of faculty working in teams, believing that teams can achieve what individual disciplinary specialists cannot.

We embrace Davis's last point wholeheartedly. To us, it takes two to tango. We feel that the only way to give students a truly interdisciplinary experience is to have a professor from each discipline present at all class

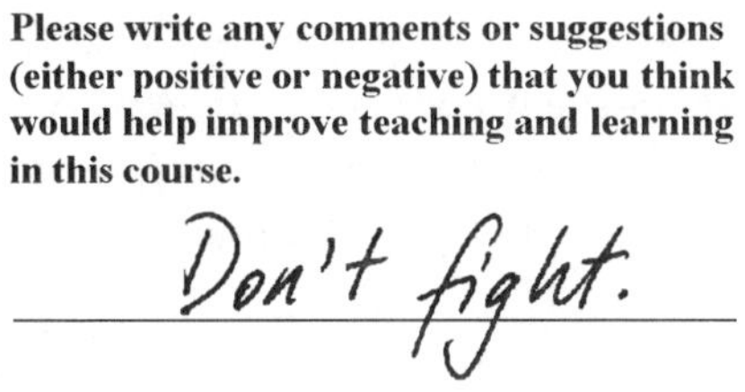

Please write any comments or suggestions (either positive or negative) that you think would help improve teaching and learning in this course.

Don't fight.

Figure 3-1:
A student comment on our teaching.

meetings. We understand the logistical problems that this presents, and we address those in a later chapter. We also understand the differences of opinion and perspective that will arise in class, but we see no need to hide those from students. As the comment shown in Figure 3-1 makes clear, we do not shy away from our differences; we embrace them.

We fought?!? Wow. We didn't think we fought. But that's how this student characterized some of our interactions on an end-of-semester Course Evaluation form. We may still have a lot to learn about how to get our different perspectives across without appearing to "fight," but teaching an interdisciplinary course is and always will be a work in progress that is full of unexpected surprises. In addition, rather than trying to homogenize our perspectives of each other's fields, we find that those differences foster a creative and fruitful environment that stimulates not only student learning but ours as well.

When those differences result in squabbles, we believe that everyone in the room—including the teachers—learns from the resolution of those differences. It almost goes without saying that throughout this work Gena has learned a lot about computing from Jesse, while she in turn has taught him to think more deeply about the sounds he hears and even the horizons of what he considers to be "music." The dual perspective of our collaboration, and our attempt to share both perspectives with students, is therefore the essence of what we define as interdisciplinary teaching.

"SYNCHRONIZED" VERSUS "HYBRID" COURSES

One of the first decisions you will need to make is whether to take the plunge into interdisciplinary teaching, either by revising and rethinking an entire course or by beginning with a small well-defined project. Our first foray was project-based and probably closer to the "additive" multidisciplinary approach. We put students together from regular classes that we were already teaching, *General Music Methods* and *GUI Programming*. (GUI stands for graphical user interface.) Our colleague Fred Martin dubbed these "synchronized" courses [8]. Students did a project that we describe later in detail, but suffice it to say at this point that the students in each course did their parts of the project independently. We professors taught our classes independently of each other, except for the few times during the semester that we brought our classes together to share, discuss, and evaluate their work as shown in Figure 3-2.

The synchronized courses showed some positive results, but we wanted more. We wanted students from different disciplines to work together throughout an entire semester. We therefore developed what Martin [8] termed a "hybrid" course, co-taught with both of us in the classroom simultaneously. This is *Sound Thinking*, focusing on the study of sound from the perspective of digital musicianship.

Like Don Marinelli and Randy Pausch at Carnegie Mellon University, Gena and Jesse "personified the mix of arts and technology; right brain/left brain, [music gal]/computer guy" [11] (p. 124). In Pausch's book *The Last Lecture*, we could easily substitute our own names for Don's and Randy's:

> Given how different Don and I were, at times we became each other's brick walls. But we
> always managed to find a way to make things work. The result was that students often got
> the best of our divergent approaches (and they certainly got role models on how to work
> with people different from themselves). [11] (p. 125)

Figure 3-2:
Usability test by an interdisciplinary Music + CS team.

As discussed earlier, we didn't try to hide our differences and differing perspectives, which led that one student to think we were "fighting" when we let our bantering go a bit too far.

LEARNING FROM EXPERIENCE

As you begin to develop your interdisciplinary experience, be mindful of setting up regular meeting times before and during the semester for planning, reflecting, and modifying some of the course details. Strong communication and the ability to evaluate one's work "in process" are essential to a successful collaboration. You and your colleague should attempt to make a conscious effort to find a common class meeting time and try to set aside specific days when the classes will meet as one. As we both learned from previous attempts at this, it's a good idea to introduce the project together and build it in phases. You may also wish to think about setting up multiple planning meetings before the beginning of the semester as well as scheduling regular meetings throughout the semester to evaluate, reflect upon, and make modifications to the project as needed.

The following comment, from one of the music education students, pretty well sums up the class sentiment when they were informed that we would be working on an interdisciplinary project with a group of computer science students.

> We were introduced to the computer science majors from Jesse's class this week. I think that the class had mixed emotions about this. A lot of people were wary because of the project that we did in tech class.

Many of these music education students had participated in a previous interdisciplinary project. They therefore initially greeted the prospect of this project with a great deal of apprehension. One student wrote in her journal:

> The first thing I thought when I saw the computer science students: Oh, great. Another team of people [who] will never get back to us and make our grades suffer.

A subsequent journal entry by this same student showed a significant change of heart:

> The computer science students know how to read symbols and try to put a meaning to them quicker than most. I enjoy having them come and participate in our classroom activities.

The music education students were quickly won over by the fact that we had arranged for so much in-class contact with the CS students, which resulted in substantial bonding between students who would normally never even come into contact with each other.

You may also wish to consider building in time for the students to evaluate each other's work. Peer-to-peer feedback is invaluable to the learning process, particularly with a diverse group of students with different strengths. As previously suggested with regard to the definition of computational thinking, we sometimes get hampered by our habits of mind and modes of thinking. Getting students to think about solutions from another person's perspective will help develop their analytical thinking skills, one of the benefits of a computational thinking mindset. In our case, when the teams were required to present their work, we did it as one class. This made it possible for CS students to comment on the work of and give feedback to the music students, and vice versa. In addition, the students developed an appreciation for the differences in thinking and learning styles and the creative thinking that formed a common link between them. This was confirmed by comments in another student's journal:

> I feel that this time we have more support from the professors involved and that the CS students are more into the idea. I like how the project has benefits for both sides. It allows us to be able to think back to the beginnings of notation and to communicate our ideas with little to no explanation to people who have no musical background. For the CS students, they get a taste of what it is like to work for a client and to interact with people to give them a final product that is efficient.

What resulted was a successful collaboration all around, based on what, for the most part, fits the definition of an interdisciplinary project. The general sentiment of the music education class with regard to this new collaboration, was summed up by one student:

> Boy, do I really like to have the CS students in our class! I feel we are really becoming one class, not just two classes in the same room. It's great to have other voices in the class, and to provide perspective from students outside the music department.

"Not just two classes in the same room." What better confirmation could we have asked for? We were pumped, but could we do it again and make it last an entire semester?

Building an entire interdisciplinary course around a long-range project or thematic idea can be a daunting task without a clear idea of your purpose for doing this in the first place. In the case of our own class, our goal was to create an entire interdisciplinary course for all students interested in music technology and how to manipulate it. Or, more to the point, we were going to have students "get under the hood" to discover how these programs work. We therefore based our strategies and projects on the interdisciplinary synchronized course module we created for computer science and music majors.

Whether you are attempting a single interdisciplinary project or developing an entire course, you may want to use the following questions to help frame your thinking and planning:

1. What is it that you hope to gain with regard to your students' learning?
2. How will this impact your own personal and professional growth?
3. What will be the overall benefits? What barriers will you have to overcome?
4. What compromises will you have to make when you enter into a long-term collaborative endeavor?
5. And, most important, how exactly are you defining interdisciplinarity with regard to your content and teaching?

In our case, our rationales for developing the new course were straightforward. For music education majors, there are few opportunities to gain immersion into areas of study outside their discipline, let alone the technologies that may support and enhance their work. Even students in our Sound Recording Technology program sometimes lack sufficient opportunities to understand the programming and visual aspects of multimedia technology that support much of their work. At the other end of the spectrum, those who design and build software applications have few opportunities to pursue in-depth study of multimedia applications from the perspectives of the audio and visual artists who are their end-users.

Whatever your rationale, one of your goals should be to break down boundaries created by compartmentalized instruction and have your students see their own work through an interdisciplinary lens. You will find that such experience is critical in preparing students for the multidisciplinary workplace, regardless of their major field. In particular, you will find that interdisciplinary experience is critical to students interested in working with and understanding digital media from the perspective of creating with sound.

BENEFITS TO STUDENTS

Boix Mansilla and Gardner [1] believe that merely teaching subject matter does not draw upon or challenge students' intuitive understandings of the world. They suggest that every discipline has its own ways of thinking about the world and communicating its ideas. In their view, "students develop a disciplined mind when they learn to communicate with the symbol systems and genres of a discipline" [1] (p. 104). In our case, that might start with musical notation or computer code. However, as one becomes immersed in a discipline, one quickly realizes the limitations of such symbol systems. After a rather detailed demonstration of the value and limitations of both traditional musical notation and more inventive graphic notation, one student commented:

> One of the things we've often debated in class is the issue of freedom [and] artistic limitations [imposed by] the method of sound production and notation. In other words, what things inhibit our ability to perform and create naturally, or what things stop us from thinking "outside the box"?

We set out to explore broad concepts through the lenses of our respective disciplines and integrate those concepts within a project-based learning environment. We put students into the position of decision makers, a role they do not often occupy [3]. Boix Mansilla and Gardner suggest that such projects give students multiple opportunities to develop "performances of understanding," in which students are invited "to think with knowledge in multiple novel situations" [3] (p. 105). They discuss at length the importance of training students to think like the practitioners in the various fields of study they encounter during their schooling.

So what does this mean for your students and why should you care? In our case, one of our goals was to give students "real-world" experiences. Perhaps the fact that we both began our careers in the world of business might have something to do with shaping our perspectives on the skills and thinking that our students will need once they leave our classrooms.

Among the many advantages of interdisciplinary courses is that these courses encourage and support creative risk taking and the ability to accept ambiguity [10]. This would seem to benefit professors, as well as students.

BENEFITS TO THE PROFESSORS

The benefits to you as teachers can be profound as well. Joint classes with a faculty member in another discipline can present significant learning experiences, breaking down the isolation that faculty sometimes feel within one's own department or discipline. Course planning conversations and project meetings are opportunities for reflective practice allowing you to explore ideas about pedagogy and the skills necessary for students to be truly well educated. The ability to revisit what you teach and how you teach with a new perspective has the potential for professional revitalization in a manner that typical professional development workshops may not always accomplish.

A River Runs Through It is not only the title of a movie but also a very real description of the physical and ideological divide that separates the left and right brain thinkers of our campus. Our university is divided by the Merrimack River, with our North Campus housing the math, science, and engineering departments on one side and our South Campus housing the arts, humanities, and social sciences on the other (see Figure 3-3). While there are many opportunities for *faculty* within a single department or college to interact in terms of committees, dinners, and research symposia, the demands of scheduling blocks, the differences in each major's curriculum requirements, and the variations in each department's promotion and tenure requirements make it far more difficult for science and arts colleagues to interact in any kind of meaningful way.

In the world of interdisciplinarity, we, Gena and Jesse, would be known as "early adopters," at least at our university. We began collaborating several years before our Performamatics project was funded by the National Science Foundation and before interdisciplinary endeavors were "the thing to do" on our campus [5]. Our paths crossed through a university-wide grant opportunity in which we developed an online practice test for the music teacher certification exam. Early in that project we discovered that even though we approached issues from differing perspectives, talking through our ideas and differences of opinion often led us to end results neither of us anticipated at the outset.

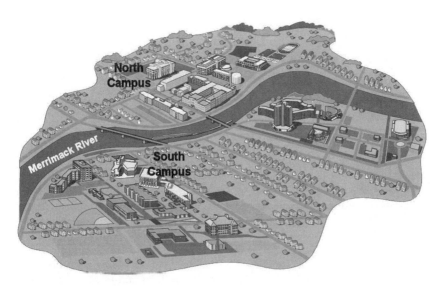

Figure 3-3:
"A river runs through..." our university.

Here are some of the benefits we experienced. We are fairly certain that others can experience these, as well:

- You will each learn a lot more about the other's discipline.
- You can attend and present your work at conferences in each other's field, further expanding your respective knowledge of the other's disciplines.
- You will most likely receive significant recognition within your own university, raising your profiles. In our case we were each invited to serve on university-level committees that may influence the future of interdisciplinary teaching at our institution.
- You will be introduced to other colleagues in your respective departments, thereby expanding the scope of your work, leading to new collaborations and possibly to grant applications.

On top of all that, if our experiences are any indication, you will quite simply have a lot of fun. This last point should not be taken lightly. The National Science Foundation program that funded our own work was conceived to "revitalize undergraduate education in computing" [9]. As we strove to achieve that goal, we found that the process revitalized us as educators. Such faculty revitalization is clearly key to educational transformation, because while faculty are not always the major source of curriculum *innovation,* they are—and for the foreseeable future will remain—the major component of curriculum *implementation.*

BIBLIOGRAPHY

[1] Boix Mansilla, V., & Gardner, H. (2009). "Disciplining the Mind." In M. Scherer, ed., *Challenging the Whole Child: Reflections on Best Practices in Learning.* Alexandria, VA: ASCD, pp. 97–106.

[2] Davis, J. R. (1995). "Reengineering Teaching for 21st Century Learning." *Educational Record* **76**(4):16–23.

[3] Greher, G. R. (2006). "Transforming Music Teacher Preparation through the Lens of Video Technology." *Journal of Music Teacher Education* **15**(2):49–60.

[4] Halbersgerg, E. (2012). "TPG Architecture Helps Global PR Firm Weber Shandwick Make the Move to a More Collaborative Mindset in Its New Chicago Offices." *Interiors Sources Magazine* **28**(5):96–101.

[5] Heines, J. M., Martin, F., Roehr, K., Jeffers, J., Greher, G. R., & Strukus, W. (2007). CPATH CB: *Performamatics: Connecting Computer Science to the Performing, Fine, and Design Arts.* www.nsf.gov/awardsearch/showAward.do?AwardNumber=0722161, accessed 4/19/2010.

[6] John-Steiner, V. (2000). *Creative Collaboration.* New York: Oxford University Press.

[7] Lattuca, L. R., Voigt, L. J., & Fath, K. Q. (2004). "Does Interdisciplinarity Promote Learning? Theoretical Support and Researchable Questions." *Review of Higher Education* **28**(1):23–48.

[8] Martin, F., Greher, G. R., Heines, J. M., Jeffers, J., Kim, H.-J., Kuhn, S., Roehr, K., Selleck, N., Silka, L., & Yanco, H. (2009). "Joining Computing and the Arts at a Mid-Size University." *Journal of Computing Sciences in Colleges* **24**(6):87–94.

[9] National Science Foundation. (2010). *CISE Pathways to Revitalized Undergraduate Computing Education (CPATH).* www.nsf.gov/funding/pgm_summ.jsp?pims_id=500025, accessed 4/19/2010.

[10] Nikitina, S. (2005). "Pathways of Interdisciplinary Cognition." *Cognition and Instruction* **23**(3):389–425.

[11] Pausch, R., & Zaslow, J. (2008). *The Last Lecture.* New York: Hyperion.

[12] Spelt, E. J. H., Biemans, H. J. A., Tobi, H., Luning, P. A., & Mulder, M. (2009). "Teaching and Learning in Interdisciplinary Higher Education: A Systematic Review." *Educational Psychology Review* **21**:365–378.

CHAPTER 4

Notation and Representation

How We Get 'Em to Crack the Code

In the beginning was the noise...
Hart & Lieberman, *Planet Drum*

GATEWAYS, BARRIERS, AND BOUNDARIES

M usic can and does exist without notation. In fact, its existence predates what we have come to accept as traditional music notation. Many musical traditions have thrived for centuries without any kind of formal codified symbol system to make musical replication easier. Music has existed, and often still exists, as an aurally transmitted art form.

The same can't be said for computers. Though the tongue-in-cheek Hart and Lieberman quote at the beginning of the chapter gets to the heart of the aural and intuitive nature of music's origins, computer code relies on complex mathematics built, amazingly, on the seemingly simple 1s and 0s of binary arithmetic. Yet just as with music, there are tools and applications that your students can use to express themselves without even thinking about the underlying mathematics. For many of your students, the act of creating, whether it's making music or developing web content, is accomplished intuitively, without formal training and knowledge of the "tools of the trade": musical notation and computer code.

Sherry Turkle asserts that "today's children are growing up in the computer culture; all the rest of us are at best its naturalized citizens" [21]. Following that line of reasoning a bit further, let's assume for a moment that for your students music and computers are ingrained components of their culture. As is sometimes the case, however, the formal acquisition of these tools can often serve as a barrier to further understanding rather than the gateway this knowledge is meant to serve: impeding rather than enabling the creative process.

Gardner feels that formal musical training can "be the beginning of the end of most children's musical development" [7] (p. 38). He believes "the challenge of musical education is to respect and build upon the young child's own skills and understanding of music rather than impose a curriculum designed largely for adults" (p. 38). Bamberger's research with college students suggests that students of any age possess musical instincts that, in the proper environment, can be developed and nurtured [1]. One of your goals, then, might be to engage students in projects that help them to investigate the *why* and *how* of the symbol systems used in both fields, as well as to understand the boundaries imposed by these systems. As suggested by Torff and Gardner, "People may be symbol-using creatures, but we do not know automatically how to make sense of symbols. We have to learn to read (decode) and create (encode) symbols" [20] (p. 98).

If musical notation isn't necessarily intuitive to your students, how might you help them learn it in a way that builds on what they already know? And rather than being an insurmountable impediment, how might you help them discover the necessity of creating a common symbol set while simultaneously recognizing its complexities and limitations? In this chapter we explore one project's evolution from its original simple acoustic inception through a variety of digital permutations and extensions.

FOUND INSTRUMENTS PROJECT: GOALS AND OVERVIEW

The Found Instruments project—within the context of a course designed for music teacher education—is focused on helping students experience acts of music exploration, intuition, creation, and composing from the perspective of a child before the imposition of formal musical training. Gena typically assigns it to music education students in their General Music Methods class but has used variations of it at a wide range of grade levels.

Students are asked to find typical household objects that can produce several pitches or timbres. They then fashion a "musical instrument" (Figure 4-1) from these "found objects" and create a musical composition (Figure 4-2) that adheres to a common musical form. Once the composition is crafted, students are asked to devise a system of creative/graphic notation to somehow "preserve" this piece of music for others to perform and enjoy.

Of course, with inexpensive, readily available digital technology, one could "preserve" the music simply by recording a performance. But the idea

Figure 4-1:
Andy demonstrating how to play his toaster as a found instrument.

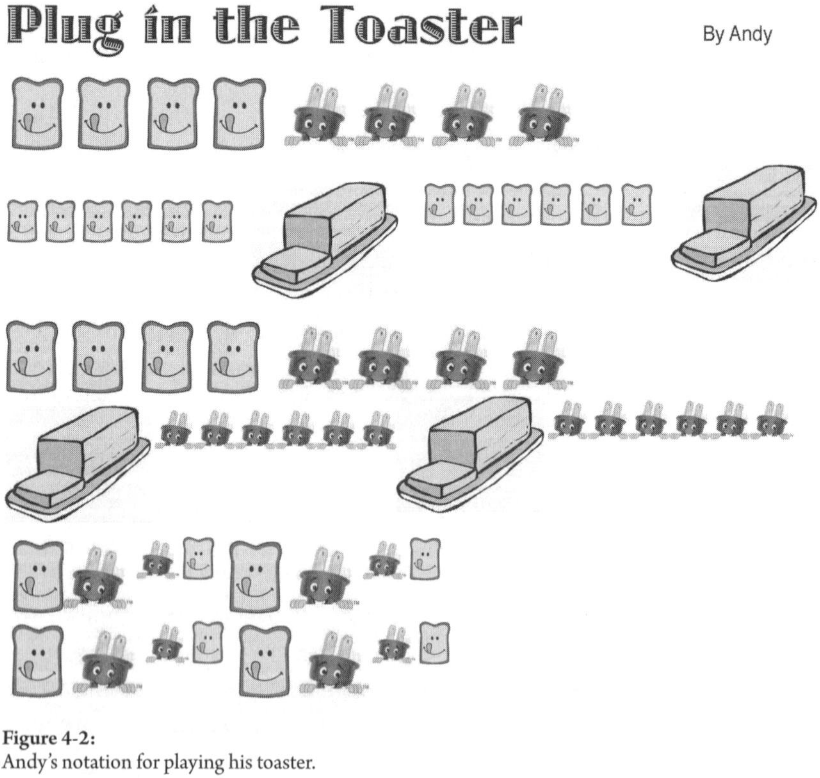

Plug in the Toaster

By Andy

Figure 4-2:
Andy's notation for playing his toaster.

is to get your students thinking about how people would have done this *before* such technology was available and *before* a formal notation system was in place. As noted earlier, learning musical notation can be an impediment to music making for many students. The Found Instruments project encourages students—particularly those preparing to be teachers of music—to think about how a total novice goes about learning a new symbol system. Through this activity, students begin to appreciate the relative simplicity of traditional music notation. They begin to comprehend the difficulties in creating a universal symbol system designed to transmit a variety of dynamic data: one that transcends languages and cultures. (See Figures 4-3 and 4-4.)

A BIT OF BACKGROUND

Experimenting and creating music with found sounds, as well as using invented notation, is by no means a new or novel practice. As composers in the early 20th century began to expand their aural palette beyond traditional musical instruments and musical structures by using found sounds and electronically generated sounds to augment more conventional ones, the need to find alternative modes of representation formed the basis for what we generally refer to as invented or graphic notation [15]. In fact, this practice still continues. Found sound compositions continue to make their way into today's concert halls such as "Kraft" written by Magnus Lindburg in 1980 and recently performed by the New York Philharmonic, and "Junkestra" written by Nathaniel Stookey and performed by the San Francisco Symphony [11, 19, 23]. In both cases, various members of each orchestra scavenged local garbage dumps and spent time exploring the various pieces of garbage for "percussion instruments" that produced just the "right" sounds. Not surprisingly, the seeds for Tod Machover's[1] inclinations toward creating music using traditional Western musical instruments as well as a greatly expanded sonic palette were planted in his youth by his mother [12]. As a toddler, through his mother's encouragement to find music within his house, he learned the basics of music composition.

> Each week, we set out on expeditions of her devising, discovering household objects that made interesting sounds that could in turn be combined to create new textures, emotions, and narratives. Then followed the task of making a "picture" of our new composition so that we could recreate it the following week. I learned to invent music from these first principles: sound, structure, score. [12] (p. 14)

The more traditional approach to music teaching generally begins with a series of learning objectives based around concepts that are unfamiliar to

Figure 4-3:
Matt playing Zori's *ZoriPhone* found instrument.

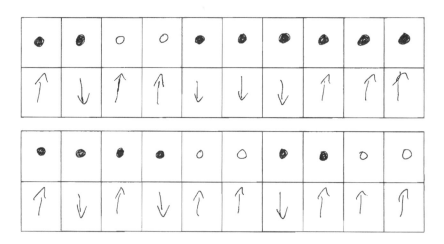

= Rest / Pause   Note: Even spacing.

● = Hole Closed

○ = Hole Open   Zori

Figure 4-4:
Zori's notation for playing his *ZoriPhone*.

most students—traditional notation—as well as skill building on traditional musical instruments, which may also be unfamiliar territory to many students. Beginning with non-traditional objects for music creation encourages students to better explore the sonic potential of materials not generally associated with musical creation. The novelty of the objects offers students an opportunity to explore and demonstrate a variety of ways to "play" them [24].

In the late 1960s, starting with the Contemporary Music Project [5, 13], a small group of musicians, composers, and educators began to advocate the inclusion of musical composition and improvisation into the more performance-oriented music curriculum. Many educators and composers at that time proposed that children needed to explore properties of sound and construct their own symbol systems in order to make meaning of what they are intuitively hearing [2, 3, 4, 16, 22]. This was in response to the traditional view of music education in which, as both Bamberger and Benson contend [2, 4], the learning of musical notation is given "privileged status" in the curriculum, minimizing the importance of other aspects of music making. As Ronald Thomas wrote in *MMCP Synthesis: A Structure for Music Education*:

> Mastery of notation, a complex system of symbolism for the transcription and recall of notes, can so dominate the study that the reason for the symbolism becomes obscured. Note reading is substituted for conceptual understanding, and rhythmic computation, often divorced from a musical context, becomes a major activity. [18] (p. 4)

Benson [4] offers two sound reasons for not emphasizing traditional notation when first introducing creative composition activities to children. The first is to remove any advantage that students already knowing notation might have over those who don't. The second, which gets closer to the heart of the problem-solving nature of our work, is to allow and encourage students to think seriously about to how best to represent their work.

There are several caveats with regard to a student's invented notation system. First, it should not resemble standard musical notation in any way, shape, or form. For music majors, this requires a great deal of "letting go" of learned habits. Second, the notation system should be understandable with little or no verbal or written direction. In reality, as your students will be quick to point out, there is a great deal of direction with regard to the learning and interpreting of notation, but the idea here is to build on what each of them believes would be intuitive. Third, you must lead students to believe that they will be performing their own compositions for the class.

This is where the "Gena Twist" comes in. Your students will come to class eager to demonstrate what they've created. Instead, ask them to hand over their found instrument and composition to a classmate who will explore it and perform the composition for the class *with no explanation from the composer.* "What's the point?" you ask. If your students first performed their own piece and then had someone else perform it, you would not readily know what was intuitive and what was remembered from the composer's performance.

The element of surprise presents a kind of challenge. Who will and will not "get" what the composer/creator intended? The "twist" is what gets to the heart of the project and gently prods the performer into analytical and critical thinking mode, foundational elements of computational thinking (CT). To decipher (or interpret) another student's symbol system, students must posit hypotheses about the symbols' meanings and then test the efficacy of those hypotheses. These are two of the basic steps in all scientific and mathematical problem solving.

This project will pose some interesting questions for your students. Music is about sound and exists in space and time, but notation is static and two dimensional. Therefore, students must ask themselves, "What symbolic representation will best convey the musical action I intend with respect to rhythm, pitch, duration, dynamics, or timbre? What other important attributes of the sound am I looking to convey? How can I best represent those?"

As one of our students pointed out,

> for students to truly comprehend standard musical notation, they must first create their own. Through that creativity and exploration, they will make the connections necessary to bridge the gap between their own creations and standardized music notation.

Another student suggested that "playing other people's instruments really made us think analytically and creatively about figuring out how to 'break the code.'" This experience, in fact, helped students reflect on the choices they made with regard to their own representations. A third student likened learning notation to learning a foreign language:

> I think we were asked to play each other's instruments so we could get an idea of what it feels like again to have to read a foreign language. When beginner students are asked to read music, they are basically doing just that, and once the skill is developed [they] can read fluently. The same goes with our compositions.

SYNCHRONIZED CLASS VERSION
Part 1: The Music Assignment

The Found Instruments project has now been through several permutations. For our synchronized classes, we paired music education majors with computer science majors for a joint project while the two groups of students were still in independent classes [6, 9]. The first axiom of interdisciplinary projects done with independent classes is that both sets of students must have equal "buy in." That is, both must have an equal commitment to the project, or at least to the part for which they are responsible. The second axiom is that both sets of students must understand the *entire* project.

To address these issues, first make it clear that the students' work in each class will be evaluated, even though those evaluations may differ significantly. In our case, the Found Instruments project was only a small part of the music course, while the implementation of the music students' notations was the major part of the CS course, which focused on graphical user interface (GUI) programming. This dichotomy caused some problems. Second, schedule a number of joint classes in which your students can work together and get to know each other. We had five such classes during the semester.

Based on our experience, we would suggest that you use the first of those joint classes to introduce the project to both the music and CS students at the same time. You may also wish to consider structuring the project in two phases. Have your music students develop their found instruments, compositions, and notations in Phase I, and have your CS students recreate those notations as computer applications in Phase II.

One way for you to get both sets of students involved with the project early is to require *all* students to come to class with some kind of household object that could produce several different sounds in terms of either pitch or timbre. We found this to be a great ice-breaker. After each student demonstrates his or her found object and the sounds it can make, have them form "ensembles" and play their objects in a spontaneous musical composition. To avoid intimidating technical students, group each such student with a couple of music students. The support each gives the other will help create an atmosphere of trust within the group.

In our class, we discovered that the CS students were very well able to hold their own during the group performances! In Figure 4-5, the student in the middle is a music major, while the other two are CS majors. In Figure 4-6, the two women are music majors, while the man is a CS major.

For your second joint meeting, have the music students bring in their full-blown creations and notations. While they will know in advance that they will be giving their notations to the CS students to perform, the CS students will be expecting to merely observe this class to gain insight into the programs they will be creating as a result.

Here you will find found sound examples from our Synchronized Class.

Will the music students be able to separate themselves enough from their musical training and embrace the perspective of a non-musician with respect to their invented notations? Conversely, will the CS students be

Figures 4-5 and 4-6:
Students playing their found instruments in ensembles.

able to write an application that makes intuitive sense to a non-CS student? By placing both sets of students in the role of a novice, you require them to intuit a symbol system, much the way children learn to read music or learn a new computer application. Concepts that are taken for granted or considered "obvious" to one group are not necessarily intuitive or easy to grasp for

NOTATION AND REPRESENTATION *(55)*

the other. Formal, disciplinary-specific training can give students "tunnel vision." One of the major goals of interdisciplinary projects is to break down the barriers that prevent students from understanding the perspectives of those not trained in their subject area, and one way to achieve this is to get them to think about novice perspectives.

The appendix to this chapter shows some of the other notation systems that our students developed for their found instruments.

Part 2: The Computer Science Assignment

In part 2 of the adaptation, ask your CS students to bring these instruments and notations to "life" in a computer-based environment similar to traditional computer-based notation programs. While your music students explore the intricacies of instrument creation and notation systems, your CS students explore user interface components and techniques such as menus, toolbars, drop-down lists, and particularly approaches to implementing drag-and-drop, with an eye toward creating interfaces that are as easy to use as possible.

The ease-of-use goal is a critically important one. It is this goal that brings the assignment full circle back to the music students. As your CS students develop their programs, they periodically get to test their usability by having their music student partners attempt to use them (see Figures 4-7 and 4-8). Such usability testing provides important insights into interface design that are impossible to gain by asking another CS student or professor to try to use the program. The interface must be tested with someone who is a member of the target user population. This is where most of the interdisciplinary student interaction takes place. In addition, repeated testing keeps program development on track and results in incremental improvements that will eventually lead to a polished product.

The CS students in our class commented that the "music students were more interested in the outcome [than the art students in the previous semester] and more excited about what we did with their notations." The CS students also "enjoyed being exposed to music concepts that they wouldn't have any insight into." Among the issues that popped up were how to represent silences (rests) and how to design the user interface so that it made sense to people firmly rooted in standard music notation.

One of the most successful computer implementations of a music student's creative notation was created by a CS student in conjunction with a music student who used his jacket as a found instrument. Figure 4-9 shows Mike playing his piece, while Figure 4-10 shows his notation. A video of a student trying to play this notation and then Mike performing his piece himself can be found at **http://www.youtube.com/watch?v=iD4dEZOTiIg**.

Figures 4-7 and 4-8:
Music students reviewing CS students' early efforts to write composing programs for their creative notations.

Figure 4-9:
Mike playing his original *Eine Kleine Jacket Musik* on his jacket.

The next six figures give a feel for the music composition program that Chris created for Mike's notation. It is interesting to note both the pros and cons of this program from a user point of view. First, in Figure 4-11, we see the toolbar at the left of the window. The icons were captured directly from Mike's original, handwritten notation. Note in particular the last icon: a blank. This was added after the initial usability test to satisfy the need for notating a rest.

Figure 4-12 shows the program after a number of icons have been dragged onto the left-hand and right-hand "staffs." Icons can also be added by double-clicking them, in which case they will be added to the right of the last icon added or the currently selected icon. (More on selecting icons in a second.)

In Figure 4-13, the user has "selected" the sixth icon in the left-hand staff of the first system. Note the cursor that appears to the right of this icon to indicate the next logical insertion point. But the user isn't going to insert another icon, he's going to delete the currently selected one by pressing the **Delete** key.

The result of that action is shown in Figure 4-14. *Note the loss of the insertion point cursor.* In Figure 4-15, the user is about to add a new icon immediately after deleting one. Figure 4-16 shows the result of that operation.

Where was the new icon added? Not where it was expected! The icon was added at the *beginning* of the staff on which the user had been working,

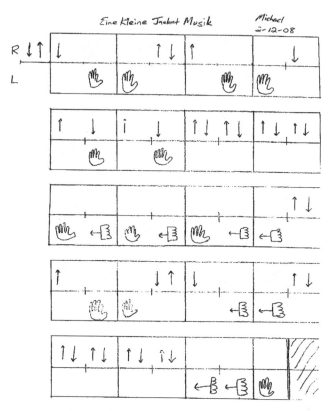

Figure 4-10:
Mike's creative notation for playing his jacket.

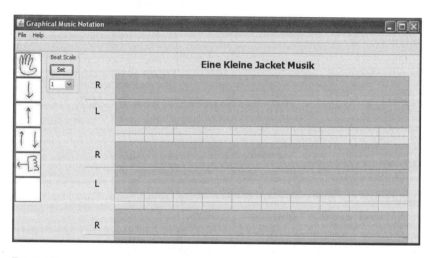

Figure 4-11:
Program for composing jacket notation (step 1), showing the icon toolbar and a series of right- and left-hand "staffs" grouped into "systems."

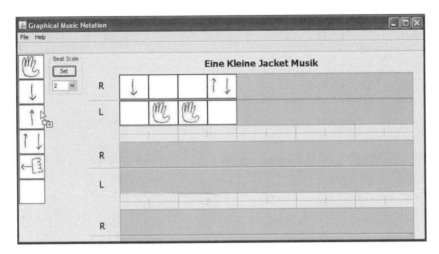

Figure 4-12:
Program for composing jacket notation (step 2), showing icons added to the first "system."

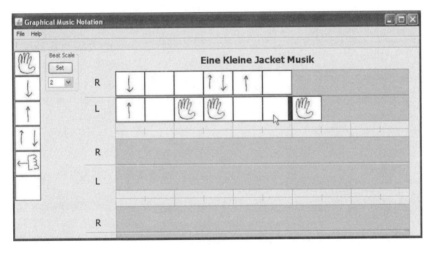

Figure 4-13:
Program for composing jacket notation (step 3), showing the result of clicking the sixth icon in the left-hand staff of the first system to "select" it.

not at the cursor position, where it should have been added. This is a user interface programming bug that provided us with a wonderful "teaching moment" when it totally confused the music students!

As this project was nearing completion, the music students were coming up with ideas for incorporating another project with the CS students into our coursework. This represented a complete turnaround in their attitudes, since they began our collaboration with a great deal of skepticism. As suggested by Seifert and Mandzuk, "learning communities do not happen automatically" [17]. In our case, the shared planning and class times were instrumental in helping our students bond and take ownership of the group experience.

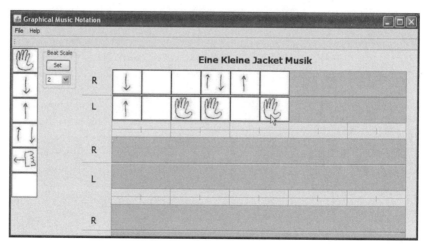

Figure 4-14:
Program for composing jacket notation (step 4), showing the result of pressing the Delete key when the program is in the state shown in Figure 4-12.

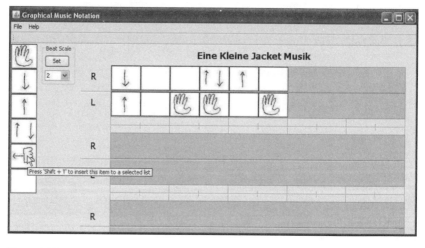

Figure 4-15:
Program for composing jacket notation (step 5), showing the user about to add a new icon after performing the deletion in Figure 4-13.

HYBRID CLASS VERSION
From Two Parts to Three

The goal for the first half of our interdisciplinary, "hybrid" *Sound Thinking* course—the general education (GenEd) version with two professors in the classroom throughout the semester—was to introduce students to the idea of initially playing with, representing, and then manipulating sound both acoustically and digitally. In planning the Found Instruments project for this class, we needed to re-think the computer-based component. Outcome

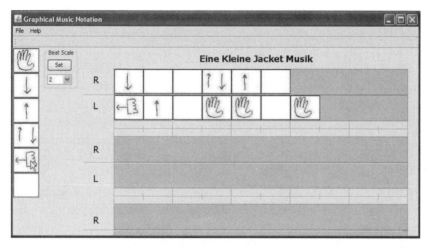

Figure 4-16:
Program for composing jacket notation (step 6), showing the result of adding the icon indicated by the mouse pointer immediately after the deletion.

expectations in a GenEd course are vastly different from those in a course for majors from a single discipline, even when the GenEd class is heavily populated with majors from mostly two disciplines: music and CS. Our projects and assignments need to allow students from *any* discipline to be successful in *all phases* of the project. Therefore, unlike the two distinct parts of the Found Instruments project in the synchronized classes, we re-configured the project so that all students could participate in all phases. We also want to expand on the idea of invented notation as something that composers and performers are still grappling with. That is, we want to stress that this is not just an academic exercise.

 You will find examples from our Hybrid Class here.

In planning your interdisciplinary course, whether you intend it to sat-isfy general education requirements or not, we suggest breaking the project into three parts. In part 1, your students should work individually as in the synchronized class version, creating compositions, coming to class pre-pared to perform their own compositions, and then being informed that their pieces would be performed by another member of the class. In part 2, have students record their "instruments" and import their recordings into Audacity (discussed in Chapter 5) so that they can edit, manipulate, and process them into a completely new composition. In part 3, have each stu-dent create a notation for another student's manipulated composition.

A subtle benefit of part 2 is that it allows you to introduce digital musicianship (using Audacity) early in the semester and within the context of a project rather than as a stand-alone activity. We have found that such context-specific activities are more effective than introducing tools on their own. As was noted by one of our students who is not a big fan of technology:

> In creating a new, digital version of my found object composition, I definitely learned how amusing it is to explore the things one can do with sounds. It is hard to imagine what something would sound like reversed until you hear it, but Audacity helped a lot in that case.

Figure 4-17 shows a screen capture of one student's Audacity project. Note the repetitions of individual sounds that were recorded from his found instrument.

During part 3, the performance class, an incident took place that illustrates the unexpected dynamics of the hybrid course environment very well. After one of the performances, Jesse innocently asked the students, "What did you like about what you just heard?" Gena immediately retorted, "Jesse, I can't believe you just asked that!"[2] As she not too subtly pointed out, Jesse's question was judgmental and one that doesn't always provide constructive criticism. A rather lengthy discussion ensued about how we should try to pose questions that will elicit thoughtful analysis rather than just whether one likes or doesn't like a composition or performance. After all, when people put themselves out there creatively, do we necessarily want to shut them down with issues of likes and dislikes, which suggest it's either "right" or "wrong"? This is an area in which

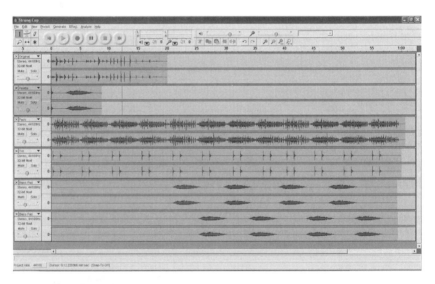

Figure 4-17:
Sounds generated by a student's found instrument as loaded and manipulated in Audacity.

music education students need to be particularly mindful. Were our philosophies and teaching styles clashing? Or was this truly a teachable moment?

Part 1, in which students were composing and creating original notation, brought to light Bamberger's observation that "our units of description come perilously close to becoming our units of perception—we hear and see what we can say" [1]. Students tended to default to simpler pieces they felt they could more easily notate. In many of the journal reflections and follow-up class discussions, students mentioned that they had come up with some complex compositions but could not figure out how they would portray their ideas through notation. Comments like this were common and confirmed our initial instincts regarding *unlinking* the composition from notation:

> When creating the new composition, I felt more free to get elaborate and not worry about how to notate. It was freeing to know afterwards that it wouldn't be my job to figure out how to relate the piece. Overall, I think everyone was much more creative.

In part 2 we wanted students to put all of their creativity into playing with the sounds, so no notation was required. Another student remarked:

> When I first started composing, I began thinking about what the notation would look like, and I really had to force myself not to think in that fashion and focus more on how I wanted it to sound. Not knowing what the program could do, this was actually a little difficult, but once I got exploring and let go of the idea of notation it was much easier.

The sound manipulation activity was quite successful on a number of levels. This statement sums up what many students felt:

> I learned how to use a new computer program (new to me at least), how to manipulate sounds, and how to notate a piece by listening carefully and repetitively (but notes help a whole bunch).

One student noted the enjoyment of manipulating sounds, though recreating his found objects piece came with some level of frustration. He discussed having to start over several times, but then noted:

> As frustrating as it was, I do not believe my piece would have come out as good as it did if I didn't redo it a number of times. Each time I restarted I had a new perspective and was able to think of better ideas and new ways to approach my piece.

The act of analysis and revision is a very important part of the composition process and one that is often difficult to motivate students to do. This student's issues highlight some of the computational thinking that was necessary to complete the project to his satisfaction. He was dealing with temporal structuring, procedural thinking, and non-destructive editing. Creating music with technology affords your students instant aural feedback, allowing for a great deal of exploration.

 You will find Audacity remixes from student found sound compositions.

In part 3, which was announced after the completion of the digital compositions in part 2, students paired up so that each created the notation for his or her partner's composition (see Figure 4-18). This activity generated a great deal of interest and engagement in the act of critical listening on a level that was much deeper than we would have anticipated. As one student noted in his reflection, "This process forced me to listen actively (this includes interpreting the sounds in a way that others can understand)." He went on to discuss his thinking process:

> I don't know why I choose one thing over the other—I just picked what seemed most natural to me, hoping others would understand…looking back on my final draft, I felt like the notation represented the music rather well (sometimes it's best to think with your senses and intuition).

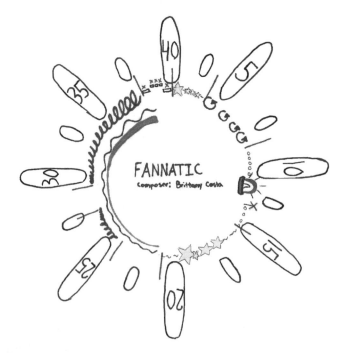

Figure 4-18:
Mary Ellen's notation for Brittany's composition.

Another student observed:

> I really liked that we did the notation process this way, writing for someone else's piece instead of your own. I feel like if I had written for my own piece, I would've been stuck on my original notation and—having created the piece—I wouldn't have been able to listen to it objectively and take the sounds in differently. Working with someone else's piece allowed me to start from scratch, listen actively, and create.

Part 3 actually had students applying skills from previous activities in terms of categorizing sounds to represent them. A student wrote:

> Coming up with notation for a piece I was not intimately familiar with was a huge challenge. I could not really even start until after I had listened to it a dozen times, just to get a sense of it and start to hear the different layers. I started to be able to categorize the sounds, hearing the bubbles, the scratches, the hums.

From Exercises to Music

It was during the part 3 activity that we really began to witness the seeds of computational thinking taking hold. All the students were exploring more. They were thinking about music and sounds differently and listening more critically. Without realizing it, they were engaging in musical analysis in the most fundamental ways. They were going through the mental processes of organizing their thinking and coming up with a plan.

Now we needed to somehow tie this back to the world of music. As luck would have it, we were both attending a concert by the JACK Quartet, a group of young string players who specialize in contemporary music (see Figure 4-19 and **www.jackquartet.com**). Since this concert was in an intimate venue, we could see some of the music, which looked suspiciously like invented notation (see Figure 4-20). Helmut Lachenmann, the composer, was present and spoke about his music, the sounds he was looking to create—which were non-traditional—and the manner in which that information was conveyed to the performers. This prompted us to think about spending a little time on the idea of musical notation, its beginnings, and some of the ways contemporary composers have found traditional notation limiting.

New music is often presented in a manner that can be off-putting to the novice listener. However, breaking down the composition and comparing aspects of the modern composition with musical elements students are familiar with can help students to listen with a more open mind. Engaging the students with performers, who are generally eager to share their musical world with others, can be an extremely valuable learning experience. As a resource, college music departments can be a treasure trove of performers, both students and faculty, with expertise in non-traditional forms of music making.

Figure 4-19:
The JACK Quartet. Copyright © 2010, JACK Quartet. *Reproduced with permission.*

In our case, we were fortunate that Ari Streisfeld, one of the JACK Quartet violinists, was in the midst of working on his doctorate in performance practices at a nearby university. We approached Ari after the concert and invited him to give a presentation on his music to our class. He readily agreed. Ari began his presentation by demonstrating the many ways in which one could interpret a classical composition by Bach even though it is written in traditional music notation. He then compared it to several contemporary compositions and explained how he goes about interpreting less traditional forms of notation.

 You can view a short video of Ari Streisfeld's performance in our *Sound Thinking* class.

One student in the class was transformed by this. She commented:

I found that whole learning experience very intriguing and I am itching to learn more about it. I am currently doing some more research into this style and have found some great compositions, like *Sonata V* by John Cage. Ari's presentation opened up a whole new world to me that I did not know existed and I want to share it with others.

The students were once again thinking and hearing differently. Another student wrote in his journal:

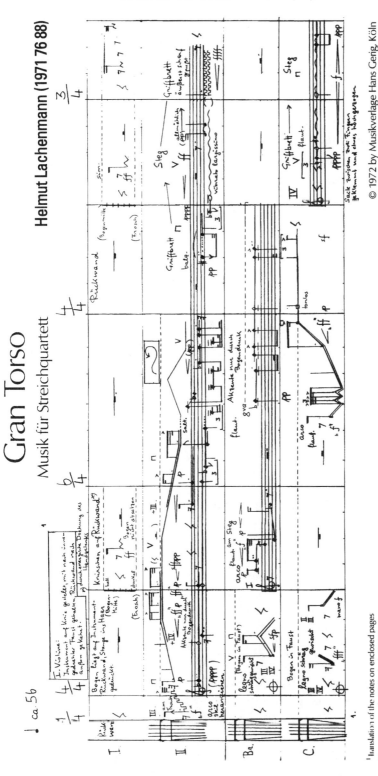

Figure 4-20:
Excerpt from Gran Torso by German composer Helmut Lachenmann, demonstrating creative notation being played today by the JACK Quartet. Copyright © 1980, Breitkopf & Härtel KG, Wiesbaden, Germany. *Reproduced with permission.*

Ari's presentation was definitely an experience I'm glad to have had recently.... [I]t definitely made me look at conventional instruments and alternative sounds that can be created with them. It was also interesting to see how a musical notation can rarely show exactly how a composer envisions their piece to be performed. There is only so much that can be explained this way. The rest is up to the performer.

Yet another student commented that "Streisfeld's time with us ... was valuable as he showed us the farthest extremes of creative sound, and [gave us] a glimpse into the rules that can be broken to do so." We could talk about this, they could read about this, they could even do their own experimenting, but seeing and hearing an accomplished musician demonstrate these concepts helped to validate their own experiences and realizations.

THEME, VARIATIONS, AND COMPUTATIONAL THINKING

As you can no doubt see, there are enough variations on this project to engage a diversity of student populations and interests. But we still expect that you will be able to devise new twists that haven't yet occurred to us. Even if you are not in a position to engage a colleague in collaborating with you on an interdisciplinary course, perhaps you will find some aspect of our experience worth looking into with your own students, getting them to explore and think creatively about sound and how to represent it in new ways. Feedback from some of our Performamatics workshop participants confirms that teachers are bringing this activity into their classes with novel results.

The key to crafting learning activities is to weave them together so that each reinforces and builds on work that has gone earlier. In a participatory course like *Sound Thinking*, where students tend to have a lot of fun, it is easy for them to lose sight of the learning objectives and *why* they're doing certain exercises. That's not necessarily a bad thing. Carnegie Mellon professor Randy Pausch referred to such diversions as "head fakes" [14]. And legendary MIT professor Harold Edgerton (who invented the electronic strobe), liked to say: "The trick to education is to teach people in such a way that they don't realize they're learning until it's too late" [10].

But while it may be OK for your *students* not to see the big picture—well, at least not *initially*—it's crucial that *you* keep the big picture in mind, and that big picture is computational thinking. To maintain that focus, have students write reflections on each activity recounting what they learned. Share these reflections in class to stimulate discussion of the activities' underlying principles. Analysis and the application of logic are a large part of CT.

Another way to reinforce CT is to have students rate the degree to which a student's performance matched the intentions of the composer. Be careful here: we are *not* suggesting that you have students rate each other's performances, and we are *not* suggesting that they rate the quality of either the composition or the performance. Rather, we are suggesting that they rate the congruence between what the composer wanted to convey in the notation and what the performer perceived. To do this, students must develop a set of criteria—what some would call a *rubric*—by which they can evaluate the degree of agreement. If they establish criteria, assign weights to them, and then score each composer/performer pair and multiply by the weights to achieve a weighted average, they will indeed be practicing computational thinking.

BIBLIOGRAPHY

[1] Bamberger, J. (2003). "The Development of Intuitive Musical Understanding: A Natural Experiment." *Psychology of Music* **31**(7):7–36.

[2] Bamberger, J. (2006). "What Develops in Musical Development?" In G. MacPherson, ed., *The Child as Musician: Musical Development from Conception to Adolescence*. Oxford, UK: Oxford University Press.

[3] Barrett, M. (2011). "Constructing a View of Children's Meaning-Making as Notators: A Case-Study of a Five-Year-Old's Description and Explanations of Invented Notations." *Research Studies in Music Education* **16**(1):33–45.

[4] Benson, W. (1973). "The Creative Child Could Be Any Child: Drawing Out Inherent Creativity in Compositional Experiences." *Music Educators Journal* **59**(8):38–40.

[5] Dello Joio, N., Mailman, M., Halgedahl, H., Fletcher, G., Beglarian, G., & Wersen, L. G. (1968). "The Contemporary Music Project for Creativity in Music Education." *Music Educators Journal* **54**(7):41–72.

[6] Feldman, D. H., Csikszentmihaly, M., & Gardner, H. (1994). "A Framework for the Study of Creativity." In D. H. Feldman, M. Csikszentmihaly, & H. Gardner, eds., *Changing the World: A Framework for the Study of Creativity*. Westport, CT: Praeger.

[7] Gardner, H. (1992). "Do Babies Sing a Universal Song?" In B. L. Andress & L. M. Walker, eds., *Readings in Early Childhood Music Education*. Reston, VA: MENC, pp. 32–38.

[8] Hart, M., & Lieberman, F. (1991). *Planet Drum: A Celebration of Percussion and Rhythm*. Petaluma, CA: HarperOne.

[9] Heines, J. M., Greher, G. R., Ruthmann, S. A., & Reilly, B. (2011). "Two Approaches to Interdisciplinary Computing+Music Courses." *IEEE Computer* **44**(12):25–32.

[10] International Institute of Photographic Arts. (2010). *Harold Edgerton*. www.iipa.org/permanent/haroldedgerton/bio.html, accessed 7/16/2010.

[11] Katz, L. (2013). *Junkestra Symphony Is Pure Garbage*. news.cnet.com/8301-17938_105-20003461-1.html, accessed 4/15/2013.

[12] Machover, T. (2011). "Objects of Design and Play: My Cello." In S. Turkle, ed., *Evocative Objects*. Cambridge, MA: MIT Press, pp. 12–21.

[13] Music Educators National Conference. (1973). "Contemporary Music Project." *Music Educators Journal* **59**(9):33–48.

[14] Pausch, R., & Zaslow, J. (2008). *The Last Lecture*. New York: Hyperion.

[15] Pogonowski, L. (2001). "A Personal Retrospective on the MMCP: A Manhattanville Music Curriculum Project Participant Reflects on Its Innovative Initiatives in Light of Current Curriculum Theory." *Music Educators Journal* **88**(1):24–27.

[16] Ruthmann, S. A., & Heines, J. M. (2010). *Exploring Musical and Computational Thinking through Musical Live Coding in Scratch.* Scratch@MIT. Cambridge, MA.

[17] Seifert, K. L., & Mandzuk, D. (2006). "Student Cohorts in Teacher Education: Support Groups or Intellectual Communities?" *Teachers College Record* **108**(7):1296–1320.

[18] Thomas, R. (1971). *MMCP Synthesis: A Structure for Music Education.* Bardonia, NY: Media Materials.

[19] Tommasini, A. (2010). "A Night for a Rhapsodic Violin and a Brake Drum." *New York Times.* October 8, 2010.

[20] Torff, B., & Gardner, H. (1999). "Conceptual and Experiential Cognition in Music." *Journal of Aesthetic Education* **33**(4):14.

[21] Turkle, S. (1995). *Life on the Screen: Identity in the Age of the Internet.* New York: Touch-Stone / Simon & Schuster.

[22] Upitis, R. (1990). "Children's Invented Notations of Familiar and Unfamiliar Melodies." *Psychomusicology* **9**(1):18.

[23] Wakin, D. J. (2010). "From Heaps of Junk, a Melodious Clang." *New York Times*, October 5, p. C1.

[24] Welwood, A. (1980). "Improvisation with Found Sounds." *Music Educators Journal* **66**(5):6.

Appendix for Chapter 4

ADDITIONAL FOUND INSTRUMENTS
AND NOTATION EXAMPLES
From the Synchronized Classes

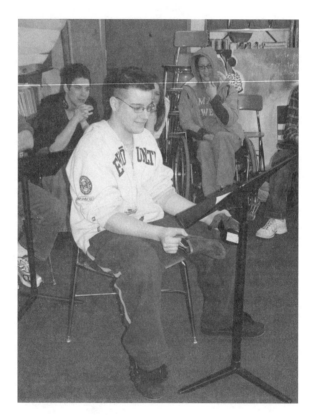

Figure 4A-1:
Creative notation for a Kristin's "shoe sonata."

Figure 4A-2:
Chase (a CS major) attempting to play Kristin's "shoe sonata."

♩ Keyboard Rock
Forte   Andante

(Enter)	X	X	_	_	X	X	
(↑Shift)	X	X	_	_	X	X	
(Space)		X					X
(Enter)		X				X	X
(↑Shift)		X		X		X	X
(Space)	X			X			

Figure 4A-3:
Creative notation for a Rob R.'s "keyboard rock."

From the Hybrid Class

Figure 4A-4:
Rob W. (a CS major) attempting to play Rob R.'s "keyboard rock."

SPL: $\frac{1}{3}$

1	2	3	4	5	6	7	8	9	10	11	12	13

40	41	42	43	44	45	46	47	48	49	50	51	52

Figure 4A-5:
Creative notation for a Eric's "lever drumitar."

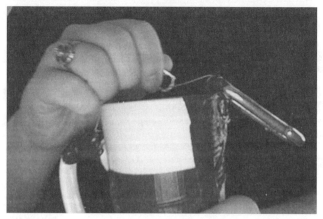

Figure 4A-6 and 4A-7:
Eric's "lever drumitar."

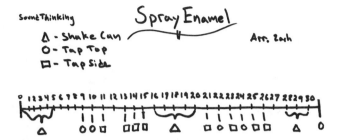

Figure 4A-8:
Creative notation for a Zach's "spray enamel can."

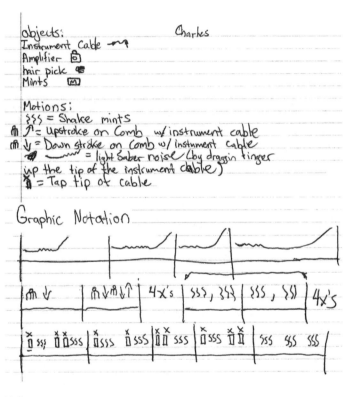

Figure 4A-9:
Creative notation for a Charles's "mints and amplifier."

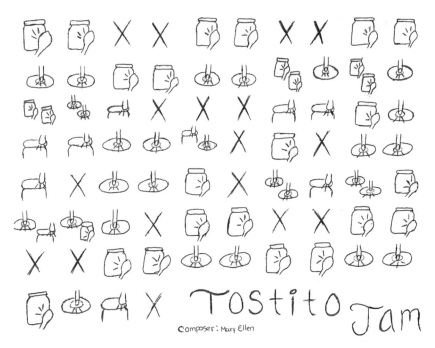

Figure 4A-10:
Creative notation for Mary Ellen's "tostito jam jar."

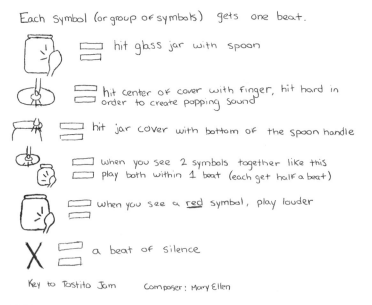

Figure 4A-11:
Legend for reading Mary Ellen's "tostito jam jar" notation.

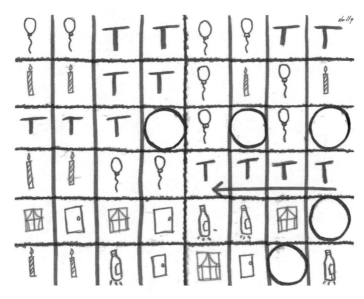

Figure 4A-12:
Holly's "conditioning style" notation.

Conditioning Style
Symbol Key
by Holly

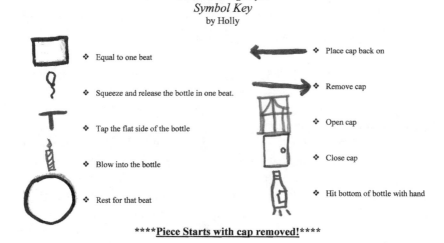

❖ Equal to one beat

❖ Squeeze and release the bottle in one beat.

❖ Tap the flat side of the bottle

❖ Blow into the bottle

❖ Rest for that beat

❖ Place cap back on

❖ Remove cap

❖ Open cap

❖ Close cap

❖ Hit bottom of bottle with hand

****Piece Starts with cap removed!****

Figure 4A-13:
Legend for reading Holly's "conditioning style" notation.

CHAPTER 5

Getting Them Started

I Didn't Know You Could Do That

with a Computer

JUST WHAT *IS* A COMPUTER, ANYWAY?

"What's an iPod?" "What's an iPhone?" "What's an Android?" Pose those questions to any gen-Xer or millennial and we guarantee you that there's one answer you *won't* get: "a small, handheld computer." We'd also be shocked if their answers included anything like "a communication device capable of connecting to a wireless or cellular network." You're more likely to hear: "It's like, a thing I use to chat with my friends, watch videos, and listen to music." They can tell you what these devices are *for*, but they would have trouble telling you what they really *are*.

Is this bad? No, not in and of itself. The computer has truly become an appliance, and some think about it no more deeply than they think about their toaster. Let's credit the geeks in Silicon Valley for making complex devices so easy to use that, as they say about driving a car, "any fool can do it, and many do." If your neighbor has a problem connecting to the Internet and comes to you for help and you ask what browser he or she uses, you just might get a blank stare. If you then try to break the ice by asking: "When you connect to the Internet (or World Wide Web) to look up something with Google or read your email, what program do you use?" An answer we commonly hear is: "I don't know. I just click on the little picture that says 'Connect to the Internet' (or 'Read Your Email,' etc.)." This assumes, of course, that your neighbor knows what you mean by "program." If not, it's probably easiest to just ask: "Tell me the steps you follow to open your email so that you can read and send new messages."

Even though we feel that everyone should know a bit more about computers than this, we applaud the developments that have made computers everyday devices. All of us drive cars, but the vast majority of us have no desire whatsoever to really understand what's going on under the hood or the physics involved in controlling a two-ton vehicle traveling at 65 miles per hour. However, understanding a bit about those things can make us better drivers, and understanding a bit about how computers work can make students better users. To begin with, recognizing that one's iPhone is a handheld computer connected to a complex network can alleviate a lot of frustration when something goes wrong. And learning how to back up one's personal files can alleviate a lot more than that when a disk goes bad.

But how do we interest gen-Xers and millennials in learning how computers work? When Jesse asked his 13-year-old niece—who uses both handheld and desktop computers constantly for communication, gaming, and doing her homework—whether she had any interest in learning to program those machines to make them do new and interesting things, she not only replied "No," she added that she didn't think any of her friends had such an interest, either. That doesn't bode well for our efforts to help students learn computational thinking.

Many children start taking music lessons very early in their lives. It's not uncommon for preschoolers to already be enrolled in music classes, and YouTube hosts an uncountable number of videos of children singing, dancing, conducting, and doing other musical things even if they've never had any training at all. Ideally, we want young musicians engaging first with actual musical materials through sound and kinesthetic explorations before being introduced to theory or the structure of notation embodied in staves, notes, and accidentals. Likewise, we want new computing students—particularly those turned off by mathematical formalities—engaging first with interesting applications before being introduced to theory and the structure of computer languages.

Our approach is therefore to start them off by getting them to use a computer to manipulate something they're familiar with, surreptitiously showing them that they can *control* a computer and get it to do what *they* want it to do. We do this by getting them to create digital mash-ups and variations of their favorite songs.

AUDACITY: THE STANDARD IN FREE MUSIC EDITING

We love Audacity [2]. It's free; it's easy to use; it has more than adequate functionality for our purposes; it runs on Macintosh, Windows, and Linux systems; and its data files are compatible across systems. Admittedly, it's not a professional quality editor like Avid's Pro Tools [3] or even a "prosumer"[1] [6] quality editor like Sony's Sound Forge [7] or Adobe's Audition [1]. However, free cost, ease of use, reasonable functionality, and cross-platform availability are critical characteristics that allow all students (and teachers) to download and run Audacity on their own systems, thus allowing them to do their assignments outside of class. These characteristics are paramount in virtually all decisions we make about what software to use in our courses.

Audacity's home page is **http://audacity.sourceforge.net**. You can download the software for Windows, Macintosh, and Linux systems from there. Once the program is installed, you can import and manipulate lots of different file types, including MP3s, but there's a bit of an issue with regard to exporting sound files in MP3 format. The appendix at the end of this chapter provides instructions to address this issue that augment those on the Audacity website itself. If you don't yet have Audacity up and running on your system with the LAME MP3 encoder, please see that appendix.

Note: All descriptions of Audacity in this book refer to Audacity version 2.0.3, released on January 21, 2013. Almost all screen shots were made on a Windows 7 system, but in most cases, the Macintosh version looks only slightly different.

GETTING MUSIC INTO AND OUT OF AUDACITY

There are many terrific things that students can do with Audacity, but we begin by building on the song flowchart work discussed in a previous chapter. Virtually all students have MP3 versions of their favorite songs, and if they do not, they can usually find an MP3 of a song they're willing to work with or make their own MP3 using a variety of tools, including Audacity. If they find a song they want to work with on YouTube, they can download that song as an MP3 using the free YouTube to MP3 converter available from DVDVideoSoft.com.[2]

The types of audio files that Audacity can import include these (see Figure 5-1):

- *WAV, AIFF, and other uncompressed file types,* most of which are playable in the Windows Media Player.
- *Ogg Vorbis files,* which are playable *without* a plug-in in the Firefox browser, but *not* in most other browsers.
- *FLAC (Free Lossless Audio Codec) files,* which are "similar to MP3s, but lossless, meaning that audio is compressed in FLAC without any loss in quality." [5]

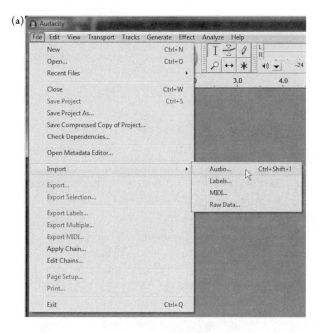

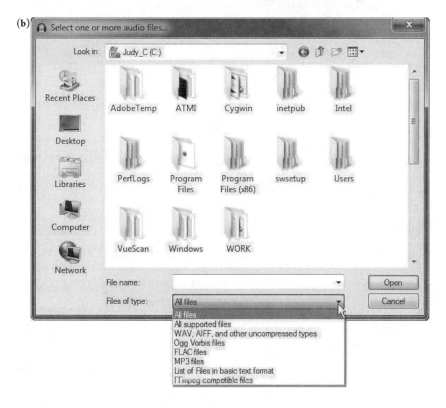

Figures 5-1a and 5-1b:
Importing an audio file into Audacity and supported import file types.

- *MP3 files*, which are playable *without* a plug-in in the Chrome, Opera, and Safari browsers, in the Internet Explorer browser with the QuickTime plug-in installed, and in QuickTime, iTunes, and the Windows Media Player.
- *FFmpeg-compatible files*, such as MPEG and FLV (Flash), which are playable in many applications, including games.

That about covers the field, so students should be able to import music in just about any file format they happen to have.

Exporting music is only slightly different. The basic process is the same in that you select **Export . . .** from the **File** menu (once you have something to export and the **Export . . .** option is not grayed out indicating that it is disabled), but the list of available file formats is longer (see Figure 5-2). The only issue here is that the **MP3** files entry will not appear in the list of available export file formats unless the MP3 encoder is installed, as mentioned previously and discussed in the appendix to this chapter.

Figure 5-2:
Supported Audacity export file types.

GAINING COMPUTATIONAL THINKING SKILLS THROUGH AUDACITY

It may at first seem strange to go into so much detail on Audacity import and export file formats in a book on computational thinking. We don't think so. As a matter of fact, understanding how to work with Audacity at more than a rudimentary level is exactly the type of thing that we believe *should* be covered in an interdisciplinary course or project on computing+music. This does *not* mean that we get into the mathematics of compression or the algorithms that allow Audacity to shape and manipulate sounds. It means that we want students to understand things like Audacity's file structure to the point that they can backup their work and move projects from one system to another. Just as musical instruments produce very different results depending upon the skill and experience of the artist who plays them, computer tools such as Audacity produce very different results—and levels of frustration—depending upon the skill and experience of the person who uses them. We don't try to make our GenEd students programmers, but we certainly do try to make them skilled, experienced, and sophisticated users who practice computational thinking (CT).

 These are recorded found objects sound files for you, the reader, to use to create your own re-mix in Audacity.

So just what CT skills can students gain by working with Audacity? Before answering this question, it's worthwhile to review Jeanette Wing's definition of CT once again:

> Computational thinking involves solving problems, designing systems, and understanding human behavior, by drawing on the concepts fundamental to computer science. Computational thinking includes a range of mental tools that reflect the breadth of the field of computer science. [9]

Also, remember that in the context of our interdisciplinary work we define CT very broadly, encompassing a wide range of problem-solving skills. Our reason for this stance is that we see problem solving as the essence of CT for students in non-technical fields. These students are just as smart as any other, of course, and they can use computer applications as well as anyone *when things go according to plan.* The issue is their ability to solve problems *when things go wrong.* Do they analyze the situation using CT, or do they throw up their hands and say "I can't do this"? Our goal is obviously to get them to do the former.

 Here you will find examples of individual student re-mixes of their found sound compositions created in Audacity, along with their notes and reflections.

HOW COULD YOU HAVE THE *AUDACITY* TO DO THAT TO MY SONG?!?

Rather than just listing and describing the CT behaviors that can be gained by using Audacity, let's explore them in the context of an assignment that might be used in a course like *Sound Thinking*. The assignment itself is conceptually simple, and it builds directly on the song flowchart project discussed previously. Here it is in a nutshell:

Part I. Load the song that you used to create your flowchart into Audacity. Using your song flowchart as a guide, break the song into chunks and store each as a separate MP3 file. Reload the MP3 files you created into a new Audacity project so that each is in a separate track. Recombine the tracks in various ways to make a new "song" from the component chunks. [*There are several ways to do this, which we would cover in class.*] Save your Audacity project so that you can come back to it later and save your composition as a new MP3 file.

Part II. Reload your composition into Audacity as a new project. Experiment with some of the sound manipulation tools provided on the Effect menu by applying them to all or part of your composition to see what they do. Remember that you can type Control-Z (**Ctrl-Z**) on Windows or Command-Z (⌘-**Z**) on Macintosh to "undo" any change that you don't like. Save your Audacity project and save this second version of your composition in such a way that you now have both your original and your manipulated versions.

 Here you will find collaborative remixes along with notes and reflections.

Do students learn CT skills by doing assignments such as these? Yes, and they have fun doing so. OK, so just what do they learn? "Let me count the ways…" [4]

(1) **Students learn about file types and data storage.** They learn that Audacity, like many other programs, has its own unique way of storing data so that users can close the program and reopen it at a later time and continue from where they left off. They learn that MP3 files are not the same as AU files.[3] They learn about hierarchical folder structures, because Audacity's

Folder Hierarchy	Contents of AudacityTestsEtc	Contents of OneToFive_data	Contents of e00	Contents of d00
AudacityTestsEtc →	OneToFive_data →	e00 →	d00 →	e00000ab.au
OneToFive_data	Five.mp3			e0000a6e.au
e00	Four.mp3			e0000b0d.au
d00	One.mp3			e0000b3b.au
	OneToFive.aup			e0000ce0.au
	OneToFive.mp3			e0000d67.au
	Three.mp3			e0000e7f.au
	Two.mp3			e0000ee7.au
				e0000f09.au
				e0000fbd.au
				e000001b.au
				e00001cf.au
				e00003d8.au
				e00006dd.au
				e00008a7.au
				e0000012.au
				e0000746.au
				e0000998.au

Figure 5-3:
Audacity folder hierarchy and typical contents of subfolders.

Icon Legend: = Folder (or subfolder)

 = MP3 file (.mp3)

 = Audacity project file (.aup)

 = Audacity sound file (.au)

critical AU files exist in a subfolder of the main folder. For example, Figure 5-3 shows an Audacity folder hierarchy in the first column, with the contents of each folder in this hierarchy expanded in the remaining four columns.

(2) *Students learn about the importance of saving intermediate versions of their work.* Audio editing can be complex, involving many steps. It is really disheartening to work on something for an hour or more and then be unable to save it or have a computer glitch wipe out one's work. It has happened to all of us, even the most techno-savvy geeks, but it can be really devastating to students who are already predisposed to dislike using computers.

To avoid such crises, we teach students to do two things. First, we caution them to save the entire Audacity project every 5–10 minutes or so and/or at critical points in their work using **File➡Save Project As . . .** rather than just **File➡Save Project . . .**, adding **-v01, -v02, -v03,** and so on to the project name each time they save it. This allows them to go back to a good, working, previous version of their project if they—or the computer—really screws something up. Second, we entreat them to take notes as they go along so that they can recall what they did to get "from here to there." One music student learned these lessons very well, with a valuable side effect. He wrote in his reflection on a related assignment:

I had stayed up till about 2:30 in the morning [working on this project]. I went to export the audio from my Audacity project and received nothing but silence. I troubleshot until about 4:00AM and then threw in the towel. Once again the computer had won. I can't explain how much I despise giving in to an inanimate object. I had no choice but to post-pone the project.

About four days later I tried a couple of last ditch efforts and then realized I would have to start the project from scratch. Luckily, having taken the advice of my knowledgeable profes-sors, I had taken notes on the original project. It was an interesting process to repeat my steps again. Not only was I able to reproduce my project, but I was also able to create a better ver-sion. I found better ways to do things and had more creative ideas as I reworked my project.

(3) *They learn techniques for and the importance of making backups.* They learn that if they want to transfer an Audacity project to another system, they must copy the entire folder hierarchy, not just the **.aup** project file in the top-level folder (a common mistake). This is an important con-cept, since hierarchical file structures are used by most other audio and video editing systems and many other types of programs, too. Backing up also involves dealing with the large sizes of the data files, which in the case of Audacity are the **.au** files in the last "leaf" of the file structure tree. Each of these is typically 1 megabyte in size. For large projects, especially those in which a lot of editing has taken place, there can literally be dozens of **.au** files that one has to copy. Therefore, if students are going to back up their projects from school systems to their personal ones, they have to plan to bring a flash or thumb drive big enough to hold all those files and make sure they have enough time to copy them before they have to run to their next classes. These may seem like trivial matters to experienced computer users, but they are anything *but* trivial to students whose only computer experi-ence involves using a device that they don't even realize is a computer.

(4) *They learn to explore and experiment.* Audacity is a rich environ-ment. It provides a wealth of manipulations that students can perform on imported audio. For starters, the number of effects that one can apply is huge, as shown in Figure 5-4.

(Note: These same effects are available on Macintosh systems, but the menu looks somewhat different because they are grouped into submenus as shown in Figure 5-5.) It is not only fun to figure out what each of these effects does, but also very *instruc*tive from both a CT and a music point of view.

To us, exploring and experimenting (with the ability to undo changes), as well as wading through sometimes sparse documentation are as much CT skills as writing program code. While students learn these skills **they also deepen their understanding of music structure and sound effects** and get to exercise a bit of creativity.

Figure 5-4:
Audacity Effect options menu (on Windows). *Note that the effects are not grouped.*

The exploratory aspect of the project can produce some wonderfully ser-endipitous results. A music student wrote:

> I experienced something while working on this project that I was not expecting. As mu-sicians and consumers of music we are all familiar with the potential music has to move people. There is a phenomenon known as a "skin response," which is the very thing I live for in music. There is simply nothing that compares.
>
> So there I was…just throwing in music and experimenting, when out of nowhere I felt this shutter [*sic*]. These four songs lined up at this one point at 2:30 in the morning. That was an amazing moment. I never would have expected to nor have I experienced this in "digital music." … This project was worth that single moment.

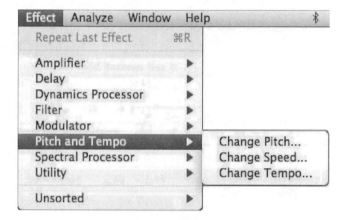

Figure 5-5:
Audacity Effect options menu (on Macintosh). *Note the difference between the Mac and Windows versions of this menu: on the Mac, the effects are grouped.*

(5) We could go on and on, but let's end on this one: **students learn to solve problems.** This is perhaps the penultimate CT goal, and it certainly involves using (in Wing's words [9]) a "range of mental tools" that are part of "the breadth of the field of computer science." The types of problems students encounter range from the mechanics of getting *this* chunk to go *there* to getting the mash-up to sound the way they want it to. The technical students in the class can help the arts students at the mechanical end of that spectrum, while the arts students can help the technical ones at the aesthetic end. It's a win-win situation that exemplifies the best characteristic of interdisciplinary work: students learn *from each other*, not just from the professors. As a matter of fact, it is common for students to come up with a trick or two that the professors don't know. The teacher-student roles are then reversed, creating one of those magical moments that make teaching so fulfilling.

AN EXAMPLE FROM OUR COURSE: THE AUDIO-ETHNOGRAPHY PROJECT

The first time we taught *Sound Thinking* we used a slightly different assignment from the one just described because we did not do the flowchart project (described in an earlier chapter) that year. However, the assignment we used was still a mash-up. We presented it to students as follows.

Audio-Ethnography: The Soundtrack of Your Life

What This Assignment Is About

The next project is a play on the term "autoethnography." According to Wikipedia, auto-ethnography is "a form of autobiographical personal narrative that explores the writer's experience of life" [8]. Autoethnography focuses on the writer's subjective experience, rather than the beliefs and practices of others.

Autoethnography is now becoming more widely used (though controversial) in performance studies, the sociology of new media, novels, journalism, and communication, as well as applied fields such as management studies.

What You Are to Do

Instead of a written narrative, you will be creating an audio narrative of who you are. Your materials will be a collection of music that describes you, reflects your interests, represents the type of music you enjoy, or anything else that will give us an idea of who you are and what makes you tick. You may also include other non-musical sound sources to enhance your presentation.

One piece of music played from start to finish will not cut it. You will need to work with at least a half dozen musical sources that you will edit, process, and layer into a cohesive musical narrative of exactly 300 seconds ... not a second more or a second less.

By requiring students' submissions to be *exactly* 300 seconds, we forced them to use CT skills to map out the timing of the songs they wanted to include rather than just including clips of arbitrary length. In most cases, one wouldn't want to start or stop a song in the middle of a phrase, although this could be done as a creative technique if it was appropriate to a student's vision of who he or she is. Clean, logically whole clips are usually much more preferable, and these had to be created of appropriate length so that everything added up to 300 seconds.

This assignment is challenging to do in Audacity for a number of reasons. The first is obviously the task of cutting the clips to the lengths one wants. Then there's the need to load each clip in the right sequence, which is easier to do if one uses separate tracks rather than trying to do everything in a single track. Next is the issue of transitions. Of course sharp cuts are acceptable if that's the effect one wants, but most of the time it's aesthetically more pleasing to hear smooth transitions between songs. Here's how a CS student described his thoughts on this issue and what he decided to do about transitions:

One major problem I had at first was figuring out a proper order of the piece. Some of the songs had the same tempo, while others were much faster or slower. I decided I wanted many of the clips to run smoothly together, but also to have a few drastic jumps within the piece to make certain clips stand out.

So putting the piece together involves trial and error with lots of "undoing" along the way to get things just the way one wants. And since this assignment is to create something that represents themselves, students take it pretty seriously. Students have to exercise their CT skills considerably to accomplish the mechanics of the assignment.

At the same time, the assignment gets students to listen critically to the music they want to use so that they can create and recombine clips in a way that makes sense. Here's what one student wrote about listening:

> Analyzing the lyrics and the melodies, a lot more than I initially realized could be discovered about me. There are certain qualities the listener could easily realize I possess just by listening to this piece. I would imagine this is exactly what an Audio-Ethnography piece should do.

To demonstrate how seriously some students took this assignment, consider that one student used 44 songs! This student wrote in her reflection:

> I spent so much time on this project. I thought about it over and over again. I actually completed it three times. The first time I had maybe only ten songs with much longer selections, but I didn't feel that it represented me. Then I shortened some so I could add more. I finished it again. This time about twenty five songs. It still wasn't enough. I finally went through and shortened each clip into only the necessary part so I could add more and more....I cannot wait for us to post these on our new websites so when I go home for Easter I can sit down with my family and play it for them and see if they will know it is supposed to represent me.

 You will be able to view other examples of student reflections.

THE VALUE OF PERFORMANCE

A major aspect of almost all projects should be an opportunity for students to share their work via informal "performances" of the students' creations. (We intentionally put the term "performance" in quotes here because we try to take a very broad view of what it means to "perform.") This is where the term "Performamatics" comes from. In the audio-ethnography project, we had students submit their creations and then we played them without telling the class who the composers were. Some of the students knew each other well and some did not. Nevertheless, we asked them to guess who had composed the pieces they heard. A computer science student wrote:

> The opportunity to listen to other people's pieces without knowing who made them...made the whole assignment come together for me, because it gave us the oppor-

tunity to see qualities of our classmates that we normally may not see. Coming from a Computer Science background and not Music, I've always found myself a little out of the loop in the classroom, so it was nice to give the class a better glimpse of who I am. It was also an interesting experience to listen to other people's works and figure out who made them based on the little I know about each student. It also let me experience qualities of people I'd never normally see or music I probably wouldn't discover on my own.

Another CS student had a somewhat different "take" on the assignment after hearing other students' creations. He wrote:

> While the musical choices themselves were important, I feel that the song order and style of transition also said significant things about the author. Some students organized their projects in a way that sounded best to them, while others tried to convey a message or idea with the order and choice of the music they included in their compositions. Some chose songs that seemed to fit and blend together, while others opted for more variety.
>
> I think that students' personalities show as much through the composition of their project as their song choices. These were important aspects of this project, and I tried tofocus on both. I used music from my library that I felt defines me as a person and reminds me of important past experiences. This project helped me to familiarize myself with my own musical tastes, further my knowledge of Audacity, and was an interesting and fun introspective exercise.

We are strong believers in the value of "performance" as a way to get students to learn from each other. In addition to playing student compositions in class, we make them available on the web. We actually do this with all assignments. It was especially interesting for students to be able to see others' song flowcharts, for example, since we didn't have time in class to show and discuss all that work. With the students' permission (they all signed waivers approved by our Institutional Review Board), we made our assignment website public. You are welcome to view their work at **compthinkinsound.org.**

> *Note:* We didn't do the audio-ethnography project in 2011, so you won't find students' compositions for this assignment there. However, you will find the Song Flowchart assignment there. Also note that the audio players that appear next to MP3 files in most browsers and OGG files in Firefox require HTML5, so you need to be using the latest version of your favorite browser to have access to these controls.

It is interesting to note two things about posting student work on a public website. First, it completely eliminates cheating. Students can't possibly copy other students' work and submit it as their own when it's all publicly accessible by everyone. Copying would stand out like a sore thumb!

Second, it fosters far more learning than can be accomplished in class, interdisciplinary or not. In regular computer science classes, for example, students seldom take a detailed look at other students' code. Music students, on the other hand, are strongly encouraged and even required to listen to many different types of music, different interpretations, and different arrangements. There is something to be learned from each one. The same is true in computer science, but we seldom require CS students to really "get into" other programmers' code other than to look at brief examples. By posting student work on a public website for all to see, students' natural curiosity is piqued to the point that at least some examine the code in detail to figure out how their peers "did that."

Developing CT skills in a collaborative environment focused on exploration and discovery can lead to many surprises. Students often come up with very different ways to approach assignments, including ways that we don't think of ourselves. They also discover features of the software that we may not have investigated and techniques that we may not have explored. Thus, not only do the students learn from each other by seeing their classmates' work, but we professors learn as well. When everyone is posting work for others to see, everyone is engaged. What could possibly be a better environment for learning?

APPENDIX
Downloading and Installing Audacity with the LAME MP3 Encoder

Audacity's home page is **http://audacity.sourceforge.net**. To download the software, click the **Download** tab and then click the appropriate link for your system. This takes you to a page with instructions specific to your system (see Figure 5-6). Click the appropriate link to download the software for your system. Once you save the installation file on your system, execute that file to begin installation.

There is one more thing you need to do before using Audacity. While *importing* MP3 files into Audacity is straightforward, *exporting* music created in Audacity as MP3 files requires an additional installation step: you need to install the MP3 *encoder*. Like Audacity, the encoder is available free of charge, but it is covered by a separate license, so it is not bundled with Audacity itself.

The good news is that downloading and installing the MP3 encoder is rather easy. Under **Optional Downloads** on the download page (see Figure 5-7), you will find a link to the **LAME MP3 encoder**. That link that takes you to a page entitled "How do I download and install the LAME MP3 encoder?" with detailed instructions for both Windows and Macintosh

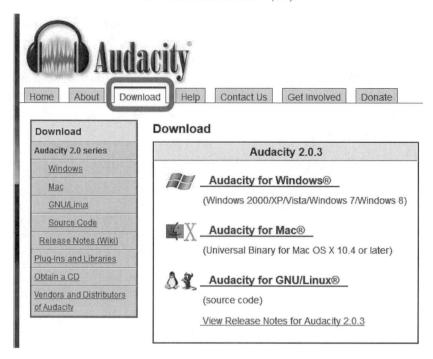

Figure 5-6:
The Audacity website Download page. http://audacity.sourceforge.net/download

Figure 5-7:
The Audacity website Download section for Windows systems, showing the locations of the links to download the program and the LAME MP3 encoder. http://audacity.sourceforge.net/download/beta_windows

systems. You click yet another link, labeled **LAME download page**, to get to **lame.buanzo.com.ar,** which is the website from which you can actually download the required. **exe** file for Windows or. **dmg** file for Macs to install the LAME MP3 encoder.[4] Once you have that file on your system, follow the directions back on the Audacity website and voilà! Audacity will then be able to export MP3 files that play on just about any MP3 device that you or your students may own.

BIBLIOGRAPHY

[1] Adobe Systems. (2011). *Adobe Audition CS5.5.* www.adobe.com/products/audition. html, accessed 8/9/2011.

[2] Audacity Open Source Development Team. (2011). *Audacity: The Free, Cross-Platform Audio Editor and Recorder.* audacity.sourceforge.net, accessed 8/5/2011.

[3] Avid Technology. (2011). *Pro Tools.* www.avid.com/US/products/family/pro-tools, accessed 8/10/2011.

[4] Browning, E. B. (1850). *Poems* ("New Edition," 2 vols.). Revision of the 1844 edition, adding *Sonnets from the Portuguese* and other poems. Sonnet No. 43. London: Chapman & Hall.

[5] Coalson, J. (2008). *FLAC - Free Lossless Audio Codec.* flac.sourceforge.net, accessed 8/10/2011.

[6] Quinion, M. (2011). *World Wide Words: Prosumer.* www.worldwidewords.org/turnsofphrase/ tp-pro4.htm, accessed 8/10/2011.

[7] Sony Creative Software. (2011). *Sound Forge Product Family Overview.* www.sonycreativesoftware. com/soundforgesoftware, accessed 8/5/2011.

[8] Wikipedia. (2010). *Autoethnography.* http://en.wikipedia.org/wiki/Autoethnography, accessed 8/21/2011.

[9] Wing, J. M. (2009). "Computational Thinking." *Journal of Computing Sciences in Colleges* **24**(6):6–7.

CHAPTER 6

Platforms and Tools

Anything You Can Do,
I Need to Do Cheaper

There is nothing like making music and messing with sound to inspire people to learn how to program.

> Wilson, Cottle, & Collins, *The SuperCollider Book*

GETTING INTO THE GAME

On their page intended to woo prospective graduate students, the Georgia Tech School of Music website says [8]:

> Successful design and development of music technology systems must be supported by knowledge of music theory, perception, composition, and performance, as well as digital media, computing, electrical and mechanical engineering, and design.

We don't disagree, but that's an awful lot to know! What's more, requiring students to have even a subset of these skills before they can "get in the game" deprives a huge percentage of them the opportunity to learn valuable computing skills through the engaging power of music.

There is no end to the money you can spend on technology to gain the ability to design and create. For certain types of projects, professional or "prosumer"[1] software applications boasting the latest bells and whistles might in fact make total economic sense in terms of functionality and time. However, we don't feel that it's necessary to jump into the higher end of the market at the beginning stages of learning computational skills. In addition, such costs are prohibitive for most undergraduates and even graduate students. Of course, you could outfit a computer lab available to students with this level of software, but then they would have to do all their assignments in the lab. This is not a practical solution for our students because so many of them are commuters or work off campus and are unable to spend significant time in our labs outside of class time.

We think it's important that students can run the same software on their own systems that is demonstrated in class and with which they are expected to do their assignments. We therefore suggest that you adopt software platforms that you can download freely from the web, but that still allow you to explore broad computing and music concepts common to the higher end platforms. We don't contend that such software is as sophisticated or as polished as its professional or "prosumer" cousins, but it is most likely fully sufficient for your teaching purposes. *Remember:* Your goal is to make the excitement of creating music accessible to students so that you can teach computing and music together in engaging ways. While this approach to computing+music is *not* about training audio engineers, virtually all the music professors we have worked with believe that every musician can benefit from knowing something about computing and recording technology.

The argument for low cost of entry is particularly compelling in elective courses at the introductory level (like ours) because most of these students will not take another course in which they might use the same tools. Thus, we readily trade a bit of quality or a lack of advanced features for free cost. In addition, "good enough" is a compelling criterion for evaluating what platforms and tools to use, especially when one considers students' pocketbooks. We also find that "good enough" does not hinder creativity or impede learning. On the contrary, it might actually enhance those outcomes. And we're sure that as we write this, new, free web-based options are being developed at higher and higher levels of complexity.

Consider this little anecdote. Jesse and his wife Bonnie went to see *Jersey Boys*, the story of the iconic Four Seasons, in Boston. The show was terrific, and on the way out Bonnie wanted to buy the CD. It was $25 at the theater, and Jesse said that they could probably buy it from Amazon.com at half that price. Bonnie acknowledged that, but said that she wanted to listen to all those great songs on the drive home. As you can probably guess, we bought the CD at the theater, and indeed we enjoyed it almost as much as the show as we sang along in the car.

Once we got home, Jesse went on Amazon.com and bought four original Frankie Valli and the Four Seasons CDs for the same $25 price. When they came a few days later, something seemed to be missing. The original Four Seasons weren't as good as the actors portraying them! Why?

Well, there are two reasons. The first is simply 50 years of improvements in recording technology. Even though the old recordings had been re-mastered, they still couldn't compare to the brilliance of the show recording. But the second reason is actually the more interesting. Just who were Frankie Valli and the Four Seasons, and what was their musical training?

Before we answer that question, consider the backgrounds of the actors who play the Four Seasons in the national touring company of *Jersey Boys* that played in Boston. Matt Bailey (who played the role of *Tommy DeVito*) has two B.F.A. degrees from the University of Arizona, one in acting/directing and the other in musical theater [1]. Joseph Leo Bwarie (*Frankie Valli*) has a B.F.A. in acting from Boston's Emerson College [5]. Josh Franklin (*Bob Gaudio*) has a B.F.A. in musical theater from Webster Conservatory for the Theater Arts in St. Louis, Missouri, and has studied music and theory with Linda Weiss, a graduate of the Juilliard School of Music and founder of the Colorado Springs Conservatory [7]. Steve Gouveia (*Nick Massi*) is the odd man out in this regard, having taken only "a few voice lessons here and there," and claiming that he was simply "blessed with a good singing voice" [9].

The original Frankie Valli and the Four Seasons, on the other hand, were just—as they say near the end of the show—"four guys under a streetlamp" making "that sound, our sound." They had little to no formal training, but they sure had style. And heart. Perhaps it was exactly that raw energy and not the formal polish that helped to propel the original group to the top of the charts, because listening to them even on compressed MP3s using tiny earbuds is enough to make even the most hardened audio engineer smile.

So while the best recording equipment and the best software may be financially out of reach for most of us—and especially for our students—all of us can still make music. Good music. What's more, it is entirely feasible to teach a lot *about* music and explore the CT techniques that complement the musical concepts we introduce in this book using "good enough" tools. And even more, when assignments are created to reinforce those concepts, or to get students to extend them by writing programs, students can do so on their own systems in their own homes or dorm rooms. For these purposes, accessibility trumps professional quality any day.

SOUND EDITING
Audacity

We have already discussed the free sound editor Audacity (**audacity.sourceforge.net**), at considerable length. This is the main sound editor we use in our classes and that we highly recommend, not only because it's free, but because it will be more than adequate for your purposes and runs well under both Windows and Mac OS. Most music students are already quite familiar with Audacity, but few have explored its capabilities thoroughly. They may have used it to record themselves and then cleaned up those recordings. For many, the most sophisticated thing they may have done beyond simple cut-and-paste editing and trimming is to normalize the waveform of a soft recording to increase its volume. Few at the beginning GenEd level understand the ramifications of clipping or the relationship between volume and decibels.

Students in other arts majors are much less likely to be familiar with Audacity. Like science and engineering majors, many of these students may have never used any sound editing software at all, including the limited applications that come with their own systems.

This is OK, of course, and we repeat that the point of this work is not to train audio engineers. But Audacity's many effects and filters provide wonderful opportunities to teach CT while students are, in the words of Dan Truman, "messing around with sound" [20]. (Dan Truman [14], along with Perry Cook, is also the founder of the Princeton Laptop Orchestra, "PLOrk" [18, 19].)

For example, when you are attempting to learn a song from a recording it is often useful to slow down the tempo. Audacity has an effect that allows you to change tempo without changing pitch (see Figure 6-1). This dialog box is very nice because it allows you to specify the change as either a positive or negative percentage or as a beats per minute value. If you enter numbers into the "beats per minute" fields, the percentage change is automatically calculated for you. The resultant length (the time to play the entire recording) is also calculated automatically.

One thing you can do with this dialog box is to have students compute the values themselves and then use Audacity to verify their answers. Or you can turn the problem on its head by slowing a recording down or speeding it up and then asking students to figure out how to reverse that change using only the "Percentage Change" field. The answer is that you have to use a reciprocal. That is, if you slow it by 50% (1/2), to get back to the original tempo you have to speed it up by 100%. But is that 2/1? No, it's not. The arithmetic gets a bit tricky here. To slow by 50%, you're really using

$$(1/2) - 1 = -1/2 = -50\% \qquad \textit{note the negative values}$$

To get back to the original you use

$$(2/1) - 1 = +1 = 100\% \qquad \textit{note the positive values}$$

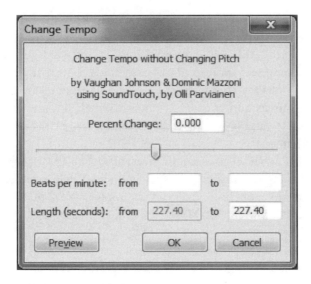

Figure 6-1:
Audacity dialog box for "Changing Tempo without Changing Pitch."

This makes it easier to see the reciprocal relationship, but some students will obviously have trouble understanding the computations. Things get even more interesting if you only want to slow it by one third, which is two thirds of the original speed. This computation becomes

$$(2/3) - 1 = -0.33 = -33\%$$

To return to the original speed, you need to use

$$(3/2) - 1 = +0.5 = 50\%$$

You can then contrast changing tempo without changing pitch with simply changing the speed, which is another Audacity effect, but one that affects both tempo and pitch. Students will clearly hear the difference between the two.

Thus, Audacity is a perfect choice for students' first sound editor. What's more, given that many music majors at least know the concepts that some of Audacity's effects implement—such as changing pitch without changing tempo and vice versa—they get an opportunity to teach the science and engineering majors. When we get into programming later in the course, the science and engineering majors typically teach the music and arts majors. This is truly *reciprocal learning* at work [2], and we consider that the best way to engage the entire class.

DVDVideoSoft Free Studio and AVS4YOU

We have also mentioned the free DVDVideoSoft suite of tools (**dvd-videosoft.com**, see Figure 6-2). These tools are mostly converters, not editors, but they are invaluable for capturing songs from YouTube and other sources and converting them to formats that Audacity can work with. As of this writing there were 48 programs in the entire package, all free!

AVS4YOU (**www.avs4you.com**, free with logos and watermarks that can be removed for a small registration fee) is a full suite of 16 editing and associated audio, video, and image editing tools (see Figure 6-3). The frequently asked questions (FAQs) section of their website states:

> The non-activated [*free and unregistered*] programs do not have any feature or time limitations. The only thing is that they have a voice logo in the output audio files (that is true for audio programs, such as AVS Audio Editor, AVS Audio Recorder, etc.) or a watermark in the output video files (AVS Video Converter, AVS Video Editor, etc.). To remove logos and watermarks you need to activate your programs [*by registering them and paying a small fee*] and reconvert your source audio or video files.

This will be fine for most educational purposes, as long as you don't mind hearing the voice logos or seeing the watermarks on student assignments. As usual, these tools are not as sophisticated as the expensive programs, but they are very impressive for the price.[2] In addition, they are very easy to use,

Figure 6-2:
DVDVideoSoft Free Studio Manager.

which is of paramount importance for students at the level we teach and useful for users at all levels.

Some of the DVDVideoSoft programs are available for the Macintosh, but as of this writing the AVS4YOU programs explicitly specify "no Mac OS/Linux support." However, you can find similar tools for the Mac with straightforward Google searches. For example, we found the free "Enolsoft Free YouTube Downloader HD for Mac" at **www.enolsoft. com/free-youtube-downloader-hd-for-mac.html** and "SoundCon-verter for Mac" at **soundconverter.en.softonic.com/mac**. And of course, you can also do basic sound editing with a number of tools that come with Macs, such as GarageBand, or others that are specifically de-signed for the Mac.

The bottom line is that in addition to Audacity, there are numerous other options for creating and editing existing or newly recorded sounds. To repeat, however, your goal in selecting tools should be to use those with a low threshold, both in terms of cost and learning curve. While computing+music is the *vehicle* for teaching computational thinking, you don't want to become so tool-centric that your students "can't see the forest for the trees." We suggest that you use tools that your students can pick up quickly, even if they don't use all of the tools' features. After all, how many of us, even those who consider themselves advanced, really use or are even familiar with *all* the features of Microsoft Word or Excel?

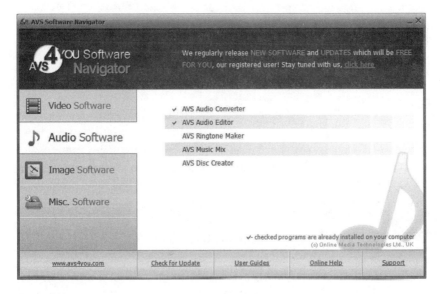

Figure 6-3:
AVS4You Software Navigator.

SOUND PROGRAMMING

The same philosophy of ease of use applies to our choice of sound programming software. To Jesse, programming is a delight. He sees it as a highly creative activity in which he gets to express himself through hundreds of small decisions about how to design and implement an algorithm and how to present information to a user. He takes real pleasure in coding elegant solutions to sometimes complex problems.

To Gena, programming is at best a black art, and at worst a black hole! She doesn't enjoy becoming engrossed in the rigid structure of computer languages as Jesse does. She has spent countless hours achieving the skill required to produce precise sounds on her violin, but she doesn't relish spending similar hours teaching a computer to do likewise. Gena believes that software for the average person should be intuitive, logical, and user-friendly. And most important, it should work—plain and simple. When it doesn't, there's little joy in the effort required to figure out why.

When we talk about these differences in professors' perspectives, you might consider them cute. But when you face an interdisciplinary class full of students from disciplines that are, at least on the surface, near polar opposites of each other, they present a real challenge for keeping all students engaged. If we program in a language or system that is comprehensible only to computer science majors, the music majors will tune out, regardless of how patient we are in explaining what's going on. If we program in a language or system that is easily grasped by the music majors but is so limited as to be seen as a "toy," not only will the CS majors tune out, but the music majors will quickly become bored, as well. The trick is to find a compromise.

Good Tools that Just Don't "Work" for Our Students

There are, of course, many programming tools and languages and libraries and systems for programming music. Some are built on standard programming languages, such as jMusic [3], which is built on Java, while others are built completely from scratch. Some are corporate products that are professionally maintained, while others are homegrown. The latter are less likely to have comprehensive documentation and rarely have any technical support.

As always, we look for free tools. As mentioned earlier, the problem is to find one that can be used by all of our students. As an example of a good tool that just doesn't "work" for our students, consider the SuperCollider

[10, 21] program in Figure 6-4.[3] Believe it or not, this program plays the famous guitar riff in Led Zeppelin's *Kashmir*. (To hear this riff, visit **www. youtube.com/watch?v=hAzdgU_kpGo.**)

It's important to stress that we are not knocking SuperCollider. On the contrary, it's a great system that some of our students and colleagues have used to produce very cool music. It's incredibly powerful in the hands of sophisticated users. Our only issue is that the large learning curve involved

```
// Select all between the parentheses and
//    press [Ctrl+KeyPad Enter] to load the synthdef
(   // The actual synth and envelope
  SynthDef( "kashmir", {
    arg sound, freq ;
    var sin, env_gen, env, freq_env ;

    env = Env.triangle( 0.2, 0.2 ) ;
       // Env.triangle has ( duration, level [, peak] ) ;
    env_gen = EnvGen.kr( env, doneAction: 2 ) ;
       // EnvGen plays back the envelope
       // when done, it frees up the space used by the synth
    sin = SinOsc.ar( freq, 0, env_gen ) + Saw.ar( freq, env_gen ) ;
       // SinOsc takes 4 arguments ( freq, phase, mul [, add] )
       // Mul is the wave multiplier, to change the amplification
       // Saw takes ( freq, mul [, add] )
    Out.ar( [0,1], sin )
       // Array enables stereo ( 0 left, 1 is right )
       // Out.ar takes 2 arguments, the busses to write out to
       //     and the source of the sound
  }).load(s);
       // The load message loads this SynthDef to the server
)

// Select all between the parentheses again and
//    press [Ctrl+KeyPad Enter] to play
(
  var x = 45, a = 6 ;
  p = Pseq([ 45, 46, 47, 48 ], inf).asStream ;
       // Pseq needs "asStream", or it won't play in sequence
       // this Pseq sequences through the notes
  q = Pseq([ 0.2, 0.2, 0.8 ], inf).asStream ;
       // this Pseq sequences the seconds to wait between notes
  t = Task({  // a task is a stream that can be paused
    loop({    // loops forever
      if( a < 6, { a = a + 1 }, { a = 1 ; x = p.value } ) ;
         // every 6 notes, x changes
      y = Synth( "kashmir", [ freq: x.midicps ] ) ;
         // calls SynthDef "kashmir" with current note
         // midicps (cycles per second) allows you to use midi
         //     numbers, which are then converted to hertz
      q.value.wait ;
         // #.wait is the number of seconds to wait
    });
  });
  t.start ;
)

// Press [Ctrl+KeyPad Enter] on line below to stop the task
t.stop ;
```

Figure 6-4:
SuperCollider program to play the Led Zeppelin Kashmir riff. Developed by undergraduate research assistant Brendan Reilly under the guidance of Profs. S. Alex Ruthmann and Jesse Heines.

in understanding the SuperCollider syntax makes it inappropriate for an entry-level interdisciplinary course in computing+music. Even with the level of documentation provided in Figure 6-4, our GenEd students would simply be blown away by the complexities of this code.

The same is true of Java with jMusic. Most (but not all) of our computer science students are familiar with Java and know how to use libraries such as jMusic, but they would have a very hard time explaining all the non-music structures to their music student partners. You can probably think of a number of other systems—some of which you may actually use yourself—that simply wouldn't be appropriate for your students. The bottom line is that we need a less intimidating, more intuitive, more user-friendly, yet still powerful, solution.

A Good Tool that Does "Work" for Our Students

The solution suggested by our computer science colleague Fred Martin and our music colleague Alex Ruthmann is Scratch, a visual programming environment developed by the Lifelong Kindergarten Group at MIT's Media Lab. Version 1.4, which Alex and Jesse adopted when they taught *Sound Thinking* together in the Spring 2010 semester, is freely download-able from **scratch.mit.edu/scratch_1.4.** This version runs on Mac OS X (version 10.4 or later), numerous versions of Windows, and Ubuntu.[4] In May 2013 the Scratch group released Version 2.0, which is completely web-based. This new version is written in Flash, so it runs directly from the web in standard browsers. It does *not*, however, run on iPads. The examples in this book were developed in Version 1.4, but they all run in Version 2.0 as well.

Although Scratch is designed for young children, it "works" for college students for a number of reasons. First, don't be misled by its stated target audience or the word "Kindergarten" in the name of the group that developed it. In experienced hands, Scratch can be used to produce very sophisticated programs. The beauty of the Scratch visual programming paradigm is that it makes the threshold of entry into the world of programming very low. That is, complete novices can do interesting things very quickly, and with the block design, students can understand the programming constructs involved considerably easier than if they were seeing them in textual code.

The "Lifelong Kindergarten Group" is not about developing software for children in kindergarten. It is about developing software that makes experimenting easy and learning by trial and error joyful, the way kindergarten children learn. The director of the Lifelong Kindergarten Group is Mitchel Resnick, a proponent of Seymour Papert's constructionist theories of learning [12]. Resnick argues that

> the "kindergarten approach to Learning"—characterized by a spiraling cycle of Imagine, Create, Play, Share, Reflect, and back to Imagine—is ideally suited to the needs of the 21st century, helping learners develop the creative-thinking skills that are critical to success and satisfaction in today's society. [15]

Thus, Scratch is not a "toy" language or system. Resnick designed it to achieve goals that he credits to Seymour Papert, as embodied in Papert's seminal book *Mindstorms* [11], and built on concepts pioneered in the Logo programming language.

> Papert argued that programming languages should have a "low floor" (easy to get started) and a "high ceiling" (opportunities to create increasingly complex projects over time). In addition, languages need "wide walls" (supporting many different types of projects so people with many different interests and learning styles can all become engaged). [16]

Resnick says that his group plans "to keep our primary focus on lowering the floor and widening the walls, not raising the ceiling," but for our purposes, Scratch already has a ceiling high enough to incorporate a number of important computer science constructs that we use to teach computational thinking: code blocks, global and local variables, lists, loops, conditionals, and subroutine-like structures.[5]

But most important for us, Scratch includes some great music functionality. First, it can play a number of built-in sounds, or sounds stored in MP3 files. You can also record your own sounds and make them available to Scratch without leaving the environment (see Figure 6-5).

But Scratch doesn't stop there. The secret to the music capabilities is that the lead programmer for Scratch is John Maloney, a gifted software developer who was a member of the team that developed Squeak (**www.squeak. org**), an experimental programming system for elementary schoolchildren headed by computer pioneer Alan Kay. Among other things, John had primary responsibility for Squeak's sound and music facilities. He integrated a number of those facilities into Scratch, particularly its ability to *generate* music using MIDI. Playing prerecorded sounds is one thing, but truly generating music it is quite another. This is the part of Scratch that we and our colleague Alex Ruthmann use most earnestly to teach CT through music programming.

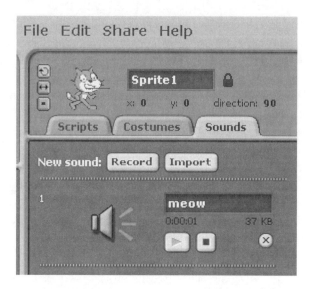

Figure 6-5:
The Scratch panel from which one can play, import, and record sounds.

TEACHING COMPUTATIONAL THINKING WITH SCRATCH
Working with Scratch

It is not our purpose for this book to be a Scratch programming manual. What's more, we are quite confident that readers of this book wouldn't even need a manual to get up and running with Scratch. You just download it, install it, and start dragging blocks around and connecting them up to form structures. For those who like a little handholding, however, we recommend the Scratch support page at **info.scratch.mit.edu/Support.**

The remainder of this chapter introduces the music capabilities built into Scratch that we use and demonstrates the scope of ways in which we use them to teach CT. We provide examples of our own work, that of students, and even some extensions created by others working in this area. However, it is impossible to cover everything. Despite its apparent simplicity, Scratch is incredibly rich. Readers who desire to see more examples are directed to the class notes and assignments on our course websites. Websites for current and previous semesters' offerings are available at **http://compthinkinsound.org**.

Handouts and sample programs from our *Making Music with Scratch* workshops are also available at **www.performamatics.org**. In addition, the programs described here can be found in the Scratch user areas, specifically these:

- **http://scratch.mit.edu/users/performamatics/**
- **http://scratch.mit.edu/users/alexruthmann/**
- **http://scratch.mit.edu/users/drjay/**

You can find examples of student work from several of their first Scratch assignments.

Generating Music with Scratch

Figure 6-6 shows the Scratch **Sound** panel, from which you can select blocks to add to your program. When you drag a `play note 60▼ for 0.5 beats` block into the Scripts area, you can change the note's MIDI value to be played by clicking the ▼ next to the note number. This brings up a piano

Figure 6-6:
The Scratch Sound panel.

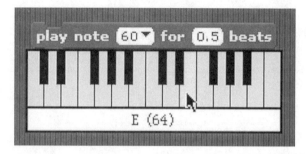

Figure 6-7:
Changing a note's MIDI value by clicking the ● and then selecting it from the popup keyboard.

Figure 6-8:
Changing a note's MIDI value by clicking the value and then typing a new value.

keyboard as shown in Figure 6-7. You can also change the note value manually by clicking it and then entering a number as shown in Figure 6-8. Using only these basic capabilities, we are able to program a linear first version of "Frère Jacques" as shown in Figure 6-9. As you can see from this example, each note is entered manually, including the notes that repeat.[6]

Coding music linearly is rather tedious, to say the least, and it isn't necessarily the way musicians think about music. Musicians more often think about music at the phrase level and look for patterns. Figure 6-10 takes advantage of the "looping constructs" in the Scratch **Control** panel (Figure 6-11) to make the coding more efficient.[7] (*Note:* In Scratch 2.0, the **Control** panel has been renamed **Data.**) As you will notice, the first four notes in our example in Figure 6-9 repeat. Placing those notes within a **repeat** block allows us to repeat that pattern as many times as we wish. We can then create subsequent loops with the next series of patterns we hear, as you see in Figure 6-10.

You can download examples of several of the demos explained previously.

The real power to generate music with Scratch comes when we replace the "hard-coded" values in the **play note** block with variables. "Hard-coded" means that actual numbers are specified in the program, such as the MIDI values 60, 62, and 64. Programmers typically avoid hard-coding whenever possible so that when they need to make a change to a program,

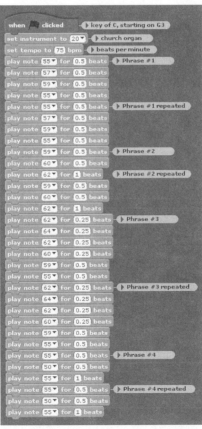

Figure 6-9:
First version of Frère Jacques with each phrase repeated in straight linear fashion. (The Scratch version is coded an octave lower than the score.)

Frè - re   Jac - ques

Dor - mez - vous?

Son-nez les ma - ti - nes

Ding   dingue   dong

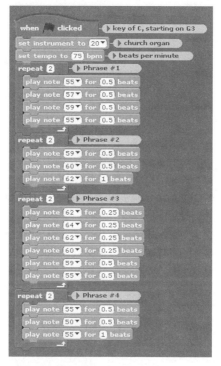

Figure 6-10:
Second version of Frère Jacques with each phrase repeated using a Scratch repeat loop. (The Scratch version is coded an octave lower than the score.)

such as changing a song's starting note, they need to make that change in only one spot. To do this, you need to use variables. If you set a variable to the starting note and each time you need that note you refer to the variable, it will be correct everywhere throughout the program.

To do this in Scratch, you display the **Variables** panel and click the **Make a variable** button (Figure 6-12a). This brings up a dialog box in which you

Figures 6-11:
The Scratch Control panel. (Note: In Scratch 2.0, the Control panel has been renamed to Data.)

enter the name of your variable (Figure 6-12b). Once a variable has been created, Scratch makes a number of operations available that you can use to manipulate that variable (Figure 6-12c).

In the program in Figure 6-13, you can use the **note** variable, which is the variable you just created when you clicked on the **Make a variable** button in the **Operator** panel. Notice that the various types of procedures one can perform in Scratch are color-coded based on how each series of blocks functions. For example, **Variables** blocks are orange, while **Sound** blocks are magenta. Most Western music is based around some kind of key structure, generally major or minor. Therefore, in the "Frère Jacques" example, we create a variable to represent the tonic, or key, note. Using this variable with the + operator available in the Scratch **Operator** panel (see Figure 6-14), you can program each **play note** block to play a note that is some offset from the tonic. That is, once you establish what the tonic of the composition will be, you can program notes based on the difference in semi-tones between the tonic and the note you want played. This allows you to program a second version of "Frère Jacques" that can play the song in any key and octave you choose.

Not only does this program introduce music majors to variables and the use of mathematical expressions (such as **tonic+7**) in programming, but it also introduces computer science students to the musical concept of transposition. Thus, the process of developing this single program demonstrates not only the power of Scratch but also an approach to teaching computational thinking in an interdisciplinary fashion.

 Student examples of transposing in Scratch can be found here.

Important Note: Scratch is built for animation. For this reason, Scratch *intentionally slows down* processing so that animations do not run too quickly on today's fast computers. However, "fast" is of course relative. What's too fast for animations is sometimes too slow for music, where precise timing is necessary. Therefore, to ensure that Scratch processes blocks as quickly as it can so that your music plays as smoothly as possible, set "single-step speed" to "turbo speed" by selecting **Set Single Stepping...** from the **Edit** menu and then clicking **Turbo speed** as shown in Figure 6-15. In Scratch 2.0, the **Turbo speed** option has been changed to **Turbo Mode** and can be found directly on the **Edit** menu.

Going Further with Scratch Music

A more advanced approach uses the Scratch list capabilities, which are series of values that can be referred to by an index value. For example, if we have a list named **CMajorNotes** that contains the notes of a C major scale

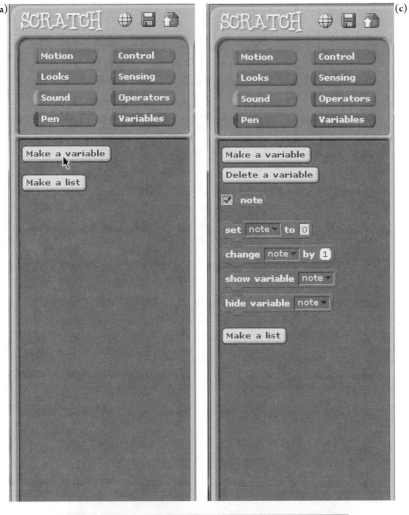

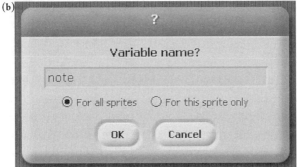

Figures 6-12:
Creating a Scratch variable named note and the operations that Scratch makes available after at least one variable has been created.

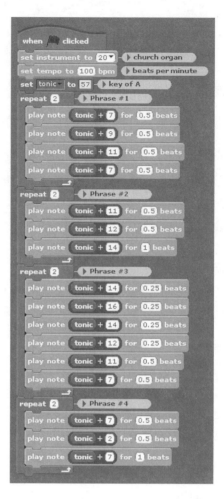

Figure 6-13:
Frère Jacques programmed using a variable for the tonic (or key) note, with each note to be played coded as an offset from the tonic. This version allows the song to be played in any key.

(60, 62, 64, 65, 67, 69, 71, 72), we can refer to the third note as "item 3 of notes." The Scratch **item *n* of *list*** block item ▼ of CMajorNotes ▼ in the **Variables** panel is intended precisely for this purpose.

Lists can also be used to teach numerous CT concepts. For example, in addition to the basic concept of an indexed data structure, a great deal can be done with computing the index of the note you want to play. When combined with loops, the structure becomes even more powerful. It is interesting to write code that plays the scale from the bottom note upward and then again from the top note back down. Or you can play every other note. Or you can pick out notes that make a chord. All such programs require computational thinking.

To make a list, you begin by clicking the **Make a list** button in the Scratch **Variables** panel as shown in Figure 6-16a. Just as when we created a variable,

Figures 6 14:
The Scratch Operators panel.

 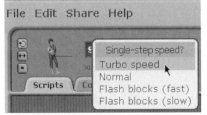

Figure 6-15:
Setting "turbo speed" to improve music timing.

this brings up a dialog box where you will name your list (Figure 6-16b). The **Variables** panel then displays a list of operations that you can do on the list (Figure 6-16c), and an empty list display appears in the stage area (Figure 6-16d).

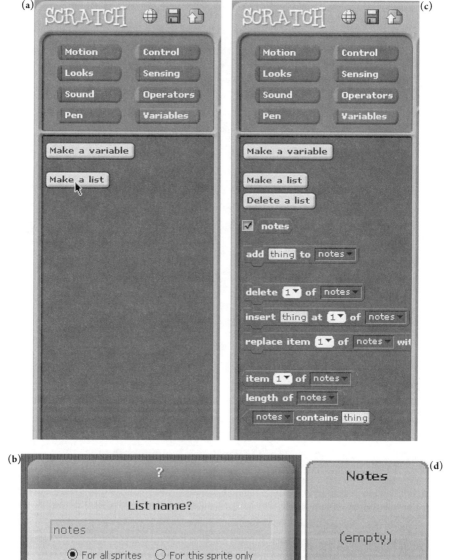

Figure 6-16:
Creating a Scratch list named notes and the operations that Scratch makes available after at least one list has been created.

There are several ways to get data into a list. The most straightforward is to enter values manually by clicking the + in the lower left-hand corner of the list display and then entering the values one at a time, pressing the **Enter** key after typing each one (see Figure 6-17). For music, however, this approach is not optimal. With a lot of MIDI note values to enter, which is the usual case, it is easy to miss a note or to enter a note twice. Editing the list in Scratch is a little tricky, so we prefer to create our lists of notes in external text files and then import those lists into Scratch.

The list to be imported into Scratch must be a simple text file with one value per line. This can easily be created using the built-in Notepad application on Windows systems or the built-in TextEdit application on Macintosh systems. If you use TextEdit, however, be sure to save your list of numbers as plain text by selecting the **Plain Text** option in the **File Format** dropdown list when you first save the file (see Figure 6-18). If you save the file as **Rich Text Format**, which is the default, you will not be able to import the list into Scratch.

Once you've created your list, right-click (control-click or two-finger click on the Mac) the list display to pop up the menu shown in Figure 6-19a. Then click the **import...** menu item. This brings up the dialog box in Figure 6-19b. Click the **Computer** button to navigate to the folder in which you stored your text file, select the file, and click the **OK** button. Your current list values will be deleted, and then the entries in the text file will populate the list. If you make a mistake, it's usually easier to change the text file and reimport the list values than to try to edit them from within Scratch.

For "Frère Jacques," we created two lists and one variable (see Figure 6-20). The first list contains all the MIDI note values, while the second contains the rhythm values (in beats). Note that whole numbers are used for the MIDI values, while decimal numbers are used for the rhythm values. This is perfectly fine: Scratch can handle them both. What's more, Scratch lists can contain strings of characters, as well.[8] These capabilities open up a world of possibilities.

Figures 6-17:
Clicking the + sign on the list display to enter note values manually.

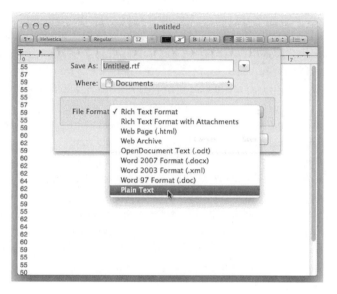

Figures 6-18:
Creating and saving a list of numbers to be imported into a Scratch list using the TextEdit application on a Macintosh system. Note that the file must be saved in Plain Text format for Scratch to be able to read it. After Plain Text format is selected, the entry in the Save As box will change to Untitled.txt, which you can then change to whatever filename you like.

We'll get to the use of the variable in a moment, but first we focus on the two lists: one for **notes** and one for **rhythms** (or perhaps the second list might be better named **durations**). Each was populated by importing values from a corresponding plain text file. It is important to note that the two lists are the same length, such that each note had a corresponding rhythm (or duration).[9]

The program that accesses these lists to play "Frère Jacques" is shown in Figure 6-21. This program uses a variable named **counter** to keep track of which loop it's on. That is, the first time through the loop the **counter** variable is 1, the second time it's 2, and so on. The **counter** variable is then used to provide access to the individual entries in the lists.

Note that you have to initialize and increment this variable yourself because Scratch does not provide access to its internal loop counter. This is not a big deal, and as a matter of fact it is a blessing to arts majors and non-programmers because it makes the way the loop works more explicit. However, it is often a stumbling point for science and engineering majors who typically know programming and realize that there *must* be an internal counter somewhere. These students get frustrated after they spend considerable time trying to figure out how to access that internal counter only to come up empty. So in this case, programming experience is a negative, not a positive! Happily, though, these students' frustration seldom lasts very long, and they get the loop working pretty quickly. For both groups of students, the trick is to remember that you have to increment the variable each time through the loop. Even we sometimes forget to do that, but the beauty

Figure 6-19:
Importing a list of numbers into a Scratch list. (a) The popup menu that appears when you right-click a list display. (b) The dialog box that appears when you select the import… menu item.

of learning to program through music is that one clearly *hears* the error. That is, if you don't increment the variable, the first note will play over and over again ad infinitum. That's clearly not what you want.

Playing Multiple Parts

As most children know, "Frère Jacques" is meant to be sung as a round. To do that, we need to play multiple parts simultaneously using combinations of the **broadcast** **broadcast and wait** and **when I receive** blocks to create subroutine-like structures. Using these blocks, you can "broadcast" a message that the **when I receive** block is listening for. When the latter block "hears" the message it's interested in, the stack of blocks that it sits above will be executed. The difference between the **broadcast** and **broadcast and wait** blocks is that the former sends its message and then allows the

(a)  (b)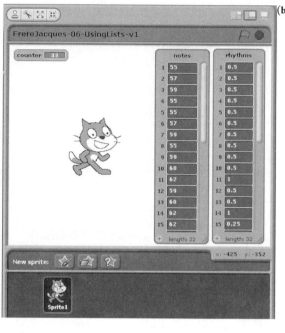

Figure 6-20:
(a) The Scratch Variables panel after creating two lists named notes and rhythms and a variable named counter. (b) The notes and rhythms lists after they have been populated by importing values from corresponding plain text files.

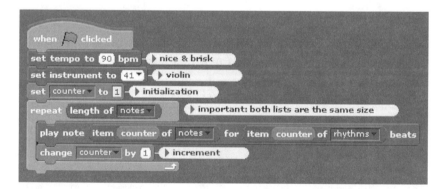

Figures 6-21:
Program to play Frère Jacques from MIDI values and rhythms stored in the two parallel lists shown in Figure 6-20.

program to continue immediately on its way, similar to when you send an email message. That is, you send an email and then go on to do something else without waiting for the recipient to respond. The latter, the **broadcast and wait** block, is more like a telephone call. It sends its message and does not go on until the stack of blocks under the corresponding **when I receive** block finishes executing. This is like waiting for the person on the other end of the line to answer before you can communicate with him or her.

To play "Frère Jacques" as a round, we first put each phrase into a separate block as shown in Figure 6-22. Each of these phrases is also stored in a separate Scratch **sprite**, a system feature that allows blocks to be organized

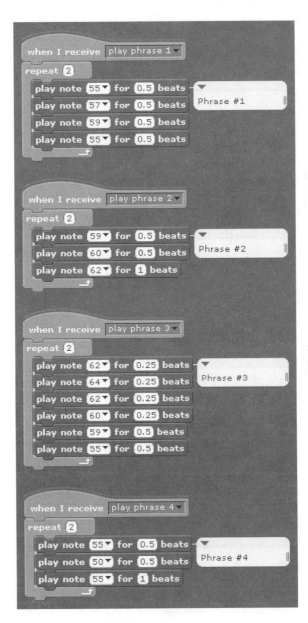

Figures 6-22:
Each phrase of Frère Jacques broken out into its own block.

into groups. When organized in this way, each part can have different volume (loudness) and timbre (instrument) characteristics, because these are "local" to each sprite rather than "global" to the entire program. Each of these stacks of blocks is executed when it receives the message it is waiting for from one of the **broadcast** blocks. Thus, we can play the song "straight" using the code in Figure 6-23.

Now, with the phrases separated and taking advantage of the fact that with the tempo set to 60 beats per minute, each twice-repeated phrase is exactly four seconds long, we can code "Frère Jacques" as a round, as shown in Figure 6-24. This is not the most elegant way to code the round, to be sure, but it is a good starting point for understanding timing and sending and receiving signals and the CT concepts embodied in doing so.

Algorithmic Music

Our uses of variables so far have been pretty simple. Things get considerably more interesting when programs are written to manipulate those variables in ways that affect the sound. Internal variables, like the one for volume, can be manipulated, too. Figure 6-25 implements a fade by manipulating the internal volume variable each time through the loop.

Manipulating one's own variables is even more interesting, and adding a `pick random 1 to 10` block makes things downright fun. In Figure 6-26 we've coded a loop that picks a random note out of a C major scale, which is coded in a list with MIDI values: 60, 62, 64, 65, 67, 69, 71, 72. The result isn't very musical, but it's interesting to hear how it changes each time the program is run. In addition, this little program can open up

Figure 6-23.
Control code to play each phrase of Frère Jacques shown in Figure 6-22.

Figure 6-24:
Control code to play Frère Jacques as a round.

fascinating discussions about *why* the result isn't very musical and how you might manipulate the algorithm to make it more musical.

Connecting to External Devices

Scratch also supports connections to external devices, specifically the Pico-Board [13] and the IchiBoard [6].[10] These devices contain a number of sensors and components recognized by Scratch, which has built-in capabilities for reading data from them. The various sensors and components

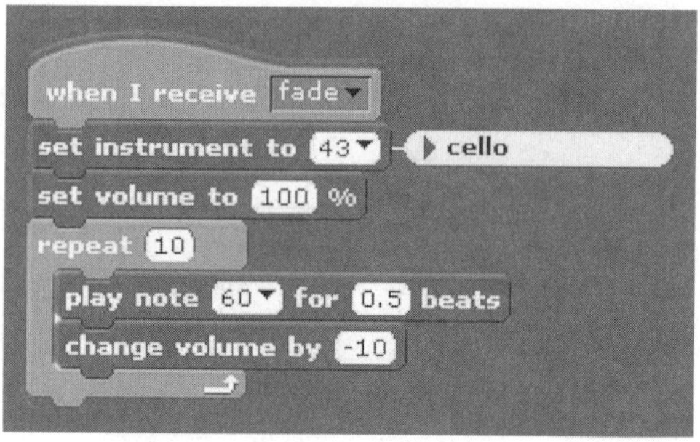

Figure 6-25:
A Scratch fader.

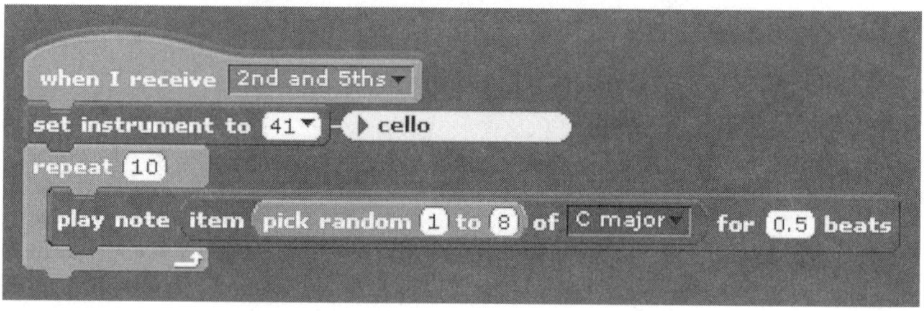

Figure 6-26:
A program that plays ten notes chosen randomly from the C major scale.

send messages and data values to Scratch that it can use within programs just like values stored in variables.

Figure 6-27 shows two views of the IchiBoard, one a photograph (a) and the other a block diagram (b). The main components are

- a slider that returns position values of 0–100
- a sound that returns volume values of 0–100
- a light sensor that returns brightness values of 0–100
- a button that returns **true** if it is pressed
- X, Y, and Z axis accelerometers that return values of −50 to +50
- four ports that take mini RCA plugs for additional connections, such as probes that measure resistance

Students use the IchiBoard to build instruments.[11] For example, one student built an electronic tympani from a simple drum head (Figure 6-28a). The IchiBoard is attached to the drum head stand, and the student manipulates the slider with a string. Scratch reads two of the IchiBoard sensor values: the sound (volume) sensor value and the position of the

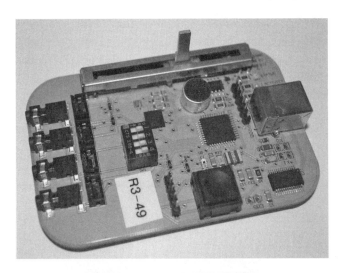

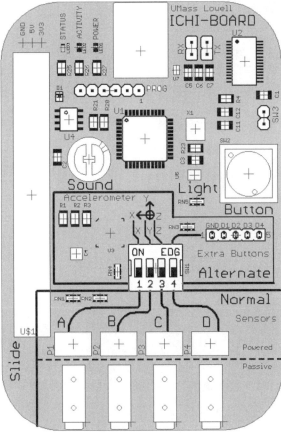

Figure 6-27:
The IchiBoard.

slider (Figure 6-28b). The sound sensor controls when Scratch triggers a note whose pitch is based on the slider position. To hear the result, listen to the first part of the video at **www.youtube.com/ watch?v=9Sec6tAZsuM**.

In the second part of that video, another student uses simple alligator clip probes attached to the IchiBoard external sensor inputs to play different tones based on the measured resistance across different pieces of fruit (Figure 6-29a) and even a classmate's face (Figure 6-29b)! Her code is very similar to the

(a)

(b)
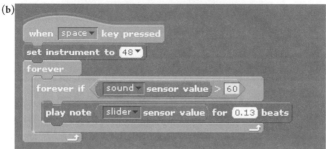

Figure 6-28:
a. An IchiBoard tympani. (Photograph courtesy of Anne Ruthmann Photography.)
b. Scratch code to control the IchiBoard tympani.

Figures 6-29:
a. Using the IchiBoard sensors to play fruit. (Photograph courtesy of Anne Ruthmann Photography.)
b. Using the IchiBoard sensors to play a classmate's face. (Photograph courtesy of Anne Ruthmann Photography.)

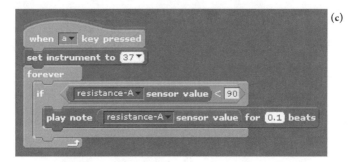

(c)

Figures 6-29:
c. Scratch code to control the IchiBoard sensors.

tympani code, but the change in sensor and the small changes to the parameters make a world of difference in the sound produced (Figure 6-29c).

 Here you will find examples of some beginning student projects using the IchiBoard.

Musical Live Coding

Far more complex music can be created, of course, with multiple parts each playing different instruments, mixing recorded and generated music, and incorporating changes that occur based on user input. For example, our colleague Alex Ruthmann likes to demonstrate to students how to make a sound get softer or louder as the mouse moves left and right or up and down, and how to increase or decrease its pitch when certain keys are pressed.

These types of interactive capabilities are the basis of *musical live coding*, the ultimate use of Scratch to generate music. Brown and Sorensen [4] define live coding as follows:

> The practice of live coding involves writing and modifying computer programs that generate music in real-time. Often this music making activity occurs in a live performance situation with the code source projected for the audience.

Scratch makes musical live coding possible because the blocks are interpreted as the program runs. Therefore, adding or removing a block or changing its parameters in a running program that is playing music will affect the sound being produced in real time. Live coding is extremely fluid, making it nearly impossible to demonstrate in the confines of a book. We therefore refer the reader to the following URLs, where videos of musical live coding in Scratch are posted.

http://www.youtube.com/watch?v=HyMXCZXjwWg
- code and live performance by UMass Lowell Professor Alex Ruthmann

http://www.youtube.com/watch?v=rDyo4p1qLuE
- code and live performance by MIT Media Lab graduate student Eric Rosenbaum using a prototype of Scratch 2.0

For further information on this topic, please see our paper *Teaching Computational Thinking through Musical Live Coding in Scratch* [17], which is linked from the book website.

 You can view and download student examples of their final projects.

Scratch, Music, and CT

We hope that our short tour of the music generation capabilities of Scratch has demonstrated the richness of what can be done with a system that appears, on the surface, to be relatively simple. To put in perspective the extent of the concepts we try to teach with our assignments, Table 6-1 enumerates all the computer science and music concepts our students are exposed to.

Many students easily make the jump from these concepts to CT skills, but some do not. The types of CT Swe are referring to include

Table 6-1. COMPUTER SCIENCE AND MUSIC CONCEPTS COVERED USING SCRATCH. (*THIS LIST WAS DEVELOPED IN CONJUNCTION WITH ALEX RUTHMANN AND JOHN MALONEY.*)

Computer Science	Music
• statements	• pitch
• sequential control flow	• rhythm (as duration)
• iteration	• melodic fragments
• conditional execution	• modes and scales
• arithmetic operators	• polyphony
• Boolean operators	• synchronization
• objects	• harmony
• concurrency	• composing
• variables	• performing
• lists	• transposition
• event handling	• balance and dynamics
• user interaction	• digital audio (as sound files)
• optimization	• MIDI representations
	• tempo
	• form and structural analysis

- breaking problems down into their components and attacking those one at a time,
- analyzing alternatives when things go wrong or don't produce the expected results, and
- creating reusable code and data structures so that they can be used again in another program.

Rather than confront these deeper (or higher level) thought processes, some students do their assignments in a mechanical way, just trying to do what they're told so that they can get the assignment finished as quickly as possible. The student reflections we have quoted throughout this book demonstrate our approach to combating these common tendencies and getting students to think about why we made a particular assignment or what they got out of it. We're sure that virtually all teachers will agree that getting students to see the deeper implications of the concepts we're trying to teach is a constant battle.

We have found, however, that letting students create and manipulate their own music using easily approachable tools like Scratch, having them work in interdisciplinary teams that foster interesting discussions, having help readily available for areas they're not familiar with, and encouraging them to release their own inner creativity all contribute to creating a fertile environment in which the development of computational thinking skills can flourish.

BIBLIOGRAPHY

[1] Bailey, M. (2011). *Bio*. www.mattbailey.info/MBI/Bio.html, accessed 11/14/2011.

[2] Baxter-Magolda, M. B. (1999). *Creating Contexts for Learning and Self-Authorship*. Nashville, TN: Vanderbilt University Press.

[3] Brown, A. R. (2005). *Making Music with Java*. South Bank, Queensland: Lulu (self-published).

[4] Brown, A. R., & Sorensen, A. (2009). "Interacting with Generative Music through Live Coding." *Contemporary Music Review* **28**(1):17–29.

[5] Bwarie, J. L. (2011). *About Joseph Leo Bwarie*. josephleobwarie.com/bio, accessed 11/14/2011.

[6] Engaging Computing Group (2012). *IchiBoard*. www.cs.uml.edu/ecg/index.php/IchiBoard/IchiBoard, accessed 1/11/2012.

[7] Franklin, J. (2011). *Resume*. www.joshfranklin.net/JoshFranklin.net/Resume.html, accessed 11/14/2011.

[8] Georgia Tech School of Music. (2011). *Prospective Graduate Students*. www.music.gatech.edu/ prospective_students/graduate, accessed 11/14/2011.

[9] Gouveia, S. (2011). *RE: Looking for information on your training*. Personal correspondence, 12/12/2011.

[10] McCartney, J. (2011). *SuperCollider*. supercollider.sourceforge.net, accessed 12/23/2011.

[11] Papert, S. (1980). *Mindstorms: Children, Computers, and Powerful Ideas*. New York: Basic Books.

[12] Papert, S. (1993). *The Children's Machine: Rethinking School in the Age of the Computer.* New York: Basic Books.

[13] Playful Invention Company. (2012). *PicoBoard - Sensor Board that Works with MIT's Scratch.* www.picocricket.com/picoboard.html, accessed Jan. 11, 2012.

[14] Princeton University. (2011). *Daniel Trueman, Lewis Center for the Arts.* www.princeton.edu/arts/arts_at_princeton/music/professor_bios/trueman/index.xml, accessed 11/19/2011.

[15] Resnick, M. (2007). "All I Really Need to Know (about Creative Thinking) I Learned (by Studying How Children Learn) in Kindergarten." *6th ACM SIG CHI Conference on Creativity & Cognition*, pp. 1–6. Washington, DC: ACM.

[16] Resnick, M., Maloney, J., Monroyhernández, A., Rusk, N., Eastmond, E., Brennan, K., Millner, A., Rosenbaum, E., Silver, J., Silverman, B., & Kafai, Y. (2009). "Scratch Programming for All." *Communications of the ACM* **52**(11):60–67.

[17] Ruthmann, S. A., Heines, J. M., Greher, G. R., Laidler, P., & Saulters, C. (2010). "Teaching Computational Thinking through Musical Live Coding in Scratch." *41st ACM SIGCSE Technical Symposium on CS Education.* Milwaukee, WI.

[18] Smallwood, S., Truman, D., Cook, P. R., & Wang, G. (2008). "Composing for Laptop Orchestra." *Computer Music Journal* **32**(1):9–25.

[19] Trueman, D., Cook, P., Fiebrink, R., & Snyder, J. (2011). *PLOrk: Princeton Laptop Orchestra.* plork.cs.princeton.edu, accessed 11/19/2011.

[20] Trueman, D. (2011, as quoted by Jacqui Cheng). *Musicians, Tune Your Keyboards: Playing in a Laptop Orchestra.* arstechnica.com/gadgets/news/2011/07/laptop-orchestras-what-are-they-and-where-did-they-come-from.ars, accessed 11/14/2011.

[21] Wilson, S., Cottle, D., & Collins, N., eds. (2011). *The SuperCollider Book.* Cambridge, MA: MIT Press.

CHAPTER 7

Logistics

"Bit by Bit, Putting It Together"

FINDING COMMON GROUND

The Sondheim and Lapine song "Putting It Together" [11] refers to the many challenges facing an artist trying to produce an artistic product and overcome the myriad obstacles to getting funding and recognition. Most people involved in the arts as creators and performers can certainly identify with the many logistical issues highlighted by the song. As the lyric so aptly states, "The art of making art, is putting it together" [11]. Creating or producing the "product" can result in a physical work of art, a performance piece, or, for the purposes of this book, a new software application. Although some may claim divine intervention or inspiration as the muse, it is generally the result of numerous fits and starts, multiple stages of development, attention to minute details, and more hours than one would care to think about. And that is just the beginning. Getting the work "out there" requires just as much attention. The goal of this chapter is to bring you into the process of "putting together" an interdisciplinary project or course, putting together a project team, and getting it and them off the ground.

Logistics is one of the many challenges in this kind of collaborative endeavor. It becomes particularly problematic at the college level for both professors and students. Professors' schedules are difficult to synchronize, but students' schedules are, too, especially when students have different majors. Gena's previous experiences with attempting interdisciplinary projects with colleagues from different disciplines, along with her experiences developing partnerships with local music teachers, informs much of how we structure our projects and negotiate our collaboration, both with each other and within the parameters of our individual departments.

It is difficult enough to attempt a project with a colleague from your own disciplinary area, so it might seem even more daunting to attempt this with someone outside your department. Perhaps as you are reading this book you are formulating an idea for the type of interdisciplinary project or class you would like to create. But finding the right collaborator is equally as important as the concept that will serve as the foundation for the course. Will you and this other person even "speak the same language," as in a shared vocabulary that can serve to help bridge any disciplinary differences? What if you don't have any idea of whom to collaborate with on your campus? Chances are, you may not get many opportunities to meet your colleagues from other departments to find out what their outside interests might be. We can assure you that becoming an expert in a second disciplinary area is not the most viable solution.

In fact, when Gena submitted a proposal to develop her licensure preparation website, she had no clue who would be the best person to work with on campus. The director of technology services for our university system suggested several people to contact. She was able to zero in on Jesse based on feedback from colleagues who knew him. After several phone conversations, she realized his love of music and continued interest in singing in a barbershop chorus would most likely result in his having a basic understanding of musical terminology and concepts that would be beneficial to their ability to communicate across disciplines. As if scheduling class times and meeting times isn't difficult enough, there are many communication issues that can arise by not always having a common technical language and symbol system where meanings and interpretations don't get misconstrued. Therefore, between Jesse's cursory knowledge of music and Gena's rather limited understanding of programming, Gena believed there was some common ground between them.

We would like to stress here that our collaboration is one that developed over time from the ground up based on our shared interests and perceived needs. There may be instances when institutional need may necessitate the creation of interdisciplinary programs and/or teams by administrative design. However, Lindman and Tahamont [4] caution that faculty are often resistant to curricular reform when it is imposed from the top. In those cases, there is the risk that each of the stakeholders may not be equally invested in the outcomes of this work. In our own experience, our collaboration came about based on projects we were each interested in exploring. As such, we feel we are totally invested personally and professionally in the outcome of this work. Yet ironically, without support from the administration, many faculty-directed initiatives may not be sustainable. Being able to articulate why this work is important and learning how to communicate this idea should be high on your agenda. Therefore, a good piece of advice is to work equally hard promoting the benefits of your project or course to your supervisors, students, and professional community as you will in creating and sustaining it.

WHY THE GEN ED COURSE MODEL?

Colleges and universities are not training schools. Virtually all two- and four-year programs at US colleges and universities require students to take courses outside their majors to ensure that they receive a rounded education. Such courses are intended to prepare students to become educated members of the "community of scholars," to which college presidents often welcome them at graduation. At many universities, including ours, these are referred to as "General Education" courses, which are commonly shortened to "GenEds." The official statement on our GenEd program's website states: "The General Education Program at UMass Lowell fosters active learning by asking students to think critically, communicate effectively, and embrace cultural diversity" [13]. What better description is there than that for what we try to do in our interdisciplinary courses?

Most colleges and universities with GenEd programs require a mix of courses. At UMass Lowell, all GenEd courses fit into one of four categories [14]:

- Arts and Humanities
- Social Science
- Science and Technology
- Mathematics

Within these categories, some courses are designated as satisfying the university ethics requirement and some as satisfying its diversity requirement. Different departments require different mixes of these courses for their degree programs. Our music studies program, for example, requires three courses from each of the first three categories. Our computer science program, and most other science and engineering programs, require three courses from each of the first two categories, since science, technology, and mathematics form the core of the courses students take within their own majors.

With most programs packed to the gills with required courses, there is very little opportunity for students to take elective courses that don't necessarily satisfy some requirement toward their degrees. For this reason, we felt that it was critical to get GenEd approval of our interdisciplinary course so that students who took it would not only get three credits but would get

GenEd credit as well, further enticing them to enroll. GenEd status also got our interdisciplinary course listed on the university's GenEd website, making it easier for students to find as they combed that list for courses to fulfill their GenEd requirements.

But where do interdisciplinary courses fit in a GenEd program? Learning about music doesn't "round out" the education of music and other arts majors, and learning about computers doesn't "round out" the education of computer science and other science and engineering majors. The key argument we made to the GenEd committee was that the *interaction* between students from different majors *itself* fulfilled the purposes of GenEd courses. We argued that the interdisciplinary classroom, as well as requiring students to work collaboratively with their peers from other majors, fostered an environment that directly supported the stated purpose of our GenEd program: to get students to "think critically, communicate effectively, and embrace cultural diversity."

The university GenEd committee didn't refute our claim, but they still didn't feel it was enough to warrant GenEd designation. In addition, they didn't know where to put our interdisciplinary course on the list. Was it mostly an arts and humanities course, or was it mostly a science and technology course? And if students from different majors worked together on projects, wouldn't the arts majors do all the artsy work and the science and engineering majors do all the computer work?

These were tough questions to answer. Fortunately, however, we were able to "stand on the shoulders of giants."[1] Our colleagues in art and computer science had successfully won GenEd approval for their interdisciplinary *Artbotics* course, which explored the intersection of art and robotics [15], by co-listing it in both the art and CS departments. Following their lead, we proposed to co-list our interdisciplinary *Sound Thinking* course in both the music and CS departments. In this way, arts students who wished to earn Science and Technology GenEd credit could register for the course using its CS department number, and science and engineering students who wished to earn Arts and Humanities GenEd credit could register for the course using its music department number. That approach, plus our guarantee to the committee that science and engineering students would indeed be required to work with music, and arts students would indeed be required to do some programming, won the day.

With this arrangement, in the five years that our interdisciplinary course has been offered, enrollments have grown from 14 mostly music and CS students to 20 to 29 to 34 to 38 students encompassing a diverse range of majors. Our current classroom forces us to cap the maximum enrollment at 38. The 38 students who enrolled in the Spring 2013 semester came from the following majors.

2 – Biology
9 – Business Administration
1 – Chemistry
1 – Community Health
4 – Computer Science
1 – Criminal Justice
1 – Electrical Engineering
1 – International Exchange Student
1 – Mathematics
1 – Mechanical Engineering
9 – Music Studies
2 – Plastics Engineering
1 – Political Science
3 – Psychology
1 – Undeclared Liberal Arts

Thus, it is easy to see that our course is truly interdisciplinary. We believe that the co-listing approach is a powerful one not only for attracting students but also because it reflects the true interdisciplinary nature of the course itself.

TEACHING DIVERSIFIED GEN ED STUDENTS

When we first offered our interdisciplinary course, Gena had never taught science and engineering majors, and Jesse had never taught arts majors. We weren't sure how we would connect to them or whether the techniques we used with our own majors would work with students in other majors. As described in this and other chapters, we therefore tried to devise a number of activities that we thought would simultaneously interest students from all majors, lend themselves to collaborative projects, and reinforce the concepts we were trying to teach.

Our class was highly diversified with respect to knowledge of music and knowledge of computing. We didn't want to go so fast with either music or computing concepts that we lost those whose expertise was in the other area, but we were also worried about going too slowly and boring some students as we introduced concepts that they had already mastered.

We therefore used several techniques to connect with as many students as possible in every class.

(1) We schedule the class for two 75-minute meetings per week rather than three 50-minute meetings. We have a big campus separated by a river, with most arts classes on one side of the river and most science classes on

the other. Thus, one faction or the other would have to make the trip across the river and back for each class. By scheduling two classes per week rather than three, we cut out 33% of the students' travel time.

(2) We keep our lecture portion to a minimum, adopting more of a "studio approach" to teaching. The longer 75-minute classes are instrumental in making this approach work, as they give us time to introduce a concept,

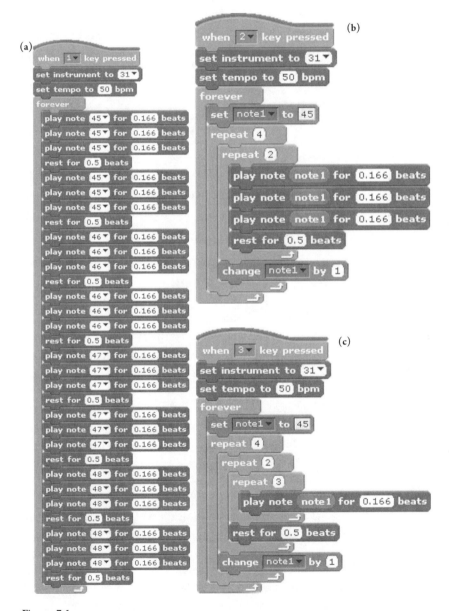

Figures 7-1:
Three versions of Jimmy Page's Kashmir riff programmed in Scratch by S. Alex Ruthmann [8].

work with students either individually or in small groups on an activity related to that concept, and then end the class with "performances" or sharing of student-created works and discussions that revisit the concepts being explored.

(3) We have adopted a "spiral teaching" approach [3], discussing topics at different levels with different students and at different times. This helps keep everyone engaged. As an illustration, consider the Scratch [6, 7] programs in Figure 7-1. All of these programs play Jimmy Page's famous guitar riff from Led Zeppelin's *Kashmir*.[2] The code in Figure 7-1a works properly and all students, regardless of background, are able to grasp the concepts of setting the instrument to be played, setting the tempo at which to play, playing a note, and looping forever.

Even on the first day that we introduce Scratch, however, many students— including many non-science majors—are able to understand how the code in Figure 7-1a can be transformed to the version in 7-1b and then to 7-1c, and that each of these programs plays exactly the same riff. But rather than trying to explain all the concepts involved to the entire class, we get them all to the point that they can start to code a song of their choice and then we work with students individually and in teams to enhance their own work.

THE COMMUNICATION FACTOR

Communication is crucial to any collaboration. Although we touched on this in previous chapters, we can't stress enough the importance of communication throughout the entire process. As mentioned previously, Gena has been involved in multiple interdisciplinary projects, and the key to the ones that were successful for both students and professors was the ability to maintain a constant two-way communication stream. Synchronizing your schedule with your colleague's will improve your ability to meet and interact regularly. Gena found through trial and error that meeting a like-minded professor and having a great interdisiplinary project idea for her students is only one piece of a more complex puzzle. We are fairly certain that if you've ever tried group projects with your students, you understand that groups that lack a strong communication ethic via phone, email, or actual face-to-face meetings have outcomes that are often inconsistent. If this can occur with students within a single class, think about how strongly the odds will be stacked against your students if they are not given an opportunity to meet with their counterparts during their normal class time. That situation will ultimately create an environment of futility and resentment among your students.

Given the social networking and collaborative tools now available, you might just as easily find yourself attempting a collaborative endeavor with a colleague from another institution as you would with someone from your own. In fact, we believe that inter-institutional collaboration will someday be the norm. In the workshops we have been offering to interdisciplinary pairs of teachers who come to Lowell from all over the country, we are starting to see some inter-institutional collaborations take hold as a result of participants meeting other like-minded people in our workshops.

Therefore, you and your colleague need to prioritize scheduling changes at the outset or your students will have a great deal of difficulty finding a common time outside of class to meet with their group mates from the other section (or institution). One of our students took part in both an interdisciplinary project where she and her partner couldn't find a common meeting time and the interdisciplinary project in our synchronized courses. In comparing both experiences, she described the first experience by saying, "But that was just a nightmare and I don't even want to think about it."

For our synchronized classes, there was a one-hour window when Jesse's and Gena's classes overlapped. We are certain that our ability to meet on a regular basis as a large group was a contributing factor to the success of this project. As we pointed out in Chapter 3, our students did not experience frustrations due to lack of communication, as the following music student's comment about having CS students in class attests:

> I think they're great. I love having them in the class. Like I said in my journal, I get the exact opposite vibe from them than I got from the other [sic] kids. These guys are really enthusiastic about what we're doing and they seem anxious to see what they can do. Unlike our other [sic] partner who found every possible excuse to never meet with us.

Consistency is another area you and your colleague must work out through communication. There needs to be a consistent set of guidelines for both groups of students regarding due dates and grading policies. In our first synchronized project, the CS students needed the graphic notations from the music students before they could proceed with their part of the project. If Gena or Jesse needed to change a due date for their students, they needed to first discuss with each other how that change would impact the other students. In Chapter 4 we mentioned that our interdisciplinary project was one of many projects in the music class but represented the final project for the CS students. It is critical to communicate with each other about how the students' grades in the interdisciplinary project affect their final course grades. As you can imagine, grading becomes more complex within a project environment between two disparate classes than within an integrated course. In situations where the assignment isn't equally weighted with regard to the percentage of the grade being affected, the grading issues can be problematic if both groups are not equally invested in the outcome. Creating a project that is intriguing to both sets of students and provides learning outcomes benefiting both your disicplines will promote "buy in" for all involved. This comment from one of the music students gets to the core of why we attempted this project in the first place:

> I love hearing different perspectives from people in totally different areas of study. It's really easy to forget what it was like to not be a musician and how you would have thought about music back then.

There is another "big picture" communication issue you need to consider before embarking on interdisciplinary projects or courses. What if you and your colleague discover you have completely different philosophical views toward grading? What effect will that have on members of your class and their perceptions of how they are doing? It is important to discuss this early in your planning process. If you don't, you may be as surprised at what develops as we were midway through our first semester teaching together.

You see, while Jesse and Gena discussed many aspects of creating this course, the particular discussion about grading never happened. To be fair, when Jesse created a formula that ranked students based on the average of their project grades, it never occurred to Gena that one little computer formula would have such negative consequences for her students. So in addition to being able to see how many points they earned toward their overall final grade, students were also able to see where they ranked in comparison to the rest of the class. Jesse created a password protected application on our website where students could access their individual grading information for this course, including their ranking.

This seemed harmless enough, and on the surface it shouldn't have been a big deal. But in any class, barring any ties, there will inevitably be one student at the top of the rankings and one at the bottom. Now it might be that the student on the bottom is separated from the students nearer the top by only a point or two. However, if you are the student who is ranked last, you are going to be fairly upset if you believe you have been working hard and doing good work and you have these grades to prove it. This is particularly true if you are a student from a program that doesn't stress rankings, such as our music program. Consequently, midway through the semester we had a near mutiny. It was a teachable moment for both of us: just because the technology allows you to do something, it doesn't necessarily mean that you should. We still use the application that allows students to access their grades for all their assignments, but we have disabled the ranking feature.

As you can see, when you embark on interdisicplinary work, you need to filter your work, processes, and procedures through multiple lenses.

HOW TO BEGIN: PROJECT OR COURSE?
Computational Thinking as a Foundation for Interdisciplinary Projects

There are many commonalities and differences between creating an interdisciplinary project and creating an interdisciplinary course, so let's start with the simpler of the two: the project. Each of you may want to take an inventory of the types of projects you currently do in your classes and think about ways each project could be extended to include aspects of the other person's discipline. In our case, we inventoried our separate projects to see what concepts they might have in common, with particular emphasis on how a new project could support the development of computational thinking.

As we outlined in Chapter 4, we began with the Found Objects project mainly because we believed it put all students on a more or less level playing field that didn't advantage students from one discipline over another. This project doesn't require students to know anything more about music than how to explore an object for its sonic qualities and then create a series of patterns using the sounds the object makes. No formal musical knowledge is necessary. Nothing more is needed than one's ears and intuitions. In fact, this activity served as a warm-up exercise for the two groups of students to get to know each other without having to step completely out of their comfort zones. The following sentiment sums up the general feelings of both sets of students with regard to the way this project unfolded.

> I enjoyed seeing everyone's found objects and I liked the fact that the CS students brought their own objects, too. We seem to already be meshing well and I am looking forward to the rest of the project.

At this point you might be thinking, "Nice project, but what does that have to do with CT?" Well, if you were to take an inventory of the kinds of thinking involved in this activity, you would come up with a fairly long list. On the music side, your students will be involved in some serious aural analysis through making decisions about timbre, rhythm, dynamics, form, and texture, not to mention the performance aspect. For the creative notation part of the project, your students will be involved in visual analysis and some serious decision making regarding symbolic representation.

The CT involved in these musical decision-making processes involves your students in temporal structuring, pattern recognition, the beginnings of procedural thinking, and categorizing.

The creative notation part of the project was where we felt the music making and computing could intersect the interests of both sets of students in a natural way. Both disciplines rely on a unique symbol system that is used to create and perform. Jesse's mind immediately gravitated toward the creation of some kind of notation software. He would have his CS students use the music students' invented notations to create notation-like software applications. From a CS perspective, his students would be required to create a project using lists and drag and drop commands, to name just a few of the computing concepts involved. Development of such programs would also highlight the difficulties inherent in translating a two-dimensional graphic symbol system meant to represent musical sounds into a functional, user-friendly, multimedia software application. As our students found out, there are certain conventions each discipline takes for granted, yet we shouldn't assume others will as well. For example, as with reading a book, we read a musical score from left to right, not right to left, up to down, or randomly, unless of course this is a contemporary piece defying traditional musical conventions. But these are all cool features computer programmers could make happen. They can make random boxes light up, too. Who wouldn't want that, right? After one student realized how his composition was being interpreted by one of the CS students, he made the following comment.

> It is good for me to see that people don't immediately understand what I am trying to portray. This way, I know that I need to have a form of communication that everyone will understand, rather than having others do the work to understand me.

Once again, issues of communication become paramount. Whether we are going to be teachers, musicians, or programmers, we need to be clear in our directions and intentions.

BEGINNING AN INTERDISCIPLINARY COURSE

It's one thing to decide as individual professors to collaborate on a project with a colleague in another discipline. Once the decision is made to expand your scope to an entire general education course, however, all kinds of questions begin to surface. Can you obtain the needed approvals from your individual departments, the college General Education committee, and possibly your faculty senate? In our case, being supported by an NSF grant was helpful for our initial offering of the course, but could we sustain this and justify to our deans that having two faculty members in one classroom was critical to the success of the course? There are ways to make this work even without a grant, but first there are some basic questions that need to be addressed regarding the rationale for offering the course in the first place, the goals and objectives of the course, and an overall outline of what you think you can accomplish. If your university's GenEd committee is like ours, you will also need to address how your learning outcomes satisfy the requirements for GenEd courses with regard to breadth of knowledge, critical thinking, and development of clear communication skills.

For breadth of knowledge, we felt that the course would help students grasp the relationship between organized sound production and its digital representation. It would also help them learn to use new tools within a context that is relevant to their needs and interests, explore problems, imagine possible solutions, express their ideas, observe, reflect, and stretch their thinking beyond "right" and "wrong" answers. For critical thinking, we believed students would be challenged to draw connections from their own major to other areas of study. They would need to solve problems in a manner that makes sense to someone else, and not necessarily from their own perspective. We hoped that they would begin thinking of solutions through the lens of another discipline. We felt that putting an emphasis on reflective journals in which they analyzed problems in music and technology as well as working in groups and being responsible for in-class presentations supported the development of communication skills.

If, like us, you do not usually teach GenEd courses, the big stumbling block will be in making the transition from thinking about how to create discipline-specific projects with defined sets of domain-specific knowledge to how to create ones that are more broadly based and appropriate for GenEd courses that are open to all students at all levels of achievement. All projects need to be designed so that any student can succeed, regardless of their major or background experience. Another issue is whether you will require any prerequisites for your course. Since our course was designed to encourage reflective journaling and discussion forums, we both believed the students should have taken and passed our university's two required core writing courses before enrolling in *Sound Thinking*. This is the only prerequisite.

COURSE STRUCTURE AND CHALLENGES

Writing the course description is actually an interesting exercise in creating a succinct description of what your course is about, but sitting down to develop the course structure is where you and your colleague will begin to wrestle with the fine details. Where do you begin the class and where do you want it to end up? How will it be structured? What concepts do you wish to cover and what types of projects will you create to address those concepts? What software will you use? Will the class be taught in a computer lab or in a regular classroom using individual laptops? And last but not least, in whose department/building will the course be offered? Once the starting and ending points are mapped out you can create the rest of your projects to scaffold the concepts needed to get successfully from the beginning of the course through the final project. To see how we structure our *Sound Thinking* course, please see the appendix to this chapter.

Another factor affecting your course structure is the decisions you make about software. This is no small matter. Before you can even begin to think about how to structure the semester, you need to address the software programs you will be using. As we discussed in Chapter 6, in a discipline-specific course geared toward teaching majors, there are certain software applications that you would expect your students to purchase as part of their coursework. However, it is one thing to require your majors to purchase a specific high-end software application that they may use in multiple courses and quite another to ask that of a non-major. We did not feel that it was right to make it all but impossible for students to complete their assignments unless they either purchased a specific software package or were tethered to our departments' computer labs. After laboring for weeks researching inexpensive software options that could closely replicate some of the more expensive programs we were considering, we had an epiphany of sorts. Using programs that were freely available online, as explained in Chapter 6, we could teach broad concepts in digital audio and computing that could serve as a foundation for working with the higher end programs that have more bells and whistles.

Once you know the tools you will be using, you can begin to zero in on the course structure and start to define the concepts and projects you will develop. Do you introduce one discipline at a time and, if so, which one will you start with? Or do you keep both intertwined throughout? The first time we offered *Sound Thinking*, we envisioned the semester being split into three phases. Phase 1 would concentrate on digital audio and Phase 2 would concentrate on computer manipulation. These two would then culminate in Phase 3: the integration of audio and video into a dynamic web application. We then drew up an assignment list (see appendix) that encompassed concepts we wanted to teach. Our Phase 1 covered form, file formats, graphic notation, sound waves, noise reduction, backing up, copying, layering/mixing, panning, compression, and effects processing. Our Phase 2 covered looping programs and simple web pages, code-driven web pages, and processing user input. Phase 3 dealt with synchronization and integration.

Feedback from our students after that first offering suggested that they wanted greater integration throughout the semester. They also wanted more hands-on programming experiences. Each semester we teach the course we still consider it a work in progress. Needless to say, the structure of our course today is vastly different from our first offering. (Please see the appendix for descriptions of our newer assignments.) Based on feedback and recommendations from our Performamatics colleagues S. Alex Ruthmann and Fred Martin, the team abandoned the interactive web pages approach after the first year. Alex pushed strongly for the adoption of Scratch as *Sound Thinking*'s primary music-programming platform, and when Alex taught the second offering of the course with Jesse, they did just that. The team is now finding a greater ability to integrate music and computing through Scratch as described in Chapter 6. We still begin the course with the same project, but we get into the computational thinking concepts almost from the beginning. You can find our most recent course syllabus, class notes, and assignment list at **http://soundthinking.uml.edu**. As you can see, there are multiple ways to structure an interdisciplinary course that integrates two disciplines.

This is a project-driven course meant to promote collaboration among non-like-minded thinkers. Therefore, we think it behooves us to have a brief discussion of how we deal with setting up collaborative groups for the class. Using the class roster, we try to pair students from disparate majors and rotate the arts and technology students through a variety of partners so that at some point everyone has the benefit of working with someone from each of the majors in the class. At the beginning of each project, Gena creates a list of pairings that we post on the class website. Even with the Found Objects project, which is an individual project, students are paired for the presentation part.[3]

You will find that there are students who are open to collaboration and others who will try every conceivable excuse to get out of working with someone else. We can't be there to police their interactions outside of class and force them to get together, so we make sure to build in time toward the end of each class to allow the pairs/teams to meet and plan. During a given project, we also encourage groups to sit together in class.

Control is also a constant issue: who likes to have it and who is more than happy to let others make decisions for them? Therefore, we also try to mix up the Type A personality types and not always pair them with a non-Type A person. Putting two or three people with similar personality types in the same group will require them to adopt an approach to working on a project involving other people that is different from what they may be accustomed to. Not every pairing will work out, but we think that replicates real life: you need to learn to work with all types of people, be willing to listen to other people's ideas, and be able to compromise.[4]

STYLISTIC DIFFERENCES

At conference presentations, Gena often introduces us using a reference to an old Macintosh commercial when she states that she's a Mac and Jesse's a PC. To the technology savvy folks attending these presentations, that short phrase immediately signals our different ways of thinking and teaching.[5] In addition to philosophical differences on grading our students, not surprisingly we have different approaches in the classroom. Jesse will outline a problem that needs to be solved and meticulously take the students step-by-step through the solution. Gena, on the other hand, is more discovery-oriented. She would rather set up a project and give the students time to explore a particular software program to figure it out and learn how it works. Actually, many students in her technology classes have described it as more of a "sink or swim" methodology, though students rarely "sink."

These differences even affect how and when we post class notes. In a typical Jesse class, he will have detailed notes available for his students to see before class so they can walk into class and hit the ground running. In a typical Gena class, the students won't be given much information beforehand, but there will be an extensive amount of student reflection after the fact to unpack the various thought processes and procedures that were uncovered through their class activities. A perfect example is how Gena conducts her Global Music Pedagogy class. The syllabus will not give students any idea of where in the world they will be musically from one week to the next. At the beginning of class, students will listen to several pieces of music to figure out what culture the music is from, what in the music makes them think that, and what musical element(s) might perhaps be consistent with the culture they explored the previous week. One style is very lecture-based, albeit a very engaging and informative lecture. The other is very much in a constructionist mode, with hands-on activities that foster inquiry and discovery. By now you are probably wondering how we can possibly make this work, yet it does.

We have found that as with most things in life, it's all about balance. Before Jesse posts any notes on the web, we discuss what can safely be revealed before class and what should wait until after class. Because so much of the class involves working in groups and working with software and concepts that might be unfamiliar, we spend the beginning third of the class discussing new concepts and leave two thirds of the class for exploration, questions, and working with one's partner. Even the mostly lecture part of the class has become more interactive, as we pose more questions that allow students to make some educated deductions based on what they are learning.

When one of us is doing the lead teaching, the other acts as an assistant when we want to demonstrate a particular point. For example, when Jesse wants to demonstrate a certain procedure for creating a loop, he will pose the question to Gena and have her come up with a solution. As we have mentioned in previous chapters, a great deal of bantering goes on between the two of us. Jesse may make a statement about a particular procedure and Gena will pepper him with a great many "what if" questions and vice versa. Or we may challenge each other in front of the students. Not in a malicious manner, of course, but in that respectful probing and questioning manner that we hope to instill in our students. It is difficult to become dual content experts and we are by no means suggesting that team teaching is not without challenges. Nonetheless, we have come to embody the notion that for integrating computing and music, two heads really are better than one.

ALIGNING WITH DEPARTMENTAL REWARD STRUCTURES
Defining What It Means to "Publish"

As we have often discussed with colleagues, there are different reward structures between those of us in the sciences and those of us in the arts and humanities. Those differences can affect how your work is perceived by people on promotion and tenure committees. This is not insurmountable, but you may need to provide additional documentation to your colleagues and perhaps have discussions with your department chair and dean.

We've all heard the age-old academic cliché: "publish or perish." To a professor in a science or engineering department, "to publish" means to get a paper accepted by an academic journal or a reputable conference, to get a manuscript accepted by a book publisher, or, in some cases, to be invited to give a prestigious lecture. To a professor in an arts department, the term "to publish" may involve a completely different set of criteria for a work to be considered valid by that college's promotion and tenure committees. In the arts, "to publish" might mean to "to perform" or "to show." The administration often looks to fine arts professors to perform musical works in prestigious venues, show their artwork in prestigious galleries, or have their words, images, or compositions included in prestigious books. On the surface, these differences may seem only semantic. But in practice, they can cause problems when two professors must follow different paths to move their academic careers forward.

One issue that can cause problems is the validity of multiple authorship. This is typical for those in the sciences but is often questioned by those in the humanities. Having numerous articles list you as one of several authors is a common practice if you are a CS professor, but it will be seriously questioned by your colleagues if you are in the arts or humanities. Yet interdisciplinary work, by its very nature, will more often than not generate research papers by multiple authors.

Another publishing-related issue concerns the types of peer-reviewed journals that are acceptable. For example, some disciplines are more disposed than others to accepting online peer-reviewed journals. If you publish in a journal that is highly regarded in your colleague's field, will that be acceptable to your colleagues within your department or college? At the time of this writing, there were few interdisciplinary journals for what we do, so it is inevitable that Gena will publish articles in computing journals and Jesse will publish in music journals. It's always a good idea to sit down with your supervisors to help them understand what you are doing and for you to get a clear picture of what their expectations are for your interdisciplinary work and how that will impact your standing within your department.

How Is Research Defined?

This type of work inevitably will blur the boundaries between teaching and scholarship. The definition of "research" itself is also problematic. Not only is this word open to different interpretations across disciplines but it is also defined differently by departments with the same name at different colleges and universities. In the sciences, the main question is whether research on, for example, computer science *education* is a viable research area for a computer science *professor*. Some administrations will answer yes, but others will answer no, taking the position that only research specific to the underlying principles of one's field is appropriate for "counting" toward promotion and tenure. There are numerous examples of professors who are famous not only for their classroom teaching but also for their educational, psychological, or other social science research on teaching (backed by numerous publications and presentations at educational conferences) who had trouble gaining promotions and tenure. For example, history professor Alan Brinkley (son of famous TV news commentator David Brinkley) was denied tenure at Harvard despite the fact that he was "judged among the best instructors by undergraduate surveys" and "won the American Book Award for his 1983 work on Huey Long and the Depression" [9].[6]

Developing, teaching, and sustaining a course such as ours can become a major research project. Since your students are your data sources, you are obligated to conduct your data gathering in compliance with your institution's Institutional Review Board (IRB).[7] One of the issues of concern to us personally is the importance of bringing the concepts we are exploring to the pre-collegiate level to impact teachers' views of the interdisciplinary nature of computing and music. Research in the classroom is fairly common in schools of education but less so for faculty in other disciplines. You may need to negotiate with your supervisors about the validity of the work you are doing.

The Value of Grants

In the sciences and engineering, at least in departments at aspiring research universities, "publish or perish" has pretty much been replaced by "bring in external grant funding or perish." Yet in the arts, sometimes even significant grantsmanship does not help one's case for promotion and tenure. As the King of Siam ponders in *The King and I*, "'tis a puzzlement" when two professors try to do something innovative and interdisciplinary. Each has to lay out his or her goals for the work clearly and honestly to ensure that their support for the project is at least compatible, if not equal. Otherwise, the collaboration will be doomed to failure somewhere down the line.

As you may be aware, outside funding in the arts and humanities is scarce, highly competitive, and most likely not as financially lucrative for your institution as grants in the sciences. As a result, at our institution, bringing in grants is not required in the arts and humanities and not prioritized when it comes to assessing a candidate's merit for promotion.

OPENING LINES OF COMMUNICATION

It probably goes without saying, but just for completeness we'll say it anyway: the first step in avoiding the disconnects discussed in the previous section is to open all the lines of communication you can with your interdisciplinary partner. The Columbia Center for New Media Teaching and Learning discusses numerous issues involved in collaborative research, including "difference in style of investigators," "difference in style of research across and within disciplines," and even "ethical considerations [that] may affect research across institutions and nations" [1]. But quoting Macrina [5], they cite the very first of six "key components of a successful collaboration" as "communication first, second and throughout." We couldn't agree more.

Set aside a standard time to meet with your interdisciplinary partner. Your meeting might be face-to-face, over the phone, or via a service such as Skype [10] or Google Hangouts [2] that allows you to make a video call.

The advantage of a video call if you can't meet face-to-face is that it allows you to show each other things that you are working on. These programs even allow you to share your computer screens, but to do that we prefer TeamViewer [12].

As mentioned previously, Gena's and Jesse's offices are on different campuses of our university, separated by a river. They are only 1.4 miles apart, but you really have to drive from one to the other. To avoid the hassle of having to go back and forth in a single day, we intentionally schedule our interdisciplinary class at 9:30 AM. Regardless of which campus the course is taught on, the early schedule means that both professors drive to the same campus when they first come to work in the morning. Although course materials and lecture notes are posted on the course website at least the night before, we meet for an hour before class to sort out any last-minute details in the office of the professor whose "home" is on the same campus as the class. If there are no last-minute details, we use this time to discuss grading, future classes, or anything else pertaining to the course or our collaboration. We then head off to class together.

If you can, we really suggest that you try to establish a similar schedule. This one has worked really well not only for us, but also for Jesse and our other music colleague, S. Alex Ruthmann, with whom Jesse has also taught *Sound Thinking*. The beauty of setting a standard time is that it establishes a "stake in the ground." That stake can be moved, of course, but without having a standard meeting schedule, time flies by and your collaboration will suffer.

The web also provides an excellent communication channel. As noted earlier, all of our class materials are at **soundthinking.uml.edu**. This is of course good for students, but it is also good for us as professors, because when one of us posts the notes planned for a future class or a draft of an assignment, the other can easily and instantaneously review them and provide feedback to the other. Even if you don't have the resources or expertise or time to create a website for your course, you can share materials instantly using one of the online services. We use Dropbox (**www.dropbox.com**) rather heavily to share files even though our university also provides an internal application to accomplish this task. However you do it, we strongly encourage you to look for ways to use the web to share documents easily and instantaneously to maximize the efficiency of your communication.

WORKING WITH THE ADMINISTRATION

We are fortunate in that our university administration has supported and encouraged interdisciplinary collaboration for a long time. We realize that this is not true at all institutions. As described in a previous chapter, *Sound Thinking* grew out of two prior interdisciplinary collaborations between Gena and Jesse, the first of which was funded by a small, exploratory grant from our university president's office.

We therefore encourage you to look for ways to start small. Try things out. Build relationships. And don't be afraid to fail. Failure can be very educational, especially when you have the opportunity to analyze your failure and figure out just what the problems were. Every honest researcher will tell you that he or she had failures that preceded breakthroughs, and we are no exception. But one breakthrough can easily wipe away ten failures in this business, and the breakthroughs often grow out of failures through refinement of techniques that didn't work. That is, don't "throw out the baby with the bath water." Instead, try to keep the good parts of your approach, figure out where things when wrong, and fix problems without sacrificing successful aspects of your course design.

And finally, seek external funding for your work. As noted prominently on our website, our work has been funded by two grants from the National Science Foundation (NSF). The first was from the CPATH program,[8] while the second was from the TUES program.[9] NSF programs come and go, but there are always programs that support educational research in some form. And of course, there are other funding agencies that support this type of work as well.

It is always nice, of course, to have funding to pay faculty summer stipends, hire students, support graduate studies, purchase materials, and support conference travel, but external funding actually gets you something that in some ways is even more important: legitimacy. If you're in a science or engineering department and you can garner external financial support for your work, you have a much better chance of that work "counting" toward promotion and tenure and other measures of scholarly activity. And despite some instances to the contrary, the same is true in arts departments, although our experience is that the type of funding we have secured does not "count" *as much* in those departments.

There is no magic formula that works in every department or in every college and university. You have to be aware of the situation at your own institution, and we encourage you to talk to your administration about your plans before investing the time it takes to get an interdisciplinary program off the ground. Clearly, there are areas where this interdisciplinary work can fall within the confines of traditional, discipline-specific research, but as you move forward you are going to find that you are pushing the envelope as well. As we stated earlier, it is all about finding the right balance and how you go about "putting it together."

BIBLIOGRAPHY

[1]   Columbia Center for New Media Teaching and Learning (2012). *Responsible Conduct of Research: Collaborative Science*. ccnmtl.columbia.edu/projects/rcr/rcr_science/foundation/index.html, accessed 8/12/2012.

[2]   Google (2013). *Google+ Features: Hangouts*. www.google.com/+/learnmore/hangouts/, accessed 4/20/2013.

[3]   Hetland, L., Winner, E., Veenema, S., & Sheridan, K. M. (2007). *Studio Thinking: The Real Benefits of Visual Arts Education*. New York: Teachers College Press.

[4]   Lindman, J. M., & Tahamont, J. (2006). "Transforming Selves, Transforming Courses: Faculty and Staff Development and the Construction of Interdisciplinary Diversity Courses." *Innovative Higher Education* **30**(4):289–304.

[5]   Macrina, F. L. (2000). *Scientific Integrity: An Introductory Text with Cases* (2nd ed). Washington, DC: American Society for Microbiology.

[6]   MIT Scratch Team. (2009). *Scratch*. scratch.mit.edu, accessed 12/21/2009.

[7]   Resnick, M., Maloney, J., Monroyhernández, A., Rusk, N., Eastmond, E., Brennan, K., Millner, A., Rosenbaum, E., Silver, J., Silverman, B., & Kafai, Y. (2009). "Scratch Programming for All." *Communications of the ACM* **52**(11):60–67.

[8]   Ruthmann, S.A. (2009). *Computational Zeppelin*. scratch.mit.edu/projects/alexruthmann/736779, accessed 1/5/2010.

[9]   Shlachter, B. (1986). "Discontent Stirs at Harvard over Difficulty of Winning Tenure for Junior Professors." *Los Angeles Times,* October 12, 1986. articles.latimes.com/1986-10-12/news/mn-2869_1_junior-professors, accessed 4/20/2013.

[10]   Skype. (2012). *Free Skype Internet Calls and Cheap Calls to Phones Online*. www.skype.com, accessed 8/12/2012.

[11]   Sondheim, S., & Lapine, J. (1884). "Bit by Bit, Putting It Together." In *Sunday in the Park with George*. New York: RCA Victor.

[12]   TeamViewer. (2012). *Free Remote Control, Remote Access & Online Meetings*. www.teamviewer.com, accessed 8/12/2012.

[13]   University of Massachusetts Lowell. (2011). *General Education Program*. www.uml.edu/Academics/undergraduate-programs/Gened/default.aspx, accessed 4/20/2013.

[14]   University of Massachusetts Lowell. (2013). *Courses Approved for General Education 2000 Program*. www.uml.edu/Academics/undergraduate-programs/Gened/Courses/Courses.aspx, accessed 4/20/2013.

[15]   Yanco, H. A., Kim, H. J., Martin, F. G., & Silka, L. (2007). *Artbotics: Combining Art and Robotics to Broaden Participation in Computing*. AAAI Spring Symposium on Robots and Robot Venues: Resources for AI Education. Stanford, CA.

Appendix for Chapter 7

SOUND THINKING COURSE WEBSITES

Sound Thinking was first offered in the Spring 2009 semester and has been offered in the spring semester of each year since then. As noted throughout this book, the course has undergone significant revision almost every year.

All of the *Sound Thinking* course websites are still publicly available. Each has links to the course syllabi, lecture notes, assignments, and class discussion forum, as well as various other course-related resources. All of these course websites are linked from **http://teaching.cs.uml.edu/~heines/teaching.jsp**.

ASSIGNMENTS USED IN THE FIRST COURSE OFFERING, SPRING 2009

http://teaching.cs.uml.edu/~heines/91.212/91.212-2008-09s/
Taught by Gena Greher and Jesse Heines

1. Found Objects Composition
2. Composition from Digitized Found Sounds
3. Looping Composition
4. AudioEthnography: The Soundtrack of Your Life
5. Creating a First Web Page on a Linux Server
6. Creating a Web Page with Embedded Sounds
7. Creating a Web Game or Lesson

Discussion

The first assignment of the Spring 2009 semester was with the Found Objects project as we have described in detail. For the second assignment, students recorded the various sounds that their found instruments could make, loaded them into Audacity, and manipulated them to create a composition. The CT concepts and skills involved in this assignment and the CT-related problems that students had to solve include

- importing and exporting sounds,
- synchronizing clips of different lengths,
- cutting-and-pasting to arrange clips in the desired order,
- using Audacity effects to enhance sounds,
- dealing with file types and understanding the Audacity file structure,
- installing drivers to allow a composition to be exported in MP3 format, and
- following explicit directions to submit their music files for grading.

The third assignment introduced the CT concept of looping by requiring students to use a program such as GarageBand (on Macintosh systems) or ACID Music Studio (on Windows systems) to arrange their sound clips into loops. This assignment laid the groundwork for later assignments that would use loops more extensively.

The fourth assignment was the AudioEthnogaphy project discussed earlier. This exercise reinforced the concepts and skills explored in the previous projects, allowing students to practice and refine those. The more precise nature of this assignment—particularly the fact that their composition had to be exactly 300 seconds long—introduces another critical CT concept: working within constraints. Virtually all productive work today is done within constrained budgets, time, resources, and/or limits of personal creativity, and learning to do the best you can within such constraints is a critical skill to acquire.

We then moved on to creating music programs on web pages. Assignment No. 5 was an introduction to simple web programming. Each student team was given a skeletal HTML file and they were to enhance that file to contain links to their compositions for the previous four assignments. This deepened their understanding of file types and utilities for copying files, and prepared them to be ready to create a web page with embedded sounds, which was the essence of Assignment No. 6. This assignment introduced a bit of web programming using utilities that we had written for the students to simplify playing sounds on the web. (Please note that doing this in 2013 is considerably easier than it was when we first started teaching it in 2009.)

The final project this year was to create a web game or lesson that incorporated sound in appropriate ways. Some students created instructional games, while others created tutorials. One of the more revealing student comments on this assignment was (paraphrased), "If you had told me at the beginning of the semester that by the end of the semester I would create an original web page that taught a simple lesson and incorporated music, I wouldn't have believed you."

ASSIGNMENTS USED IN THE SECOND COURSE OFFERING, SPRING 2010

http://teaching.cs.uml.edu/~heines/91.212/91.212-2009-10s/
Taught by S. Alex Ruthmann and Jesse Heines

1. Creating a Composition from Digitized Sounds in Audacity
2. Creating a Song Flowchart
3. Creating a Music Sequence in Scratch
4. Creating a MIDI Composition in Scratch
5. Implementing Live Coding
6. Working with Sensors
7. Final Project and Performance

Discussion

This was the first semester that we incorporated Scratch into our course per students' requests for more programming depth. It was also the first semester that Jesse taught the course with Alex rather than Gena. Alex added a fresh look at the materials Gena and Jesse had developed and worked with us to refine those and develop some new assignments based on Scratch.

For the first assignment of this semester, Alex and Jesse used the second part of the Found Instruments project and had students record found sounds rather than sounds made by instruments they created. The assignment required students to arrange their found sounds into a composition using Audacity.

We then used a new assignment based on the idea of flowcharting a song, inspired by Jeannie Harrell's work [3] as discussed in Chapter 1. The idea behind this assignment is to get students involved with CT even before they start to write computer code. The assignment involves

- critical listening,
- "chunking" (breaking music down into its component parts),
- listening for repeated sections and thinking about loops,
- using new software to produce the flowchart or using known software (such as PowerPoint) in new ways,
- solving layout problems to avoid as many crossed lines as possible, and
- addressing sequencing issues to ensure that the flowchart correctly represents the chosen song.

With this introduction to programming under the students' belts, Alex and Jesse then introduced students to Scratch. Our first assignment using Scratch (the third project of the semester) followed from the sequencing aspect of the flowchart assignment. It required students to rearrange the clips they used in Assignment No. 1, but this time using Scratch. They could use the various control structures to implement repeats and even play different clips in different loop iterations. We found this an excellent way to expose students who had never coded before to basic CT concepts, including

- sequencing,
- looping,
- conditional statements,
- Boolean expressions,
- counters, and
- variables.

Our fourth assignment introduced students to MIDI. This was a new concept even for many of the music majors in the course. Even though some of them might have heard of MIDI, very few had ever worked with it. Our first assignment with MIDI had students sequence at least the melody any song that they knew. We introduced the CT concepts of signals through Scratch's **broadcast** and **receive** features, and we also introduced the CT concepts of local and global entities through the fact that volume and instrument are local to Scratch sprites, while tempo is global to an entire Scratch program. These concepts proved difficult for some students to grasp at first, but their "feel" for them increased as they revisited them in later assignments.

Alex is a strong proponent of "musical live coding" [1, 5, 6], so our fifth assignment attempted to give students a feel for creatively manipulating music code in real time [4]. This proved to be quite difficult for the students, and we did not use this assignment in later years, although we continue to demonstrate this to students in the course and Alex works with students individually who express an interest in doing live coding. For a video of Alex performing live coding, please see **http://www.youtube. com/watch?v=HyMXCZXjwWg**.

Our sixth project of this course offering required students to work with the IchiBoard developed by our Computer Science Department's Engaging Computing Group [2] and discussed in detail in Chapter 6. This assignment led into the final assignment of the semester, original projects in which various students incorporated virtually all of the techniques explored throughout the semester.

ASSIGNMENTS USED IN THE THIRD COURSE OFFERING, SPRING 2011

http://teaching.cs.uml.edu/~heines/91.212/91.212-2010-11s/
Taught by Gena Greher and Jesse Heines

1. Creating a Composition for a Found Objects Instrument
2. Creating a Composition from Digitized Found Sounds
3. Creating a Song Flowchart
4. Sequencing Sounds with Scratch
5. Creating a Composition Based on Major Seconds and Perfect Fifths
6. Transposing with Scratch
7. Using IchiBoards and Sensors
8. Final Sound Thinking Project and Performance

Discussion

In the third iteration of our course, Gena was once again teaching with Jesse. We went back to the Found Instruments project (under a slightly different name), but we broke it into two assignments. In the first, students created their instruments and devised their notations. In the second, we had them use Audacity to create a composition out of the sounds generated by their instruments.

The third and fourth assignments this semester were identical to those in the previous semester: "Creating a Song Flowchart" and "Sequencing Sounds with Scratch." Gena then devised a new assignment for introducing MIDI: having students create a composition using only major seconds and perfect fifths. This gave us the opportunity to introduce not only the important music concept of intervals but also the following CT concepts:

- basic algorithms
- randomization
- constraints
- ranges
- reinitialization

We built on Gena's "seconds and fifths" assignment by teaching what it means to transpose music from one key to another. For this assignment, we introduced Scratch lists, which are actually indexed, dynamic data structures somewhat equivalent to the Java **ArrayList** data type. We showed students how to create lists consisting of either absolute note values or intervals, where those intervals could be differences from the starting or tonic note or differences from the preceding note. They then used loops with index variables to step through the list of notes and play them one at a time. To control rhythm, students also created a list of note durations and stepped through that synchronously to read the corresponding duration of each note in the list of note values. To transpose, we showed students how to use offsets in the Scratch **play note** block. This assignment therefore truly married music with computing, as it taught important music as well as CT concepts. It was the assignment that generated the vast majority of "Ah-ha!" moments in the students' learning, and we have used it every year with great success ever since.

The final two assignments of this semester were the same as in the previous semester: "Using IchiBoards and Sensors" and putting it all together into a "Final Sound Thinking Project and Performance."

ASSIGNMENTS USED IN THE FOURTH COURSE OFFERING, SPRING 2012

http://teaching.cs.uml.edu/~heines/91.212/91.212-2011-12s/
Taught by Gena Greher and Jesse Heines

1. Creating a Composition for a Found Objects Instrument
2. Creating a Composition from Digitized Found Sounds
3. Creating a Song Flowchart
4. Sequencing Sounds with Scratch
5. Creating a Composition Based on Major Seconds and Perfect Fifths
6. Transposing with Scratch
7. Using IchiBoards and Sensors
8. Final Sound Thinking Project and Performance

Discussion

We used exactly the same assignments in our fourth iteration of the course as we did in the third. This gave us an opportunity to make small refinements to our assignment write-ups and "tweak" the directions for clarity.

ASSIGNMENTS USED IN THE FIFTH COURSE OFFERING, SPRING 2013

http://teaching.cs.uml.edu/~heines/91.212/91.212-2012-13s/
Taught by S. Alex Ruthmann and Jesse Heines

1. Designing and Performing an Original Musical Instrument Using a MaKey MaKey Board

2. Creating a Composition from Digitized Found Sounds
3. Creating a Song Flowchart
4. Sequencing Sounds with Scratch
5. Creating a Composition Based on Major Seconds and Perfect Fifths
6. Transposing Using Scratch Lists
7. Final Sound Thinking Project and Performance

Discussion

Our fifth course iteration saw Alex and Jesse teaching together for the second time, and once again Alex brought an innovation to the assignments that we had been using. Instead of having students build an instrument from found objects, Alex had them build an instrument using MaKey MaKey boards created by Jay Silver and Eric Rosenbaum of the MIT Media Lab, the same lab that created Scratch. A wonderfully creative video demonstrating the capabilities of this board is posted at **http://video.mit.edu/watch/makey-makey-11520/**, and the board itself can be found at **http://www.makeymakey.com**. The Makey MaKey kit consists of the components shown in Figure 7A-1, and Figure 7A-2 shows the board "hooked up" in our of our students' creations.

To use the MaKey MaKey board in our first project we had to give students skeleton Scratch code. We did that without really explaining how it works, but students were still able to create some very clever "instruments." Figures 7A-3 through 7A-6 show a few of these creations, and much more in-depth information about the board itself is provided at **http://web.media.mit.edu/~ericr/makeymakey/**.

The remainder of the assignments we used in the Spring 2013 semester were the same as those in the Spring 2012 semester, except that some students used the MaKey MaKey boards in their final projects, which of course did not occur in previous semesters.

Figure 7A-1:
MaKey MaKey kit components.

Figure 7A-2:
MaKey MaKey board "hooked up" to its alligator clips and USB cable.

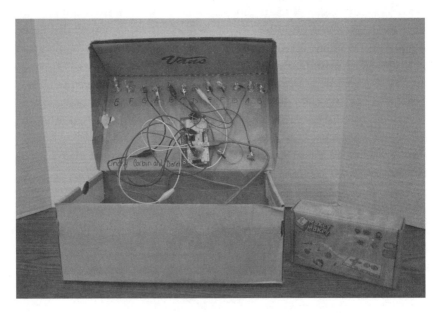

Figure 7A-3:
Internal view of a MaKey MaKey board piano.

FINAL THOUGHTS

We will, of course, continue to add innovations as we discover them, but after five offerings our *Sound Thinking* course is now quite stable. However, as you can see, it took a while for us to get it so. The course still has a some-what different feel when Jesse teaches it with Gena versus when he teaches

Figure 7A-4a:
External view of a student-created MaKey MaKey board game board.

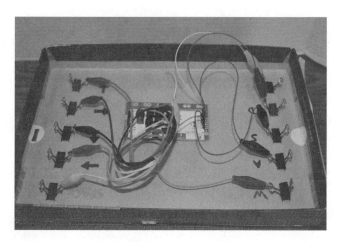

Figure 7A-4b:
Internal view of a student-created MaKey MaKey board game board.

it with Alex, but we do not want to remove that variation because it helps keep the course "alive."

As all teachers know but no one seems to understand, some years the students will get excited about a specific assignment, while in other years that very same assignment will fall flat. We continue to try to identify the factors that contribute to such variation and modify our projects to achieve wider student engagement. You may always find the latest version of those assignments as well as all course materials at **http://soundthinking.uml.edu**.

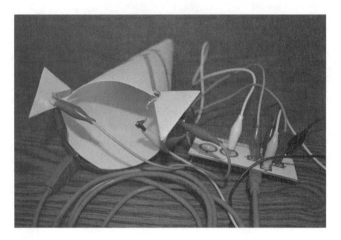

Figure 7A-5:
A student-created MaKey MaKey board trumpet.

Figure 7A-6:
Collection of student-created MaKey MaKey board instruments.

BIBLIOGRAPHY

[1] Brown, A. R., & Sorensen, A. (2009). "Interacting with Generative Music through Live Coding." *Contemporary Music Review* **28**(1):17–29.

[2] Engaging Computing Group. (2012). *IchiBoard*. www.cs.uml.edu/ecg/index.php/ IchiBoard/IchiBoard, accessed 1/11/2012.

[3] Harrell, J. (2009). *Koufukuron ("On Joy")*. jeannr.tumblr.com/post/165291081/i-made-a-flow-chart-that-we-might-better, accessed 12/25/2009, reproduced courtesy of the author.

[4] Ruthmann, S. A., & Heines, J. M. (2010). *Exploring Musical and Computational Thinking through Musical Live Coding in Scratch*. Cambridge, MA: Scratch@MIT.

[5] Sorensen, A. C., & Brown, A. R. (2007). "Aa-cell in Practice: An Approach to Musical Live Coding." *Proceedings of the International Computer Music Conference*, Copenhagen, Denmark.

[6] Wang, G., & Cook, P. R. (2004). "On-the-fly Programming: Using Code as an Expressive Musical Instrument." *Proceedings of the 2004 Conference on New Interfaces for Musical Expression*, pp. 138–143. Hamamatsu, Shizuoka, Japan, National University of Singapore.

CHAPTER 8

Assessment

Making the Grade

HOW I GRADE STUDENTS VERSUS
HOW YOU GRADE STUDENTS

All students know that different professors grade differently. We'd be willing to bet that your experiences in this area mirror ours, and that you'd agree that the differences go much deeper than we could have imagined. It's not just a question of one professor being a tough grader while the other is easy, or one grading on established intervals (93–100 = A, 90–92 = A–, 87–89 = B–, 83–86 = B, etc.) while the other grades "on the curve." It's more a question of style: how much feedback students receive on their work and in what form, how the various components in any individual assignment are evaluated to make up an overall grade for that assignment, and how final grades are computed, especially if the computing involves grades of differing weights. There also appear to be quite different "cultures" concerning grades in the sciences and the arts. While students in all disciplines are understandably concerned about their grades—if for no other reason than to maintain the grade point average (GPA) required to keep their financial aid or to avoid a clash with parents—those in the sciences seem to desire more precise accounting than those in the arts. Add to these factors that students in an interdisciplinary course are, by definition, constantly being put into situations outside their comfort zone, and it's easy to see that the wave of students complaining about grading can be a tsunami waiting to happen.

One can discuss grading philosophies forever, but we begin from the premise that if students put reasonable amounts of effort into the coursework, they should get "paid" with a decent grade, which we consider to be B– or better. In fact, one of us believes that all students walk in with an

A and it's the student's responsibility to maintain that grade. This is especially true in an experimental course such as our *Sound Thinking*, where we know that some of the assignments and our expectations of students' work may come across as a bit "fuzzy." If our own experience can be used as a benchmark, you will find that many times your students will come up with solutions and approaches that you haven't even thought of yourself. As discussed previously, as teachers you want to encourage that creativity, which you can do by taking into consideration students' willingness to take risks and try something new, even if the final result doesn't work out exactly as planned. However, no matter how "fuzzy" the assignment, it's pretty easy to tell an assignment that was done on the way to class from one that a student really put some thought into. Things get trickier with assignments that are done in teams (which most of ours are; more on this later), but "the cream still rises to the top" when it is truly present. Thus, you will want to set up a grading scheme that includes subjective evaluation of students' effort as well as objective evaluation of what they produce.

GRADING CRITERIA

As a case in point, we devised a system for setting up all of the assignments for our *Sound Thinking* course that we believe can be applied to any type of course. (All of our assignments can be viewed by going to **soundthinking. uml.edu** and selecting **Assignments** from the menu.) Each assignment write-up includes four sections:

- What This Assignment Is About
- What You Are to Do
- Submitting Your Assignment for Grading
- How You Will Be Graded

The last of these should indicate the qualities you will be looking for when you grade your students' submissions. As an example, typical lists of criteria for two of our assignments are shown in Tables 8-1 and 8-2.

It has been our experience, however, that regardless of how carefully you attempt to explain your grading criteria, there are always student misunderstandings. Some students, of course, may not even read the write-ups, but there's little that one can do about that. We suspect that in our case the major cause of misunderstandings might simply be the interdisciplinary nature of the course itself. Despite our best efforts to provide comprehensive instructions, students in different majors will sometimes interpret criteria differently, causing them to be surprised at their grades. In addition, some students seem

---

Table 8-1. CRITERIA FOR ASSIGNMENT NO. 2: CREATING
A COMPOSITION FROM DIGITIZED FOUND SOUNDS.

- For the Sounds you recorded and the Composition you created
  - Clarity — Did you record a few different sounds clearly or just one or two with considerable distortion?
  - Chunks — Did you use large, unwieldy clips or did you break them down into manageable sizes for maximum flexibility?
  - Creativity — Did you just rearrange the sounds or did you try to put together a truly new composition with some interesting characteristics?
  - Problem Solving — Was it evident that you put some thought into this assignment?
  - Structure — Did you use sounds from both (or all three) students' found instruments and create a piece with a clear form and a variety of musical elements such as textural changes, dynamics, rhythmic variety, melodic elements, etc.?
  - Submission — Did you save your work in MP3 format and submit the correct file?

- For the Notes on what you did
  - Screen shot — Did you submit a screen shot of your Audacity project window?
  - Clarity — Could someone else reproduce your work from your notes?
  - Comprehensiveness — Could you yourself reproduce your own work 6 months from now?

- For the Reflection you wrote
  - Content — Did you discuss the computational concepts involved?
  - Effort — Did you leave this until the last minute or is it clear that you thought about what you wanted to write and put some effort into doing the writing?
  - Professionalism — Were you mindful of formatting, grammar, spelling, etc., or did you just throw a few sentences up on the website in a sloppy manner?

Table 8-2. *CRITERIA FOR ASSIGNMENT NO. 4: SEQUENCING
SOUNDS WITH SCRATCH*

- For the Program you created
  - Do the musical chunks match the melodic structure?
  - Are the additional chunks your created appropriate for the composition?
  - Is your program as short as possible?
  - Did you compensate for some of the major timing issues?
  - Did you add comments to the program to identify the major sections?

- For the Reflection you wrote
  - Did you think about the various aspects of this assignment and their relation to musical composition?
  - What did you learn about music and what did you learn about computing?
  - What did you learn from the experience of working with this partner?
  - Was your writing and its formatting, grammar, spelling, etc., done professionally?

to think that just showing up and turning in all the assignments—regardless of quality—should get them an A. That's not true in our course, and we'd be willing to bet that it isn't true in yours, either.

The pairing of students will help this problem, as students from different majors are generally able to help each other understand all aspects of the assignments. But what if there aren't enough technical students enrolled to pair every arts student with a technical student, or vice versa? In these cases, we suggest that you try to pair a tech-savvy student with one who may not be as tech-savvy. As noted earlier, in the case of our *Sound Thinking* course, all of the assignments after the first were done by students working in pairs or, in a very few cases, a group of three. We also suggest that you set up a listserv where students can ask and answer questions about assignments.[1] And finally, although it probably goes without saying, we suggest that you make sure that students know your email addresses, phone numbers, and office hours. In our case, unfortunately, few students seem to take advantage of these resources, but hope springs eternal.

As you may come to realize, it is often extremely difficult for students in interdisciplinary courses to get together outside of class. Arts students tend to have very different schedules from science and engineering students, many students may work part time and have little flexibility in their schedules, and some may live off campus. To address these issues, you may wish to give students as much time as you can to work together during your normal class time. For example, suppose your class meets for 75 minutes twice a week for 15 weeks. In this case, there will be only 30 classes per semester. On paper that may sound like a lot of time, but it goes very quickly, especially if, like us, you are trying to cover considerable breadth as well as depth and have students do a number of assignments to reinforce what you teach. We are learning that this approach is in direct conflict with a desire to increase the amount of time allocated to students presenting their work and looking at that of others. Given that aspects of two distinct disciplines are being fused into a coherent whole, the class sessions really need to model a studio approach to teaching rather than relying on the more traditional lecture format [1].

The bottom line is that we ourselves don't yet have a complete solution to the time allocation problem. However, based on our experiences we recommend that you limit the number of assignments you give and that you make every effort to facilitate student interaction both in and out of class. If that means rethinking possible "pet" topics, you may want to consider ways to incorporate those within the working sessions during class or perhaps provide more detailed information through video and web links on your course website. It is easy to forget just how difficult it is and how much time it takes for some arts majors to grasp computer science topics and some science and engineering majors to grasp music concepts. We believe that cutting down the course breadth to allow more time to delve more deeply into basic concepts yields a net positive trade-off, particularly when computational thinking is involved. You will find that it is virtually impossible for students to develop CT if they don't fully grasp basic concepts. And the better they grasp the basic concepts, the better they will understand your grading criteria and, ultimately, the better they will do in the course.

REFLECTIVE JOURNAL/BLOG POSTS
Philosophy

One of the tools that we use to evaluate effort and cognitive growth (among other things) is the reflective journal or blog posts that students are required to write for each assignment. We've included quite a few quotes from students' reflections in this book so far, but of course those were all well-written ones. It's not really worth quoting the poorly written ones. However, we mention them here because we're sure it's easy for you to imagine that not all students are as articulate as the ones we've quoted, and we don't want to give the false impression that they are.

We're equally sure that regardless of discipline, you'll agree that being articulate, that is, being able to express oneself in clear and effective language, is a critical component of success in any field. Therefore, we grade spelling, grammar, sentence and paragraph structure, and presentation (formatting) on students' reflections just as we would on any paper. Interestingly, this caused us some problems with our university's Institutional Review Board (IRB). That's an interesting story...

When we initially submitted our documents for IRB approval, which included the fact that students' reflections would be graded, the board came back with the recommendation that the reflections not be graded for the following reasons.

> We are fine with having the reflection as a course requirement, but the statement about evaluation based on the "clarity of expression and their insight into the assignment" is what we are concerned about.
>
> What if any particular student (or group) is not good at expressing themselves in writing? We would assume that they would receive a lower grade and we don't think that is your intent here.... We think if this were, for example, an English course, grading their ability to express themselves in the reflection would be appropriate.

We couldn't have been more incensed by the last statement. The previous sentence—in which they said that they didn't think it was our "intent" to penalize students who write poorly—was bad enough, showing that they seriously misunderstood our intent. But the last sentence showed a complete lack of understanding of the importance of communication in our disciplines.

We tried to write tempered responses, but we stated categorically that we "think all of us have an obligation as professors to help our students develop their oral and written communication skills." We explained that when employers talk to us about the qualities they are looking for in students they want to hire, we hardly ever get questioned about technical skills. Those skills are taken for granted, as we have quality programs and students who graduate from them are assumed to be technically competent. The biggest question that employers have about our young graduates is whether they can **communicate.** That's why we evaluate students' reflections for grammar as well as content, and that's why we strongly objected to the assertion that "students [should] not be penalized if they are poor communicators." We believe that they absolutely *should* be penalized if they spend two minutes writing a few flippant sentences and consider that a "reflection" rather than thinking deeply about the issues and writing a few cogent paragraphs. They should also be penalized if they carelessly misspell words over and over, write in all lowercase without punctuation, use abbreviations as if they're sending a text message, and so on. Even though our main disciplines are music and computer science, we still care deeply and indeed feel that it is our **obligation** to stress the importance of good writing.

Nuts and Bolts

At this point we'd like to offer a tip based on a set of guidelines we've devised that seems to finally solve the problem of how to get students to write substantive reflections that are more than a few sentences. Good students can of course do this without any scaffolding, but average and certainly below average students have trouble addressing all the salient issues without significant structure.

We suggest that for each assignment you create questionnaires with specific questions that you want students to address. We use the free Google Forms (part of the Google Drive facility, see **drive.google.com**), but of course there are other viable web-based tools that may be just as or even more appropriate for your use. Figures 8-1a and 8-1b show an example of the form we created for our Assignment No. 6, which dealt with transposing a piece of music using Scratch. Note that the form provides structure, but it stops short of asking really specific questions on the assignment content itself. There's a fine line here, and we have gone back and forth across it a number of times. Yes, we want to provide structure, but we also want students to think for themselves.

73.212 / 91.212 Reflections for Assignment No. 6: Transposing with Scratch

Please use this form to post your reflection for the assignment named above. Responses to the questions marked with an asterisk (*) are required.

* Required

Please enter your full name: *

Please enter your partner's full name: *

If there was a third partner on your team, please enter his or her name:

Please enter your notes and reflection by answering the following questions.

Please make sure that your writing and its formatting, grammar, spelling, etc. are done professionally.

(1) Please document what you did to complete this assignment as if you were writing directions for another student to duplicate your work. *

(2) What do you think about the various aspects of this assignment and their relation to musical composition or performance? *

Figures 8-1a:
Google form for students to submit their reflection on Assignment No. 6.

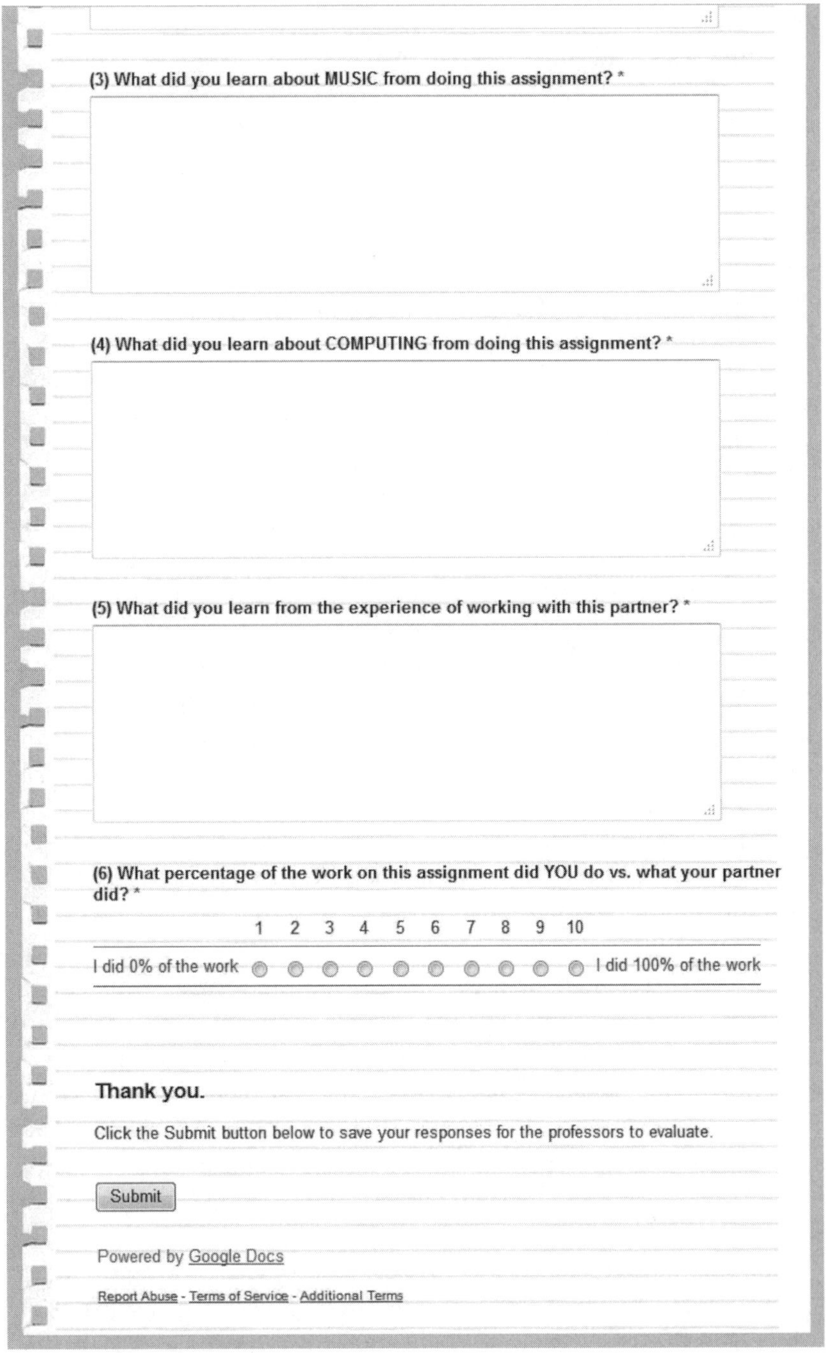

(3) What did you learn about MUSIC from doing this assignment? *

(4) What did you learn about COMPUTING from doing this assignment? *

(5) What did you learn from the experience of working with this partner? *

(6) What percentage of the work on this assignment did YOU do vs. what your partner did? *

	1	2	3	4	5	6	7	8	9	10	
I did 0% of the work	⊙	⊙	⊙	⊙	⊙	⊙	⊙	⊙	⊙	⊙	I did 100% of the work

Thank you.

Click the Submit button below to save your responses for the professors to evaluate.

Submit

Powered by Google Docs

Report Abuse - Terms of Service - Additional Terms

Figure 8-1b: Google form for students to submit their reflection on Assignment No. 6 (continued).

Notice that we also included a rating scale at the end of the form so that students could indicate their own assessment of how much they personally contributed to the assignment. In grading collaborative assignments, it's often difficult to assess who contributed what. We generally assign all contributors to a particular assignment the same grade, but we have found that in some cases, one person drops off the radar screen, leaving it to her or his partner to complete the work. Even without the rating scale, the person left doing the work will often, but not always, make note of their partner's absence within the text of their reflection. In any event, we don't believe that the student who contributed little or nothing to the assignment should receive the same grade as the one who did all of the work, and we suspect you would agree with that philosophy.

It's hard to say exactly where the line should be drawn, but the result for us has been almost revolutionary. With the use of the form and the rating scale, more students submitted the reflection part of the assignments, the submissions themselves were *much* longer and more detailed, and the quality of the writing improved, as well. We're not exactly sure why this is so. Maybe students felt more comfortable writing online. Maybe the minimal structure we provided was all they needed to get their written thoughts flowing. Or maybe the simple presence of a form tripped some conditioned response that if you're presented with a form, you react by filling it out. We have not really explored why the forms worked so well, but we were of course happy to see such positive changes in the students' reflections. As a result of these experiences, Gena is even using this approach in her other classes where reflections are part of the classwork grade.

You will discover though, that processing the forms introduces another wrinkle. When students write multiple paragraphs it is hard to view the entire reflection on a single screen (see Figure 8-2). Comparing reflections submitted by partners in the same pair or team also becomes difficult online, because to do that you have to jump all around the spreadsheet. The Google Form's "show summary of responses" is of little help either, as that only displays the first hundred or so characters of text responses.

To display the data in an easier-to-read format, you may wish to download the Google Forms spreadsheet as an Excel spreadsheet. That makes the voluminous text much easier to read because you can more easily expand columns. In addition, Excel appears to be a more stable environment for reading. If you and your partner have the technical skills, you can write Visual Basic macros to convert it to an even more readable form, such as that shown in Figure 8-3.[2] This makes the information much easier to process and digest.[3]

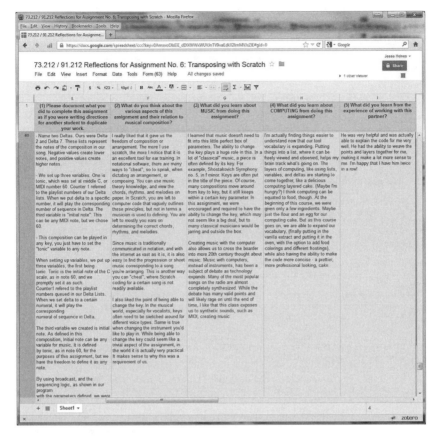

Figure 8-2:
Lengthy student reflection text responses as they appear in the spreadsheet that Google uses to store submitted form data.

ACCEPTING MULTIMEDIA STUDENT SUBMISSIONS

We tried a number of ways to handle students' multimedia submissions. We experimented with a number of websites that allow program and sound files to be uploaded to them, but none was quite right for our purposes.[4] For those of you who are teaching at schools that have easy to navigate course websites, this may not be an issue. In our case, we set up our own system using the following procedure.

1. We created a new Gmail account for our course.
2. We instructed students to email their submissions for each assignment to the course account after naming their files in a standard manner. For example, the file name for the Scratch file submitted for Assignment No. 6 needed to be in the format:

    YourLastName_YourFirstName_PartnerLastName_Partner-FirstName_Assn6_TransposingUsingLists.sb

Submission No. 26

Submission Time Stamp: 4/10/2012 10:13:41 AM

 Student Name: (name removed for publication)
 Partner Name: (name removed for publication)
Third Partner: None

Percent of Work Claimed to be Done by This Student: 40 %

Response to Question 1:
Please document what you did to complete this assignment as if you were writing
directions for another student to duplicate your work.

    - Name two Deltas. Ours were Delta 2 and Delta 7. These lists represent the
    notes of the composition in our song. Negative values create lower notes,
    and positive values create higher notes.

    - We set up three variables: One is tonic, which was set at middle C, or
    MIDI number 60. Counter 1 referred to the playlist numbers of our Delta
    lists. When we put delta to a specific number, it will play the
    corresponding number of sequence in Delta. The third variable is "initial
    note". This can be any MIDI note, but we chose 60.

    - This composition can be played in any key, you just have to set the
    "tonic" variable to any note.

    When setting up variables, we put up three variables, the first being
    tonic. Tonic is the initial note of the C scale, as in note 60, and we
    promptly set it as such.

    Counter1 referred to the playlist numbers queued in our Delta Lists.
    When we set delta to a certain numeral, it will play the corresponding
    numeral of sequence in Delta.

    The third variable we created is initial note. As defined in this
    composition, Initial note can be any variable for music. It is defined
    by tonic, as in note 60, for the purposes of this assignment, but we
    have the freedom to define it as any note.

    By using broadcast, and the sequencing logic, as shown in our program
    with the parameters defined, we were able to compose a musical piece
    in Scratch.

    Any key can be played by our program, one simply has to define the
    tonic to that specific note, and our initial note will start with said
    directions.

Response to Question 2:
What do you think about the various aspects of this assignment and their
relation to musical composition?

    I really liked that it gave us the freedom of composition or arrangement.
    The more I use scratch, the more I notice that it is an excellent tool for
    ear training. In notational software, there are many ways to "cheat", so to
    speak, when dictating an arrangement, or composing. You can use music
    theory knowledge, and view the chords, rhythms, and melodies on paper. In
    Scratch, you are left to computer code that vaguely outlines these
    principles, but not in terms a musician is used to defining. You are left
    to mostly you ears on determining the correct chords, rhythms, and
    melodies.

Figures 8-3a:
Lengthy student reflection text responses as they appear after processing by Excel macros.

Since music is traditionally communicated in notation, and with the Internet as vast as it is, it is also easy to find the progression or sheet music corresponding to a song you're arranging. This is another way you can "cheat", where Scratch coding for a certain song is not readily available.

I also liked the point of being able to change the key. In the musical world, especially for vocalists, keys often need to be switched around for different voice types. Same is true when changing the instrument you'd like to play in. While being able to change the key could seem like a trivial aspect of the assignment, in the world it is actually very practical. It makes sense to why this was a requirement of us.

Response to Question 3:
What did you learn about MUSIC from doing this assignment?

I learned that music doesn't need to fit into this little perfect box of parameters. The ability to change the key plays a huge role in this. In a lot of "classical" music, a piece is often defined by its key. For example, Shostakovich Symphony no. 5, in F minor. Keys are often put in the title of the piece. Of course, many compositions move around from key to key, but it still keeps within a certain key parameter. In this assignment, we were encouraged and required to have the ability to change the key, which may not seem like a big deal, but to many classical musicians would be jarring and outside the box.

Creating music with the computer also allows us to cross the border into more 20th century thought about music. Music with computers, instead of instruments, has been a subject of debate as technology expands. Many of the most popular songs on the radio are almost completely synthesized. While the debate has many valid points and will likely rage on until the end of time, I like that this class exposes us to synthetic sounds, such as MIDI, creating music.

Response to Question 4:
What did you learn about COMPUTING from doing this assignment?

I'm actually finding things easier to understand now that our tool vocabulary is expanding. Putting things into a list, where it can be freely viewed and observed, helps my brain track what's going on. The layers of computing, like using lists, variables, and deltas are starting to come together, like a delicious computing layered cake. (Maybe I'm hungry?) I think computing can be equated to food, though. At the beginning of this course, we were given only a few ingredients. Maybe just the flour and an egg for our computing cake. But as this course goes on, we are able to expand our vocabulary, (finally putting in the vanilla extract and putting it in the oven, with the option to add food colorings and different frostings), while also having the ability to make the code more concise -- a prettier, more professional looking, cake.

Response to Question 5:
What did you learn from the experience of working with this partner?

He was very helpful and was actually able to explain the code for me very well. He had the ability to weave the points and layers together for me, making it make a lot more sense to me. I'm happy that I have him twice in a row!

Figure 8-3b:
Lengthy student reflection text responses as they appear after processing by Excel macros (continued).

3. We then moved the files to a web server where we could both access them (see Figure 8-4). If you are not teaching with a partner, or if you have a small class, you might find this additional step unnecessary.

4. This procedure worked very well for us. It gave us both access to all student submissions from home as well as from our university offices, and it allowed us both to look at a specific submission as we discussed it on the phone, which we did more often for excellent submissions than for poor ones.

Figure 8-4:
Website for assignments to be graded.

We have also found that sites such as Edmodo (**www.edmodo.com**) will let students upload their multimedia files if they are smaller than 100 MB.

GRADING LOGISTICS

We have now described how you might access all of the components of your students' assignments, including their reflections. The next step, of course, is to actually go about grading all their work. How do two instructors teaching an interdisciplinary course together communicate what they're thinking and agree on what grade to award to each student team?

The first answer to that question is that it isn't easy. To begin, the instructors need to discuss their expectations before they start grading. The discussion actually begins at the point the assignment parameters are created, by carefully reviewing the "How You Will Be Graded" section discussed previously. Since time—or lack thereof—is a critical issue for professors as well as students, finding the time to sit down together to review each assignment is probably not feasible. More often than not you will find yourselves grading these assignments separately and at odd hours. Our solution is to create a shared Google Docs Spreadsheet like that shown in Figure 8-5, with columns for each of the major grading criteria and comments from each of the graders. This not only lets both of you work on the grading at the same time but also allows each of you to see the other's comments instantaneously, so that you can sometimes refer to the other's comments in your own.

Note particularly Column J in Figure 8-5, which shows the difference between the total scores we each assigned to individual students. When the

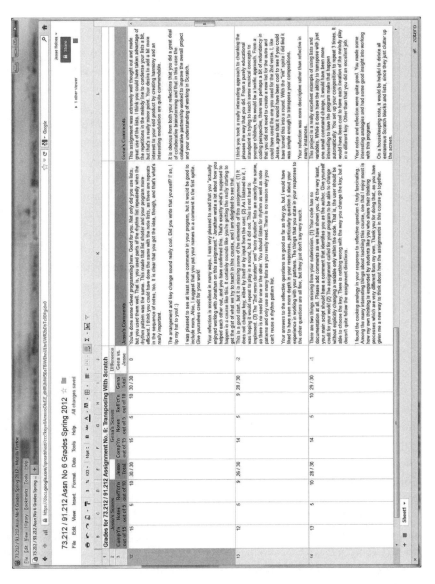

Figure 8-5:
Google Docs grading spreadsheet.

difference is 0, we had given the same score. When it was negative, Jesse had given a lower score than Gena. When it was positive, Gena's score was higher.

When we first started teaching together, we wanted to give students one grade that was awarded by both of us. But as we gained experience, we decided to keep our grades distinct so that students could see the difference in our perspectives. We don't want the difference to be too large, however, so we agreed that we would leave differences of plus or minus 2 points alone, but if we differ by more than 2 points, we discuss that student's work to try to understand why we see it differently. In these cases, one of us typically adjusts his or her grade to be within 2 points of the other's. It is a very rare occurrence when our differences are so large that we both have to adjust our grades.

As with student reflections, the information entered into the Google Docs spreadsheet has to be transformed into a more readable form to provide students with feedback. In addition, we obviously needed to extract each student's grades and comments so that we could email these to students individually. It wouldn't be too big a job to do this manually for a small class, but we devised an automated procedure similar to that for the students' reflections: we downloaded the Google Docs spreadsheet as an Excel file and processed it using Visual Basic macros to write out text files that we could email to each student. Figure 8-6 shows a sample grade report generated for the second student in Figure 8-5.

GRADING THE PROFESSORS

It is customary to think of grading in terms of evaluating the performance and progress of students. However, grading can also be a means for educators to evaluate how well they themselves are conveying course concepts. Assuming that we are not victims of grade inflation, we are probably safe in assuming that if we have few seriously low or failing grades, we have done a reasonably good job of teaching.

Most colleges and universities also have a system of student evaluations of teaching (SETs) that are administered at the end of each semester, as ours does. Our standard SET form is geared toward a professor's performance, demeanor, effectiveness, availability for help, and classroom environment. Given that *Sound Thinking* is breaking new ground in many areas, we were looking to determine the effectiveness of the course itself as well as changes in students' thinking and beliefs about the course content. Toward this end, and with the help of our Performamatics colleagues including our evaluators, we created pre- and post-course surveys in an attempt to assess overall course effectiveness and identify areas of weakness. While we adopted this pre/post survey approach as part of our NSF research, we think it's a

Subject: 73.212 / 91.212 Grade Report

Assn. No. 6: TRANSPOSING WITH SCRATCH

  Date Due: April 12, 2012

Student: (name removed for publication)

GRADES

    Scores from Jesse
      Composition: 12
            Notes: 5
       Reflection: 9

    Scores from Gena
      Composition: 14
            Notes: 5
       Reflection: 9

    Total Grade: 54 out of 60

COMMENTS

    From Jesse:
      This is a good start, but it is missing some of the elements of
      this assignment. (1) It does not change key, either by itself or
      by input from the user. (2) As I listened to it, I was hoping it
      would repeat to play in a round, but it did not. This is not
      hard to implement. (3) The "2nd verse duration" and "outro
      duration" lists are exactly the same, so there is no need for one
      or the other. You should listen for rhythm as well as note
      patterns and only use as many lists as you really need. There is
      no reason why you can't reuse a rhythm pattern list.

      Your answers to the reflective questions are good as far as they
      go, but I would have liked to have seen more depth in your
      responses, particularly question 5 about your experience in
      working with your partners. The things that you state in your
      responses to the other questions are all fine, but they just
      don't say very much.

    From Gena:
      I think you took a really interesting approach to chunking the
      phrases the way that you did. From a purely educational
      standpoint in trying to teach some musical concepts to younger
      children, this would be a terrific approach. From a coding
      perspective, there was perhaps a bit of redundancy in that you
      did not need to create a new list for the outro and could have
      used the one you used for the 2nd verse. I, like Jesse, agree
      that it would have been cool to see if you could have turned this
      into a round. With the "init" sprite I did find it was simple
      enough to transpose your compositions.

      Your reflection was more descriptive rather than reflective in
      many instances.

Figure 8-6:
Sample individual student grade report generated by Visual Basic macros run on the Google Docs
grading spreadsheet in Figure 8-5. This is the form in which the report is emailed to students.

good idea for anyone attempting something new in one's course and teaching. Doing this has given us incredible feedback on course content, teaching techniques, project designs, and learning effectiveness that often can't be captured using more standardized evaluation forms.

Like our project reflection forms, we created these surveys using Google Forms. (The actual forms used are included as an appendix to this chapter.) In the pre-course survey, we also asked students questions about their majors and whether they were taking the course specifically to fulfill their GenEd requirement. Other questions were designed to give us student perceptions on how balanced the course was between music and computing content and what projects were particularly effective, and to provide their views on creating music using computers. Finally, we asked some technical questions to give us insight into how well the students internalized some of the key concepts they learned in the course.

To develop the surveys, we started with material we had developed for our workshops and then refined the questions to make them specific to our course. With regard to how well *Sound Thinking* met students' expectations, overall we found the results to be positive. The results of our post-course survey indicate that students feel they

- learned new ways of making music and composing,
- gained more knowledge of computing and programming,
- learned to collaborate with people outside their major,
- were more willing to take risks in this course,
- felt their ability to communicate ideas was improved, and
- learned to think more creatively.

We then asked the students to elaborate on their perceptions of the changes they underwent during the length of the course. As expected, many students did not feel that they changed at all. However, comments such as this—"By taking risks, we are asked to apply our knowledge base to create new applications and original developments to unsolved problems"— were fairly typical of those who felt they had changed.

In terms of computing+music and ways of thinking, we found that, in general, students' comfort levels working with computers and music increased and most believed that one can create music with very little formal training and work with computers with little knowledge of programming languages. Students felt an increased ability to break down problems to their component parts, diagnose problems, recognize patterns, and work through some of the frustrations that one inevitably encounters when learning new concepts and technologies.

Jesse and Gena both advise undergraduates, and students come in asking if they can take *Sound Thinking* because they heard it was "cool"—suggesting that the "word on the street" about the course is fairly positive. This anecdotal evidence is corroborated by survey results in which more students than not say they got a great deal out of the collaborative nature of the projects and working with a diverse group of people. Our external reviewer reported similar comments in post-course interviews. They also say that they learned many of the core concepts that were taught, are beginning to appreciate the integration of music and computing, and realize the similarities between musical and computational thinking.

At the beginning of each semester in which we teach this course, we review survey results to inform the content and delivery methods for the next iteration of *Sound Thinking*. We believe that evaluating our work each time we teach the course helps us continually improve the experience for our students, and we highly recommend this practice if you decide to undertake interdisciplinary teaching. We consider this course and our collaboration to be "works in progress," and as such we will continue to evaluate our own performance as well as that of our students.

BIBLIOGRAPHY

[1] Hetland, L., Winner, E., Veenema, S., & Sheridan, K. M. (2007). *Studio Thinking: The Real Benefits of Visual Arts Education*. New York: Teachers College Press.

Appendix for Chapter 8

Sound Thinking Pre-Course Survey

This survey is designed to give us information about who you are as a class and to help us assess what the class learns and how attitudes change as a result of taking this class. There are no right and wrong answers, nor are some answers better or more desirable than others. We are interested in your honest and complete assessment of the learning experience.

We will administer a survey similar to this one at the end of the semester. The surveys are therefore numbered so that we can compare your answers on the two surveys. However, your responses will not be individually evaluated or have any effect on your grade in this course. Our analysis will not relate your responses to your name. The numbers will only allow us to track changes over time.

YOU THEREFORE NEED TO REMEMBER YOUR NUMBER! PLEASE WRITE THIS NUMBER DOWN somewhere so that you get the corresponding survey at the end of the semester. Thank you for your understanding on this.

To ensure that these policies are adhered to, we will not look at the results until after final grades have been submitted to the Registrar, following the same procedure as end-of-course student evaluations.

* Required

1. Your ID Number
Please enter the last 4 digits of your student ID number: *

2. Your Major
Please select your major: *

If other:

3. Your level in college
How many semesters of college have you completed? *

4. Your Reasons for Taking This Course

For each item below, please choose one of the six radio buttons to indicate how much each factored into your decision to take this course.

(a) I need an Arts & Humanities (AH) GenEd. *

        1   2   3   4   5   6
a little ◯ ◯ ◯ ◯ ◯ ◯ a lot

(b) I need a Science & Technology (ST) GenEd. *

        1   2   3   4   5   6
a little ◯ ◯ ◯ ◯ ◯ ◯ a lot

(c) I am really interested in computers. *

        1   2   3   4   5   6
a little ◯ ◯ ◯ ◯ ◯ ◯ a lot

(d) I am really interested in music. *

	1	2	3	4	5	6	
a little	○	○	○	○	○	○	a lot

(e) I want to learn more about computers. *

	1	2	3	4	5	6	
a little	○	○	○	○	○	○	a lot

(f) I want to learn more about music. *

	1	2	3	4	5	6	
a little	○	○	○	○	○	○	a lot

(g) I like one or both of the professors. *

	1	2	3	4	5	6	
a little	○	○	○	○	○	○	a lot

(h) I thought this would be an easy course. *

	1	2	3	4	5	6	
a little	○	○	○	○	○	○	a lot

(i) I want to challenge myself. *

	1	2	3	4	5	6	
a little	○	○	○	○	○	○	a lot

(j) I want to learn how music and computers relate. *

	1	2	3	4	5	6	
a little	○	○	○	○	○	○	a lot

(k) I heard that these professors are easy graders. *

	1	2	3	4	5	6	
a little	○	○	○	○	○	○	a lot

5. Your Expectations for This Course

What do you expect to learn from this course? For each item below, please choose one of the six radio buttons to indicate how much each factored into your expectations.

(a) more about music and composing *

	1	2	3	4	5	6	
a little	○	○	○	○	○	○	a lot

(b) more about computers and programming *

	1	2	3	4	5	6	
a little	○	○	○	○	○	○	a lot

(c) more about the integration of computers and music *

	1	2	3	4	5	6	
a little	○	○	○	○	○	○	a lot

(d) how to work diverse groups *

	1	2	3	4	5	6	
a little	○	○	○	○	○	○	a lot

(e) how to collaborate with others in my major *

	1	2	3	4	5	6	
a little	○	○	○	○	○	○	a lot

(f) how to collaborate with others outside my major *

	1	2	3	4	5	6	
a little	○	○	○	○	○	○	a lot

(g) to be more creative *

	1	2	3	4	5	6	
a little	○	○	○	○	○	○	a lot

(h) to be more communicative *

	1	2	3	4	5	6	
a little	○	○	○	○	○	○	a lot

(i) to be more willing to take risks *

	1	2	3	4	5	6	
a little	○	○	○	○	○	○	a lot

6. Your Perceptions of Yourself

Please choose one of the six radio buttons between each pair of words or phrases to indicate how well you think those words or phrases describe you.

Artistic/Technical *

	1	2	3	4	5	6	
artistic	○	○	○	○	○	○	technical

Left-Brained/Right-Brained *

	1	2	3	4	5	6	
left-brained	○	○	○	○	○	○	right-brained

Creative/Uncreative *

	1	2	3	4	5	6	
creative	○	○	○	○	○	○	uncreative

Do Not Take Risks/Take Risks *

	1	2	3	4	5	6	
do not take risks	○	○	○	○	○	○	take risks

"Big Picture"/"Detail" *

	1	2	3	4	5	6	
"big picture" person	○	○	○	○	○	○	"detail" person

Generalist/Specialist *

Please Note: A generalist is a person with broad general knowledge and skills in several areas. A specialist is a person whose knowledge and skills are primarily focused in one specific field.

	1	2	3	4	5	6	
generalist	○	○	○	○	○	○	specialist

Your Opinions on Computing and Music and Ways of Thinking

Please choose one of the six radio buttons for each item to indicate your level of agreement with each statement.

(1) Students in south campus majors (arts, humanities, and social sciences) are more creative than students in north campus majors (science, math, engineering, and business). *

	1	2	3	4	5	6	
Strongly Disagree	○	○	○	○	○	○	Strongly Agree

(2) I enjoy creating my own music. *

	1	2	3	4	5	6	
Strongly Disagree	○	○	○	○	○	○	Strongly Agree

(3) I enjoy working with computers. *

	1	2	3	4	5	6	
Strongly Disagree	○	○	○	○	○	○	Strongly Agree

(4) Creating music requires formal training. *

1 2 3 4 5 6

Strongly Disagree ○ ○ ○ ○ ○ ○ Strongly Agree

(5) You need to know how to read music to create music. *

1 2 3 4 5 6

Strongly Disagree ○ ○ ○ ○ ○ ○ Strongly Agree

(6) I am confident using a computer language to accomplish complex tasks. *

1 2 3 4 5 6

Strongly Disagree ○ ○ ○ ○ ○ ○ Strongly Agree

(7) Programming requires extensive and detailed knowledge of a computer language. *

1 2 3 4 5 6

Strongly Disagree ○ ○ ○ ○ ○ ○ Strongly Agree

(8) I know what it means to create music. *

1 2 3 4 5 6

Strongly Disagree ○ ○ ○ ○ ○ ○ Strongly Agree

(9) I am confident in my ability to express myself through music. *

1 2 3 4 5 6

Strongly Disagree ○ ○ ○ ○ ○ ○ Strongly Agree

(10) I am good at breaking a large problem down into its components and attacking those one at a time to solve the bigger problem. *

1 2 3 4 5 6

Strongly Disagree ○ ○ ○ ○ ○ ○ Strongly Agree

(11) I am good at diagnosing problems and formulating solutions. *

1 2 3 4 5 6

Strongly Disagree ○ ○ ○ ○ ○ ○ Strongly Agree

(12) I get frustrated when things don't go as I expect. *

1 2 3 4 5 6

Strongly Disagree ○ ○ ○ ○ ○ ○ Strongly Agree

(13) North campus majors generally have a narrower view of things than south campus majors. *

1 2 3 4 5 6

Strongly Disagree ○ ○ ○ ○ ○ ○ Strongly Agree

(14) North campus majors don't know much about music and the arts. *

1   2   3   4   5   6

Strongly Disagree ◯ ◯ ◯ ◯ ◯ ◯ Strongly Agree

(15) South campus majors don't know about computing and other technical endeavors. *

1   2   3   4   5   6

Strongly Disagree ◯ ◯ ◯ ◯ ◯ ◯ Strongly Agree

(16) Computers can be used to create cool music. *

1   2   3   4   5   6

Strongly Disagree ◯ ◯ ◯ ◯ ◯ ◯ Strongly Agree

(17) I enjoy working with people who are very different from myself. *

1   2   3   4   5   6

Strongly Disagree ◯ ◯ ◯ ◯ ◯ ◯ Strongly Agree

(18) I enjoy working on group projects. *

1   2   3   4   5   6

Strongly Disagree ◯ ◯ ◯ ◯ ◯ ◯ Strongly Agree

(19) When I have problems that I need to solve, I try to do so in a general way so that I can apply the same solution if I have a similar problem in the future. *

1   2   3   4   5   6

Strongly Disagree ◯ ◯ ◯ ◯ ◯ ◯ Strongly Agree

(20) There is a deep connection between music and computer science. *

1   2   3   4   5   6

Strongly Disagree ◯ ◯ ◯ ◯ ◯ ◯ Strongly Agree

(21) I'm good at spotting patterns in larger bodies of work. *

1   2   3   4   5   6

Strongly Disagree ◯ ◯ ◯ ◯ ◯ ◯ Strongly Agree

(22) Musicians rely more on inspiration than those in the computing field. *

1   2   3   4   5   6

Strongly Disagree ◯ ◯ ◯ ◯ ◯ ◯ Strongly Agree

(23) A well-designed computer program is artistic. *

1   2   3   4   5   6

Strongly Disagree ◯ ◯ ◯ ◯ ◯ ◯ Strongly Agree

(24) I enjoy doing puzzles and solving puzzle-like problems. *

1   2   3   4   5   6

Strongly Disagree ◯ ◯ ◯ ◯ ◯ ◯ Strongly Agree

(25) **Computer programming is fun.** *

      1   2   3   4   5   6

Strongly Disagree ○ ○ ○ ○ ○ ○ Strongly Agree

(26) **Standard musical notation is a form of code.** *

      1   2   3   4   5   6

Strongly Disagree ○ ○ ○ ○ ○ ○ Strongly Agree

(27) **Writing music down is similar to writing a computer program.** *

      1   2   3   4   5   6

Strongly Disagree ○ ○ ○ ○ ○ ○ Strongly Agree

(28) **Programming a computer is difficult.** *

      1   2   3   4   5   6

Strongly Disagree ○ ○ ○ ○ ○ ○ Strongly Agree

(29) **I can apply ideas learned in one situation to another situation.** *

      1   2   3   4   5   6

Strongly Disagree ○ ○ ○ ○ ○ ○ Strongly Agree

(30) **I'd rather watch a game show than a sitcom.** *

      1   2   3   4   5   6

Strongly Disagree ○ ○ ○ ○ ○ ○ Strongly Agree

(31) **When I watch a game show, I try to play the game along with the contestants.** *

      1   2   3   4   5   6

Strongly Disagree ○ ○ ○ ○ ○ ○ Strongly Agree

(32) **I would rather go to Museum of Fine Arts than the Museum of Science.** *

      1   2   3   4   5   6

Strongly Disagree ○ ○ ○ ○ ○ ○ Strongly Agree

(33) **When something I own breaks down, I try to figure out what's wrong before calling someone for help.** *

      1   2   3   4   5   6

Strongly Disagree ○ ○ ○ ○ ○ ○ Strongly Agree

Thank You.

Submit

Never submit passwords through Google Forms.

Powered by Google Docs

Report Abuse - Terms of Service - Additional Terms

Sound Thinking 2012 Post-Course Survey

This survey is designed to give us information about how well the class worked and to help us assess what you learned. It is also designed to help us assess how attitudes changed as a result of taking this class. There are no right and wrong answers, nor are some answers better or more desirable than others. We are interested in your honest and complete assessment of the learning experience.

As you may recall we administered a survey similar to this one at the beginning of the semester. The surveys are therefore numbered so that we can compare your answers on the two surveys. However, your responses will not be individually evaluated or have any effect on your grade in this course. Our analysis will not relate your responses to your name. The numbers will only allow us to track changes over time.

You therefore need to enter the same number that you entered at the beginning of the semester. This is the last 4 digits of your student ID number. This is very important, as it will allow us to compare the responses on the pre- and post-course surveys. Thank you for your understanding on this.

To ensure that these policies are adhered to, we will not look at the results until after final grades have been submitted to the Registrar, following the same procedure as end-of-course student evaluations.

* Required

1. Your ID Number *
Please enter the last 4 digits of your student ID number.

[   ]

2. Your Major *

[-- Please Choose One --   ‡]

2a. If you answered "other" to question 2, please enter your major. *

[   ]

3. Your level in college *
How many semesters have you completed?

[   ]

4. Changes That Occurred From Taking This Course

For each item below, please choose one of the six radio buttons to indicate how much each factored into your perception regarding the changes that took place.

(a) As a result of this course, I want to learn more about computers. *

	1	2	3	4	5	6	
Strongly Disagree	○	○	○	○	○	○	Strongly Agree

(b) As a result of this course, I want to learn more about music. *

	1	2	3	4	5	6	
Strongly Disagree	○	○	○	○	○	○	Strongly Agree

(c) This course was harder than I thought. *

	1	2	3	4	5	6	
Strongly Disagree	○	○	○	○	○	○	Strongly Agree

(d) This course challenged me to think differently. *

	1	2	3	4	5	6	
Strongly Disagree	○	○	○	○	○	○	Strongly Agree

(e) I am starting to understand the connections between computing and music. *

	1	2	3	4	5	6	
Strongly Disagree	○	○	○	○	○	○	Strongly Agree

5. How Well Did This Course Meet Your Expectations?

For each item below, please choose one of the six radio buttons to indicate the degree to which your expectations were met.

(a) I learned new ways of making music and composing. *

	1	2	3	4	5	6	
Strongly Disagree	○	○	○	○	○	○	Strongly Agree

(b) I gained more knowledge about computers and programming. *

	1	2	3	4	5	6	
Strongly Disagree	○	○	○	○	○	○	Strongly Agree

(c) I understand more about the integration of computers and music. *

	1	2	3	4	5	6	
Strongly Disagree	○	○	○	○	○	○	Strongly Agree

(d) I learned how to work in diverse groups. *

	1	2	3	4	5	6	
Strongly Disagree	○	○	○	○	○	○	Strongly Agree

(e) I learned how to collaborate with others in my major. *

	1	2	3	4	5	6	
Strongly Disagree	○	○	○	○	○	○	Strongly Agree

(f) I learned how to collaborate with others outside my major. *

	1	2	3	4	5	6	
Strongly Disagree	○	○	○	○	○	○	Strongly Agree

(g) I learned to think more creatively. *

	1	2	3	4	5	6	
A Little	○	○	○	○	○	○	A Lot

(h) I learned to be more communicative. *

	1	2	3	4	5	6	
Strongly Disagree	○	○	○	○	○	○	Strongly Agree

(i) I am more willing to take risks. *

	1	2	3	4	5	6	
Strongly Disagree	○	○	○	○	○	○	Strongly Agree

6. Were Your Perceptions About Yourself Altered as a Result of This Class?

Please consider each pair of words or phrases below and indicate how what change, if any, you see in yourself as a result of taking this course.

(a) Artistic/Technical: Has your perception changed? If so, which way and why? *

(b) Left-Brained/Right-Brained: Has your perception changed? If so, which way and why? *

(c) Creative/Uncreative: Has your perception changed? If so, which way and why? *

(d) Do Not Take Risks/Take Risks: Has your perception changed? If so, which way and why? *

(e) "Big Picture"/"Detail": Has your perception changed? If so, which way and why? *

(f) Generalist/Specialist: Has your perception changed? If so, which way and why? *
Please Note: A generalist is a person with broad general knowledge and skills in several areas. A specialist is a person whose knowledge and skills are primarily focused in one specific field.

7. Your Opinions on Computing + Music and Ways of Thinking

Please choose one of the six radio buttons for each item to indicate your level of agreement with each statement.

(a) My perceptions regarding students in south campus majors (arts, humanities, and social sciences) being more creative than students in north campus majors (science, math, engineering, and business) have changed. *

	1	2	3	4	5	6	
Strongly Disagree	○	○	○	○	○	○	Strongly Agree

(b) I enjoyed projects where we had to create music. *

	1	2	3	4	5	6	
Strongly Disagree	○	○	○	○	○	○	Strongly Agree

(c) As a result of this course I am more comfortable working with computers. *

	1	2	3	4	5	6	
Strongly Disagree	○	○	○	○	○	○	Strongly Agree

(d) It is possible to create music with little formal training. *

	1	2	3	4	5	6	
Strongly Disagree	○	○	○	○	○	○	Strongly Agree

(e) It is possible to create music without knowing how to read music. *

	1	2	3	4	5	6	
Strongly Disagree	○	○	○	○	○	○	Strongly Agree

(f) I am now more confident using a computer language to accomplish complex tasks. *

	1	2	3	4	5	6	
Strongly Disagree	○	○	○	○	○	○	Strongly Agree

(g) Programming does not always require extensive and detailed knowledge of a computer language. *

	1	2	3	4	5	6	
Strongly Disagree	○	○	○	○	○	○	Strongly Agree

(h) I know what it means to create music. *

	1	2	3	4	5	6	
Strongly Disagree	○	○	○	○	○	○	Strongly Agree

(i) I am more confident in my ability to express myself through music. *

	1	2	3	4	5	6	
Strongly Disagree	○	○	○	○	○	○	Strongly Agree

(j) As a result of this course I am better at breaking a large problem down into its components and attacking those one at a time to solve the bigger problem. *

	1	2	3	4	5	6	
Strongly Disagree	○	○	○	○	○	○	Strongly Agree

(k) As a result of this course I am better at diagnosing problems and formulating solutions. *

	1	2	3	4	5	6	
Strongly Disagree	○	○	○	○	○	○	Strongly Agree

(l) I am learning to work through frustrations when things to go as expected. *

	1	2	3	4	5	6	
Strongly Disagree	○	○	○	○	○	○	Strongly Agree

(m) My views on whether North campus majors generally have a narrower view of things than south campus majors have changed. *

	1	2	3	4	5	6	
Strongly Disagree	○	○	○	○	○	○	Strongly Agree

(n) My view that North campus majors don't know much about music and the arts have changed. *

	1	2	3	4	5	6	
Strongly Disagree	○	○	○	○	○	○	Strongly Agree

(o) My view that South campus majors don't know about computing and other technical endeavors have changed. *

	1	2	3	4	5	6	
Strongly Disagree	○	○	○	○	○	○	Strongly Agree

8. Potential Benefits of Taking Sound Thinking

Please choose one of the six radio buttons for each item to indicate your level of agreement with each statement.

(a) I believe computers can be used to create cool music. *

	1	2	3	4	5	6	
Strongly Disagree	○	○	○	○	○	○	Strongly Agree

(b) I discovered I enjoy working with people who are very different from myself. *

	1	2	3	4	5	6	
Strongly Disagree	○	○	○	○	○	○	Strongly Agree

(c) I now appreciate the benefits of working on group projects. *

	1	2	3	4	5	6	
Strongly Disagree	○	○	○	○	○	○	Strongly Agree

(d) When I have problems that I need to solve, I try to do so in a general way so that I can apply the same solution if I have a similar problem in the future. *

	1 2 3 4 5 6	
Strongly Disagree	○ ○ ○ ○ ○ ○	Strongly Agree

(e) I am now seeing a deep connection between music and computer science. *

	1 2 3 4 5 6	
Strongly Disagree	○ ○ ○ ○ ○ ○	Strongly Agree

(f) I'm better at spotting patterns in larger bodies of work. *

	1 2 3 4 5 6	
Strongly Disagree	○ ○ ○ ○ ○ ○	Strongly Agree

(g) My view that musicians rely more on inspiration than those in the computing field have changed. *

	1 2 3 4 5 6	
Strongly Disagree	○ ○ ○ ○ ○ ○	Strongly Agree

(h) I have come to believe that well-designed computer program is artistic. *

	1 2 3 4 5 6	
Strongly Disagree	○ ○ ○ ○ ○ ○	Strongly Agree

(i) I enjoy doing puzzles and solving puzzle-like problems. *

	1 2 3 4 5 6	
Strongly Disagree	○ ○ ○ ○ ○ ○	Strongly Agree

(j) Computer programming is now more fun for me. *

	1 2 3 4 5 6	
Strongly Disagree	○ ○ ○ ○ ○ ○	Strongly Agree

(k) I now see the connection between standard musical notation computer code. *

	1 2 3 4 5 6	
Strongly Disagree	○ ○ ○ ○ ○ ○	Strongly Agree

(l) Writing music down is similar to writing a computer program. *

	1 2 3 4 5 6	
Strongly Disagree	○ ○ ○ ○ ○ ○	Strongly Agree

(m) Programming a computer seems less difficult *

	1 2 3 4 5 6	
Strongly Disagree	○ ○ ○ ○ ○ ○	Strongly Agree

(n) I can apply ideas learned in one situation to another situation. *

	1 2 3 4 5 6	
Strongly Disagree	○ ○ ○ ○ ○ ○	Strongly Agree

(o) I'd rather watch a game show than a sitcom. *

	1	2	3	4	5	6	
Strongly Disagree	○	○	○	○	○	○	Strongly Agree

(p) When I watch a game show, I try to play the game along with the contestants. *

	1	2	3	4	5	6	
Strongly Disagree	○	○	○	○	○	○	Strongly Agree

(q) I would rather go to Museum of Fine Arts than the Museum of Science. *

	1	2	3	4	5	6	
Strongly Disagree	○	○	○	○	○	○	Strongly Agree

(r) When something I own breaks down, I try to figure out what's wrong before calling someone for help. *

	1	2	3	4	5	6	
Strongly Disagree	○	○	○	○	○	○	Strongly Agree

9. What were some of the challenges you had with your own creative process in this course? *

10. Is there one particular activity you can recall where the connections between computing and music began to gel for you? *

○ Yes
○ No

10a. If you answered "yes" to question 10, please describe what it was.

Lessons Learned in Sound Thinking This Semester

Please Indicate your level of agreement with each of these statements

There was too little music content in this course. *

	1	2	3	4	5	6	
Strongly Disagree	○	○	○	○	○	○	Strongly Agree

There was too little computer content in this course.

	1	2	3	4	5	6	
Strongly Disagree	○	○	○	○	○	○	Strongly Agree

I found the assignments interesting. *

	1	2	3	4	5	6	
Strongly Disagree	○	○	○	○	○	○	Strongly Agree

The assignments built on each other in a logical manner. *

	1	2	3	4	5	6	
Strongly Disagree	○	○	○	○	○	○	Strongly Agree

I found the course had a good balance between music and computer science. *

	1	2	3	4	5	6	
Strongly Disagree	○	○	○	○	○	○	Strongly Agree

Please describe what an "interval" is. (Remember that we are not evaluating you, we are evaluating how well we taught this concept.) *

In terms of Intervals, what do we mean when we talk about that interval's "inversion?" *

Please describe what a "delta" (or "offset") is in terms of the relation between two notes. *

When we create a loop, what we are really doing is *

○ going around in circles.

○ creating a repetitive pattern.

○ creating a new event.

○ transposing a melody.

When you created the Scratch project using lists to "transpose," what were you actually doing to the music? *

We have seen that some settings affect only the sprite in which they are running and others affect an entire Scratch program. The former are called "local," and the latter are called "global." Name at least one musical characteristic that falls into each category. *

A whole step in music is equal to how many half steps? *

○ 1
○ 2
○ 3
○ 4

A chromatic scale has how many notes? *

○ 6
○ 8
○ 10
○ 12

Thank You!

Gena & Jesse

[Submit]

Powered by Google Docs

Report Abuse - Terms of Service - Additional Terms

CHAPTER 9

The Performamatics Model of Sharing and Networking

We're All Connected

These young people are among the first to grow up with an expectation of continuous connection: always on and always on them.
  Turkle, *Alone Together: Why We Expect More from Technology and Less from Each Other* (p.17)

INTERCONNECTEDNESS AND WHAT WE ARE LEARNING

By now you must have realized that we do not shy away from using technology, whether directly in our teaching or in the administration of our *Sound Thinking* course. A great deal of time, thought, and effort goes into maintaining a very detailed course website where students can access the course syllabus, obtain contact information for each other, review class notes, retrieve assignment parameters, check their grades for each assignment, and find links to a host of resources to help them succeed in the course (please see our course website at **soundthinking.uml.edu**). Since we also wanted our course website to serve as an archival repository, until recently (more about this later) we linked it to a social networking site. The additional site provided opportunities for student input.

The purposes of all the web support is to enable students to interact with us and their peers beyond the classroom and to facilitate their ability to post their reflections, respond to instructor-initiated questions, pose questions themselves and answer questions posed by other students, upload and share music and video links with the class, and post their completed projects so that everyone can see what everyone else did on a given project. In addition, each class is videotaped, archived, and linked to our course website.

Our Philosophy behind the Connectivity

Our goal in making all of this information readily available is to ensure that everything a student needs to know regarding any aspect of the course can be accessed anytime, anywhere. If, for whatever reason, a student can't be in class, the assignments, notes on what was covered in class, and an actual video of a particular day's class are always available 24/7. We all know that on many levels, and for different people at various times in any course, there will be those moments when the learning curve will seem insurmountable. Those moments are most likely to occur at 2:00 AM.

To that end, we encourage you to adopt some form of course website as an extension of your face-to-face meeting time. If you have the time, interest, and expertise to build it yourself, that's great. But if you don't, there are several good course website software platforms and free hosting sites readily available, and your school probably already has a license for at least one of them. A course website can provide your students with asynchronous, step-by-step tutorials to help them work through issues whenever and wherever they arise. In theory, with all this online support there should be no excuse for students not knowing when assignments are due and what the parameters of those assignments are. We will have more about that "theory" later.

We use two different websites for our course—the result of two professors coming together and combining aspects of their teaching approaches into a single, cohesive, whole. It is, to a certain degree, a reflection of our different teaching philosophies and styles. Jesse creates a very detailed website for each of his classes (see Figure 9-1). His websites include comprehensive class notes that are posted before each class (see Figure 9-2). He teaches directly from those notes, and they remain online so that his students can refer to them after class. Gena prefers a more spontaneous element of discovery in her classes. We therefore worked out a way to compromise on how much information gets posted before class and how much after.

Gena also prefers using discussion boards and other interactive media to extend her class discussions. She sets up a web space where students can reflect on the readings and class activities, and also where students can upload their work. Her goal is to promote and encourage reflective and critical thinking among her students. She sees the discussion forum as an

Figure 9-1:
The *Sound Thinking* course home page.

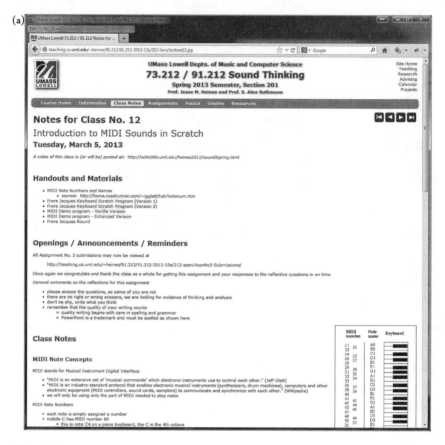

Figure 9-2a:
Sound Thinking class notes.

opportunity for students not only to answer her questions but also to answer those of other students and to pose questions of their own. As of this writing, the class discussion forum that we use in our course is Piazza (**piazza.com**).

Since both approaches have educational merit, we decided early on that it made sense to incorporate both types of web-based interactions. It is easy to link each site to the other rather seamlessly. Many of your schools most likely have licenses with course website providers, so you may find it easiest to work within your school's system. When we began teaching *Sound Thinking*, our school's website did not offer some of the media-rich capabilities we were looking for. In addition, we wanted to have access to the site well after the semester had ended. To that end, we found a social networking site that provided the features we wanted and had an easy-to-navigate interface at no additional cost, so we went with that.

Figure 9-2b:
Sound Thinking class notes (continued).

SOCIAL NETWORKING AND THE SOCIAL CONSTRUCTION OF LEARNING

Brown, Collins, and Duguid argue that "learning, both outside and inside school, advances through collaborative social interaction and the social construction of knowledge" [4] (p. 40). As suggested in earlier chapters, we contend that there is great value in developing a collaborative classroom environment through group projects. We also believe that opportunities for social interaction should extend beyond the classroom through these online exchanges, where questions might arise when students begin delving into their projects.

Our colleague, S. Alex Ruthmann, in his work with Steve Dillon, who was a Senior Lecturer at Queensland University of Technology, advocates a practice of relational pedagogy "where teachers actively design musical experiences informed by their students' musical and technological experiences" [11] (p. 177). Ruthmann proposes projects where students are "actively engaged in social music making with technology" [11] (p. 177).

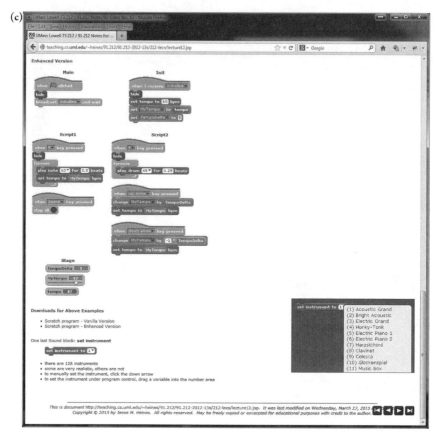

Figures 9-2c:
Sound Thinking class notes (continued).

He suggests that such activities not only give students a sense of pride in their work but also help bring the students in the class together as a community. From a music teacher educator's perspective, creating a sense of community within the class is a major focal point for modeling student/ teacher interaction. From a CS teacher's perspective, classroom community models behaviors that pave the way for students to participate in collaborative work environments well into the future.

Over the time we have been teaching this course, we have used two different social networking sites. After our original site changed the terms of use and made many of the multimedia functions fee-based, we migrated to another site. However, during the last semester we taught this course, that social networking site unexpectedly ceased operations. Interestingly enough, it was during the semester the site went down that we noticed less cohesion among the students compared to previous semesters. We attribute that partly to the decrease in opportunities for students to share their work and ideas as a result of not having a social networking component. Consequently, that sense of community we experienced in past semesters never fully developed.

Further evidence of the importance of creating a community can be found in the Scratch programming environment. The Scratch mantra "imagine, program, share" [3] (p. 2150) gets to the heart of why their programming environment has been such a hit with students and educators alike. In addition to a fairly intuitive visual programming environment, another hallmark of Scratch is its web-based gallery and forum where programmers at any level of expertise can share their creations, get feedback, and comment on and contribute to one another's projects [3].

An area of great interest, where the power of Scratch to develop computational thinking is particularly prominent, is how this online social space supports members' initiatives to "re-mix" other people's projects. This re-mixing often sparks new ideas that the original programmers might not have been able to come up with on their own, or helps to extend ideas toward more complexity than the original creators had thought of. In their case studies of the different types of Scratch programmers, the authors contend that "sharing was an essential aspect of each Scratcher's development as an interactive media creator" [3] (p. 2155).

As you might guess, there is great potential for connectivity and interactivity to take place. However, "potential" is the key word here, as Gena and Jesse have learned. To paraphrase a great movie quote, "Just because you build it, they won't necessarily come."[1] We have experienced aspects of our experiments in social networking and connectivity that are extremely beneficial to the educative and collaborative process, as well as the many challenges inherent in doing so. We have also fallen victim to some of the faulty assumptions we professors may harbor concerning technology and the role it plays in our students' lives.

THE DIGITAL NATIVE AND OTHER MYTHS
Our Perceptions

If your students are anything like ours, they most likely spend a great deal of their time "being connected" through their cell phones or other digital devices. We have reached the point where for our students, the computer is most often the preferred device for entertainment, reading, writing, and creating [5]. In addition, our students are no longer hampered by issues of location and time [1, 5, 8, 9, 10]. There are even studies to suggest that on certain campuses, the majority of distance-learning classes are actually taken by students who are mostly on campus [7]. As Turkle points out, these students would "'rather text than talk" [12] (p. 1).

All of these alternatives to real-time interaction provide us, as well as our students, with much greater flexibility and control over our interactions. If we follow much of the research on technology and how it is shaping our lives, the assumption is that putting all this information out there is a "slam dunk" in favor of our students readily participating, perusing, interacting, discussing, and reflecting on the information we put online. In fact, many of them are doing just that, but perhaps not in ways that we think or hope they are.

Their Realities

Turkle points out how technology allows us to communicate with a network of "friends" we may never actually have met face-to-face, while we may simultaneously be disengaging from our real-life interactions [12]. How many of us have sat in restaurants observing two people on a date of some sort, interacting with their cell phones instead of each other? How many of us have actually done that? As for those students who are physically in class, is all this connectivity contributing to the learning environment or is it an invitation to *appear* to "multitask," but actually to engage in non-class related activities? Are they really taking notes? Or are they shopping, texting, blogging, or checking/updating their status on Facebook?

Turkle suggested to her students at one point that they close their laptops and take notes with paper and pencil to eliminate the temptation to stray from the topic at hand. She admits that that experiment did not last beyond a one-semester trial. She and several colleagues, however, have not too surprisingly observed that the students sitting behind open laptops in class generally do not do as well as the others [12]. Yet in computer science classes, where the computer is a necessary tool, the temptation to wander from the task at hand is something that comes with the territory. However, in a computer lab where all machines are under your control, as opposed to a classroom where students bring their own laptops, there are software applications that can give the instructor access to everyone's screen. In such situations, the students must beware.

If everything out there is available online and our students are seemingly tethered to their digital devices, you would think there would be no excuse for not posting required reflections, or knowing what the assignments are about, or when they are due. Over the years we have been teaching this course and others that regularly include web-based interactions, we have observed that there is a fairly sizable group of students who do actively participate. In general, these are the motivated students who take part in class discussions and do their assignments in a thorough and timely manner. These are the students who use and refer to the class website on a regular basis. We have also observed there is always a group who post required assignments late if at all, and when they do, they may miss half of the required parameters. But as we both realized long ago, for many students an *assignment*, regardless of how you deliver it, is still going to feel like *school work*, and it just won't have any traction unless your students are personally motivated and invested in the work [6].

So yes, today's students use technology, but often mindlessly, at least in their everyday personal interactions. For many of our students, navigating our websites and working with required software programs might feel like more of a time-consuming burden. The medium of delivery is irrelevant for these students. With all the technology in the world instantly available at most everyone's disposal, we professors just may not be able to compete with the lures of the Internet, no matter how engaging we might be.

WHAT ARE WE LEARNING FROM THIS?

School assignments versus Facebook, iTunes, YouTube, gaming, online shopping, and a host of other digital distractions is, like it or not, the "new normal." As Gena observed during our first collaboration, which was the creation of a remedial website for her music students to use in preparing for their music teacher licensure exam, just putting the information out there does not necessarily guarantee that students will refer to it [6]. We need to be more proactive in giving students a reason to go to the website. Perhaps we can think about running the class completely paperless, with no handouts. This might just create the necessity for students to "check in" on the website on a regular basis. Creating more discovery opportunities through linkages between in-class activities and the website, where perhaps we embed new information not covered in class and vice-versa, can pique student curiosity.

As suggested by Brennan, Monroy-Hernández, and Resnick, we should not assume that just because our students grow up surrounded by and immersed in interactive media they are predisposed toward understanding how these technologies function [2]. Nor, as the authors suggest, are our students inherently interested in becoming *creators* rather than *consumers* of technology. But we believe that if an assignment can appeal to students' personal interests on some level, the temptation to participate in the creation process will overtake their initial resistance.

We encourage you to provide opportunities for your students to present their work. However, we are also aware that the reality of having multiple complex projects, combined with the sheer number of students you may have and the limited number of class hours, may make it infeasible to do presentations during class time. An online forum can go a long way toward resolving the conflict. In the absence of a viable alternative to the social networking site we were using, the most important aspects we discovered for fostering class participation and inter-personal connectivity, particularly when the class is made up of students from a variety of majors, are being able to post assignments online and to see what their classmates have done. These activities get to the crux of the Performamatics experience: the performance/sharing phase of creating and programming.

PERFORMANCE AS COMPUTATIONAL THINKING IN ACTION

There is a great deal of discussion these days regarding learning outcomes and the need for students to demonstrate what they've learned. A common paper and pencil exam that might include combinations of short answers and long form essays typically serves as the tool for assessing student learning outcomes over the course of a semester. But is this necessarily the best approach? Where does the synthesis and application of knowledge enter the picture in this assessment? This traditional method is certainly quicker to administer and grade. However, in thinking back on our own work experiences in the world of business, when we were asked to present ourselves, our ideas, and our work, it was never in the form of a paper and pencil test. We therefore feel quite passionately that we should be giving our students experiences closer to the reality of the world beyond school. Performance assessments should mirror the types of presentations students will need to give to their supervisors, colleagues, and potential clients in the future.

For the purpose of our interdisciplinary approach, we define "performance" as presentations of our students' creations in a public forum. Sharing work online is one viable performance method in this sense, but we also believe that it is paramount for today's students to be able to present, and in many cases actually *perform*, their creations before a live audience. The importance of developing and honing presentation skills and the ability to effectively communicate one's work or concepts—as well as the presence of mind to think on the fly in front of a group of one's peers and/or strangers—cannot be overstated. As mentioned previously, it is easier than ever for your students to retreat into their digital devices and disengage from communicating in real time with real people.

A major part of this interdisciplinary work between music and computing is to develop computational thinking skills in our students. But another equally important focus is to develop in our students the ability to express themselves, collaborate with, and communicate ideas to a variety of people who may not have their same skill sets or think about things in quite the same way. Several components go into how we measure these skills:

1. the way they approach, develop, and reflect on their projects;
2. their ability to share ideas and collaborate with their teammates; and
3. their ability to articulate the concepts underlying their projects verbally and to demonstrate the project in action.

While all these modes of assessing students' CT skills are at play in all projects, it is in the final project where the third component is most emphasized in our Performamatics model. We make a very big deal out of the final project presentations. These are done in a public showcase where we either go out into the local community or invite the community onto our campus. Using the Artbotics class as a model (**www.artbotics.org**) [14], we schedule our presentations in the evenings at local art galleries and in museum spaces. We provide food, advertise the event, and have students create titles for their projects so that we can put together a program as we would for any performance (see Figures 9-3).

What we refer to as the "performance" aspect of the course creates an aura around the final project that goes beyond the fact that it will be weighted more heavily than the rest of the class assignments. The prospect of an audience larger than just their peers fuels a level of motivation in our students different from only getting through the end of the semester with a passing grade. We have observed that students put a great deal more time and effort into these projects. They want to "look good" and not come off looking foolish. They are also invested in really personalizing these projects to their own interests. We have now lived through several semesters of angst, doubts, bursts of creative flashes, and "ah-ha" moments from our students. We believe that the whole final project package, in terms of creation, demonstrating computational thinking, presenting, and performing, is a terrific opportunity for students to synthesize everything they have been working on during the semester. In addition, as a result of the various collaborations throughout the semester and their final project performances, they came together at the end of the semester as a community, to share and support each other [11, 13].

But that is our view, that is, the perspective of the professors. What ultimately matters is how this impacts the students' perspectives on the merits of this interdisciplinary approach. Therefore, this might be an appropriate time to let our students "speak" for themselves.

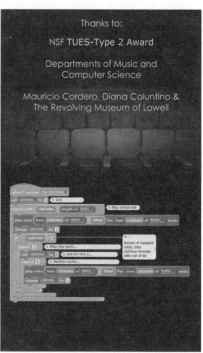

PROGRAM

1 – DORA THE SCRATCH EXPLORER – By Erin McDermott + Anthony Prestigiovanni + Kristen Keymont

2 – ICHIFUN – By Kevin St. Onge + James Sheets

3 – FEELING KIND OF ICHI – By Joshua Tracy + Georgio Broufas

4 – DIFFERENT PERSONALITIES – By Ran Guo + Roosevelt Langlois + Kofi Omane

5 – CHICKEN SCRATCH – By Chris Southwick + Elizabeth Avila + Olivia Stiling

6 – TEXT PAINTING WITH TECH – By Savannah Marshall + Nick Darling + Derek Tanch

PROGRAM

7 – INSTRUMENT & COMPUTER INTERPLAY – By Sean Harrington + Joe Prieto + Dan Faria

8 – SOMETHING CONTEMPORARY – By Barry Davis + Channate Phauk + Rachel Zelinka

10 – H'ICHI-HOP – By Ian Schaeffer + Tye Smith + Kevin Velez

---

11 – ICHI PENDULUM – By Anson Airoldi + Jonathan Bouquet

12 – DUBSTEP – Paul Karcher + Ryan O'Grady

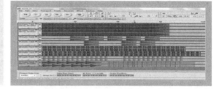

Figures 9-3:
Program for *Sound Thinking* Final Project Presentation Night.

IN THEIR OWN WORDS
On Performance

At the end of the semester our students are asked to post their reflections of their final project as the last blog for the course. They are asked to think back on what they had hoped to accomplish and then to describe what they learned both musically and computationally. In addition, they are asked to reflect on how the collaborative nature of the project affected the outcome, and to express their thoughts on the performance aspect as well. With regard to what the performance aspect contributed to the final project, one student aptly stated:

> Our project would have been nothing without the performance. Our program is actually dependent on our being there to move the execution along. It's very unlike a lot of the other projects we have completed over the course of the semester, in which a single click of the mouse or tap of the space bar will send the whole code running through itself on its own. So my thoughts? All positive. It was great fun.

The student goes on to discuss the performance aspect and how it contributed to the fun he had working on the project. As the following statement attests, he and his partners did a great deal of debugging, but the specter of having to "perform" for an audience heightened their motivation.

> We were sure to make fail-safe code, as well as run countless tests so [that we could] rest assured that nothing would go wrong. And it turned out great. We got some laughs and threw in a few last minute surprises of our own in regards to how endless the possibilities were. I would not have had as much fun with this final assignment had it not been performance-based.

We all know how crucial it is for students to be motivated. The next comment speaks to the importance of making the information you are trying to impart relevant to the students.

> I think we learned how to take our prior knowledge of Scratch and apply it to what we actually like.

A student commented on how much she learned through everyone's presentations:

> Using Scratch as an interactive accompanist was so cool! I would never have even thought to incorporate live music with Scratch. This really opens the door for using technology as a performance element in the general music classroom.

One of the CS students had the following sentiment with regard to the performance aspect of the final project.

> This project was an obvious closing assignment to the semester because it allowed us to do really anything we wanted, with the only restrictions that we use what we had learned. It makes sense to have a project that incorporates using the program to write code that will support a performance, because that completes the circle that is the construction of the instrument, and the performance with the instrument.

In discussing the musical dimensions of this project, one student wrote:

> It made me think about the hierarchy of understanding in music. We think about music in different levels of abstraction. Underlying most of it is the beat, which lies inside the bar, which lies inside the form. Tonality is made up of scales and chords. By having these concepts exist in the code, the computer is able to start to interpret things similarly to how we interpret it.

Another student looked at the ways this project stretched his thinking through its conceptualization and culmination in a performance:

> The aspects of this project [took] everything we had been learning about coding with Scratch throughout the semester and brought it to full fruition. We not only had to code, but to combine that into a live presentation with things going on outside of the coding. We had to take concepts which in live performance on an instrument are pretty basic, but putting them into code proved to be difficult.

Not every learning experience is a positive experience, however. When we ask our students to stretch their thinking and take risks, there is always the possibility that things will not go according to plan. No matter how much preparation we put in, there is always the possibility of the unexpected, as this student's comment suggests:

> I also learned that with computing there's a ton of room for hiccups and technical difficulties. Again, it was extremely disappointing that our project didn't work correctly at the Revolving Museum, but unfortunately that's just the way computers and technology go.

Another student wrote:

> I learned that performing music live is one of the most nerve-racking experiences imaginable.... I also learned that there is a big difference between practicing music alone and performing live. When you are live things don't always go as planned.

These are important life lessons for everyone, in that things won't always go smoothly, whether you are a performer, programmer, or teacher. Learning to deal with problems and mistakes in the moment and not get flustered is an invaluable skill to develop.

On Collaboration

Group projects can add an additional layer of stress for many students as well as for the professors. Certain students often need the entire semester to adjust to the idea of not working on a project solo or to acknowledge that other people's opinions might be equally as valid as their own. The following student statement really drives home the importance of the value of collaborative work:

> I learned that everybody has something to offer.

This sentiment was echoed by another student:

> It's always interesting to work with other people because we have different ideas.

But even those sharing common ground can find collaborating a beneficial experience:

> From working with my partner I learned how easy it can be when both partners have the same idea for what they want the project to be. Both my partner and I wanted to make an interactive instrument, and we both had ideas contributing to the final project.

But what about the person who generally hesitates to speak up for fear of getting his or her idea shot down by others? One of our students learned an interesting lesson:

> At first we had no idea what we were going to do, but once we threw ideas out onto the table we came up with one idea that combined all of our ideas together. I learned that when you have ideas it is best not to keep quiet, because they can be implemented into a project and it could possibly make it better.

The project she is referring to was truly collaborative, with everyone making an equal contribution to the outcome.

For students planning on teaching, working with someone who does not share your background can help alter your approach to how you might teach, as suggested by this student:

When I want to work with more advanced concepts and my partner(s) are not of the same musical level, I have to find new ways to describe my western classical training to someone without any or only a little.

Another student who had worked before with a particular partner made an interesting observation about him:

Things that I showed him in previous assignments he brought up during production of this one, which made it easy because he retained any programming tricks I showed him. Scratch may be crude coding to more experienced programmers, but it is still obvious that the central ideas ultimately sink in.

Not all collaborations will work well and some will invariably work better than others. Often one negative experience can leave students with the idea that group projects aren't workable. This comment from one student who was becoming disillusioned with group projects is particularly rewarding since, like everything else in life, learning to work with others takes time and patience:

When we encountered a problem with the code, we all took part in the problem solving. I was happy that my partners were interested in making our project the best it could be. In past projects, I sometimes felt as though when my partner and I encountered a problem, my partner would give up and leave the problem solving up to me. This project showed me that three people working together can achieve much more when they all care about the finished product.

Getting students to care about their work, particularly in a general education class, is no small feat. Designing learning experiences that allow enough flexibility to find and express shared interests when working on group projects will help to increase student motivation.

On Computational Thinking

The next student's comment speaks to the importance of fun in the learning environment. Not only were she and her teammates having fun, they were problem-solving computational issues:

This was such a fun project to do. The challenge was to give the program many facets while still keeping the coding and physical operation through the program simple.

Another student identified learning the value of modularization:

I learned that if you break down what it is you want to accomplish, then the tasks become much more manageable to figure out.

He continued by elaborating on the goals for his group's project:

> I chose to do this project because I thought that it would be interesting to see how many different musical elements the IchiBoard could handle at once. I learned that even a simple device can control and change an extraordinary number of musical elements.

Learning and problem-solving computing issues through music—and music issues through computing—help students develop the habits of mind needed to be successful, as expressed in the following sentiment:

> I learned how much you can push the boundaries of music in this assignment. The project was able to manipulate the song a lot and also do it in real-time while the song was playing. This taught me a lot about what it might be like to do a live performance with a real instrument.

Throughout a semester, our students learn a great deal about music, about computing, and about working with others. Perhaps the crux of why we do what we do is best explained by this student:

> This assignment, I feel, was more than just [about] musical compositions or performances. There were so many unique and different outcomes from every other group. It was amazing how some made a storytelling more enjoyable while others made a simulation of learning Spanish with Dora. I think this assignment shows that there can be a lot done with just one program and one IchiBoard. As long as you let your imagination run wild and free, anything can be accomplished. This assignment let us do our own thing and decide what we wanted to do. It may have been a bit difficult to decide what we wanted to do, but when [we] decided, it made the project/assignment more enjoyable.

Letting students tap into their imaginations and reconnect with the sense of curiosity they had as children are what we hope to foster through the various projects.

 You can view more detailed blog responses here.

MAKING CONNECTIONS

The term "making connections" has multiple implications in the context of our interdisciplinary work. We talk about connecting to things, to people, to concepts as well as making connections between one domain and another, and to the wider world. Sometimes we are referring to connecting to and through technology and at other times we are referring to the interpersonal connections that are needed to be successful in any endeavor of significant size and impact.

Throughout the semester our students also began to make connections to their future career paths. They had multiple opportunities to understand how many of the encounters they had working with people with varying levels of experience and expertise would be similar to how it might be to teach or work with and for people who did not share their domain-specific knowledge and skill set. They saw firsthand how their ability to mentor a classmate impacted the outcome of a project. They experienced what it feels like to work with both motivated and unmotivated colleagues and, we hope, to learn strategies for either helping to motivate their fellow classmate or positively coping with those who have little interest. This type of knowledge seriously augments the fact-based knowledge that one typically associates with school-based learning. We strongly believe that our students need to experience this type of learning to be successful when they go out into the world upon graduating.

We are confident that taking an interdisciplinary approach to computing and music will yield opportunities for you and your students to make multiple connections to music and computing content, to other areas of interest, and, most important, to other people. As you already know, it is easier than ever to connect with people, places, and things. It is our hope that the information in this book helps to make those connections more meaningful for you and your students and opens up new possibilities and ways of thinking.

BIBLIOGRAPHY

[1] Bauer, W. I. (2001). "Student Attitudes toward Web-enhanced Learning in a Music Education Methods Class: A Case Study." *Journal of Technology in Music Learning* **1**(1): 20–30.

[2] Brennan, K., Monroy-Hernández, A., & Resnick, M. (2010). "Making Projects, Making Friends: Online Community as Catalyst for Interactive Media Creation." *New Directions for Youth Development* 128:75–83.

[3] Brennan, K., Valverde, A., Prempeh, J., Roque, R., & Chung, M. (2011). "More than Code: The Significance of Social Interactions in Young People's Development as Interactive Media Creators." *Proceedings of World Conference on Educational Multimedia, Hypermedia and Telecommunications.* Chesapeake, VA: AACE, pp. 2147–2156.

[4] Brown, J. S., Collins, A., & Duguid, P. (1989). *Situated Cognition and the Culture of Learning,* pp. 32–42. http://www.ilt.columbia.edu/ilt/papers/JohnBrown.html, accessed 9/1/01.

[5] Frand, J. L. (2000). "The Information-Age Mindset: Changes in Students and Implications for Higher Education." *EDUCAUSE Review* **35**(5):14–24.

[6] Greher, G. R. (2007). "If You Build It…: A Distance-Learning Approach to Music Teacher Licensure Test Preparation." *Journal of Music Teacher Education* **16**(2):61–74.

[7] Johnstone, S. M., Ewell, P., & Paulson, K. (2002). "Academic Currency and Distributed Education." In *Distributed Education: Challenges, Choices and a New Environment.* Washington, DC: American Council on Education/Educause.

[8] Levine, A., & Sun, J. C. (2002). "Barriers to Distance Education." In A.C.o.E.C.f.P.A. EDUCAUSE, ed., *Distributed Education: Challenges, Choices and a New Evironment.* Washington, DC: American Council on Education. http://www.acenet.edu/bookstore/pdf/distributed-learning/distributed-learning-06.pdf.

[9] Natriello, G. (2005). "Modest Changes, Revolutionary Possibilities:Distance Learning and the Future of Education." *Teachers College Record* **107**(8):1185–1904.

[10] Oblinger, D. G., Barone, C. A., & Hawkins, B. L. (2001). "Distributed Education and Its Challenges: An Overview." In A.C.o.E.C.f.P.A. EDUCAUSE, ed., *Distributed Education: Challenges, Choices and a New Environment.* Washington, DC: American Council on Education.

[11] Ruthmann, S. A. (2012). "Engaging Adolescents with Music and Technology." In S. L. Burton, ed., *Engaging Musical Practices: A Sourcebook for Middle School General Music.* Lanham, MD: Rowman & Littlefield.

[12] Turkle, S. (2011). *Alone Together: Why We Expect More from Technology and Less from Each Other.* New York: Basic Books.

[13] Wenger, E. (1998). *Communities of Practice: Learning, Meaning, and Identity.* New York: Cambridge University Press.

[14] Yanco, H. A., Kim, H. J., Martin, F. G., & Silka, L. (2007). *Artbotics: Combining Art and Robotics to Broaden Participation in Computing.* AAAI Spring Symposium on Robots and Robot Venues: Resources for AI Education, Stanford, CA.

ENDNOTES

CHAPTER 1

1. Musical Instrument Digital Interface file format, which associates each semitone note with a number.
2. Audio Interchange File Format, which is popular on Macintosh systems.
3. WAVeform audio file format, which is popular on Windows systems.
4. A music-specific eXtensible Markup Language (XML), which is supported by numerous systems.
5. "Loops, if statements, and broadcasts" are all components of the Scratch programming environment, a media-rich visual programming system developed by the Lifelong Kindergarten Group at the Massachusetts Institute of Technology Media Lab. We use Scratch throughout our interdisciplinary *Sound Thinking* course, and it is freely accessible from **scratch.mit.edu.** We discuss Scratch and how we use it more extensively later, but we think you will be able to grasp the essence of the examples in this chapter without a formal introduction. Many of our examples of student work were built using Scratch.
6. Many of the examples in this section were produced in the semester that S. Alex Ruthmann first taught *Sound Thinking* with Jesse.
7. It is not a coincidence that both of these flowcharts depict songs by the Beatles, as so many of our students chose to work with music by that iconic group. We find that fascinating, especially when we remind ourselves that none of these young people were even alive in 1980 when John Lennon was killed.

CHAPTER 2

1. Using 2nds and 5ths as a composition springboard is a creative music strategy drawn from the work of Professor Lenore M. Pogonowski, Teachers College, Columbia University.
2. We're not really sure whether this story is completely true, but as Jesse's dad liked to say, "Never ruin a good story with the truth!"

CHAPTER 4

1. Tod Machover is head of the MIT Media Lab's Opera of the Future group and is a composer and inventor.
2. That last sentence was written by Gena, and she's softened the story a bit. What she really said was: "Jesse, if you were a student in one of my music ed classes and asked that question, I would have flunked you!" That got a good laugh from the class, except perhaps from the student who thought that we were fighting (see Chapter 3). I laughed, too, but I thought, "Good thing I've already got tenure!" Interdisciplinary classes are seldom dull! JMH ☺

CHAPTER 5

1. "Prosumer" = near professional, very high-end consumer.
2. **http://dvdvideosoft.com**. This site provides a huge number of image, audio, and video converters, editors, and associated tools, and they're all free. We don't know how they can afford to provide all this functionality for free, but we're very glad they do!
3. AU comes from "audio," not "Audacity." This file type was developed by Sun Microsystems, the company that gave birth to the Java computer language. Audacity is programmed in Java, so that's why the AU file type is used to store Audacity's data.
4. Be aware that the LAME download page looks nothing like the Audacity webpages, so don't be surprised when you click the link and end up on what appears to be a personal, rather unprofessional-looking page with lots of ads and requests for donations. Just scroll down until you see "LAME LIBRARY DOWNLOADS BELOW." When this book was written, the current version of the LAME encoder for Windows was 3.99.3, while the one for Macs was 3.98.2.

CHAPTER 6

1. "Prosumer" = near professional, very high-end consumer.
2. As of this writing, the price for a permanent license with unlimited upgrades was $59, but of course you should check the website for current pricing.
3. This code was developed by Brendan Reilly, one of our undergraduate computer science research assistants, under the guidance of Professors S. Alex Ruthmann and Jesse Heines.
4. Ubuntu is a free, open-source operating system for PCs (www.ubuntu.com/download) that many of our CS students prefer to Microsoft Windows due to its speed (particularly on small computers) and the abundance of free apps.
5. Real subroutines are available in Scratch 2.0 and an "advanced offshoot" of Scratch called BYOB (for "Build Your Own Blocks," also known as "Snap!") developed by Jens Mönig and Brian Harvey at the University of California Berkeley. See **byob. berkeley.edu.**
6. The "progressive examples" presented in this chapter were developed by Jesse Heines and S. Alex Ruthmann with input from John Maloney and were inspired by the Scratch Cards developed by Karen Brennan. See **http://info.scratch.mit.edu/Support/Scratch_ Cards**.
7. "Looping constructs" are programming techniques that cause groups of statements to be repeated. In Scratch, these are the blocks that enclose other blocks and cause the enclosed blocks to be executed a number of times (the **repeat** block in the Scratch **Control** panel), while a condition is **true** (the **forever if** block), or until a condition becomes **true** (the **repeat until** block).
8. Strings of characters are series of letters. In addition, programmers typically refer to a word or a phrase as a "string." The fact that lists can contain strings is important because this allows programs to use data other than just numbers. For example, you might have a list that contains "do," "re," "mi," etc. and display those syllables when the corresponding notes are played.
9. *Note to geeks:* Two lists are needed because Scratch does not support two-dimensional arrays.
10. The Ichiboard was developed by UMass Lowell graduate student Mark Sherman working under the direction of Professor Fred Martin.
11. The use of the IchiBoard in *Sound Thinking* was introduced by Professors S. Alex Ruthmann and Jesse Heines.

CHAPTER 7

1. We believe that this phrase is most correctly referenced as being first used by Sir Isaac Newton in a letter to Robert Hooke written in 1676.
2. This sequence of successive refinements was developed in conjunction with our music department colleague S. Alex Ruthmann.
3. When Jesse teaches *Sound Thinking* with our other music colleague S. Alex Ruthmann rather than Gena, Jesse and Alex do not assign project partners directly as is done when Jesse and Gena teach together. However, Jesse and Alex require students to work with different partners (in either pairs or at most trios) on all projects except the final one, where they may work with whomever they choose.
4. For more on group work and group brainstorming, see Sawyer, R. K. (2007). *Group Genius: The Creative Power of Collaboration.* New York: Basic Books.
5. At the time of this writing, Jesse has broken down and now owns a Mac as well as numerous Windows machines. ☺
6. Back in the early to mid-1990s, when the World Wide Web was brand new and course websites were rare, Jesse published a number of papers on web development and its applicability to course websites. This work was not seen as CS research by his departmental promotion and tenure committee because the journals in which these papers were published or the conferences at which they were presented focused on CS education rather than a direct subfield of CS. The work was therefore not considered relevant to an application for promotion at that time. One administrator simply wrote it off as "part of Jesse's teaching duties." It is interesting to note that the Association for Computing Machinery's Computing Classification System added "Computer and Information Science Education" as subset area K.3.2 under "Computing Milieux" in 1991 (see http://www.acm.org/about/class/ccs98-html).
7. For readers unfamiliar with IRBs, this is a university office that is responsible for ensuring, among other things, that students in experimental courses such as ours are not taken advantage of. For example, students must first be fully informed that their enrollment in the course makes them part of a research study. They must voluntarily agree to take part, and they must be allowed to opt out of certain aspects of the study such as our use of their work and likenesses in our publications and presentations. IRB approval is required for all research at our university, particularly research that involves using students as subjects and is funded by the National Science Foundation.
8. CPATH stands for CISE Pathways, where CISE stands for the Directorate for Computer & Information Science & Engineering. See www.nsf.gov/funding/pgm_summ.jsp?pims_id=500025&org=CISE, but note that this program is no longer active. The award page for our original grant is at www.nsf.gov/awardsearch/showAward.do?AwardNumber=0722161.
9. TUES stands for Transforming Undergraduate Education in STEM, where STEM stands for Science, Technology, Engineering, and Mathematics. See www.nsf.gov/funding/pgm_summ.jsp?pims_id=5741. The award page for our second grant is at www.nsf.gov/awardsearch/showAward.do?AwardNumber=1118435.

CHAPTER 8

1. We used Google Groups for quite a while in our classes, but we have now found that Piazza, a free service available at **www.piazza.com**, or Edmodo, another free service at **www.edmodo.com**, are particularly well suited for online class discussions.
2. Gena likes to say, "It's so nice to have a real CS prof on the team." ☺
3. The macros we used to do this are freely available from the book website.

4. We do not want to list all the websites we tried to use for our course, as we don't want to "bad mouth" them. Some might be totally appropriate for others' use, but they didn't work well for us.

CHAPTER 9

1. The original quote "If you build it, they will come" is from the movie *Field of Dreams* released in 1989 from Universal Pictures, directed by Phil Alden Robinson and starring Kevin Costner.

INDEX

UNIVERSITY OF ST THOMAS LIBRARIES

UNIVERSITY OF ST. THOMAS LiBRARIES